CHASING
OLIVER
HAZARD
PERRY

CHASING OLIVER HAZARD PERRY

*Travels in the Footsteps of the
Commodore Who Saved America*

Craig J. Heimbuch

CLERISY PRESS

For further information, contact the publisher at:
Clerisy Press
P.O. Box 8874
Cincinnati, OH 45208-0874

www.clerisypress.com

Library of Congress Cataloging-in-Publication Data
Heimbuch, Craig J.
Chasing Oliver Hazard Perry: Travels in the Footsteps of the Commodore Who Saved America/by Craig J. Heimbuch.
p. cm.
ISBN 978-1-57860-345-9
1. Perry, Oliver Hazard, 1785–1819. 2. Lake Erie, Battle of, 1813.
3. Ship captains—United States—Biography. 4. United States. Navy—Officers—Biography. 5. Perry, Oliver Hazard, 1785–1819—Influence.
6. Perry, Oliver Hazard, 1785–1819—Monuments. 7. Perry, Oliver Hazard, 1785–1819—Homes and haunts—Erie, Lake, Region.
8. Erie, Lake, Region—Description and travel. 9. Heimbuch, Craig J.—Travel—Erie, Lake, Region. I. Title.

E353.1.P4H45 2010
973.5'254—dc22   2010003141

Distributed by Publishers Group West
Edited by Jack Heffron
Cover designed by Stephen Sullivan
Interior designed by Angela Wilcox

The photos on the following pages are reprinted courtesy of the Library of Congress: 12, 28, 55, 56, 254. The photos on page 199 appear courtesy of the Great Lakes Brewing Company. All other photos are the property of Craig J. Heimbuch.

For Dad, thanks . . . for everything.

For Rebecca, Jackson, and Dylan,
thanks for letting me love you as much as I do.

Acknowledgments

This book was written under the influence of Miles Davis and gas station coffee. Late at night, in my office at the magazine, in my friend Curtis Zimmerman's office, and anywhere I could situate myself for a few hours after the kids went to bed. My wife, Rebecca, was patient and allowed me to slip away from home every evening for several months to avoid distraction and avoid the call of our warm, comfortable bed. She waited for me every night, falling asleep on the couch watching reruns of soap operas. I promise to use some of the proceeds of this book to purchase her a new couch before I start my next book. I carried this book with me wherever I went, on a two-gigabyte Cruzer Micro memory stick that I bought on sale at Walmart one evening early in the process. It never left my pocket, and, thank God, it never went through the wash.

There are a few people I'd like to acknowledge for helping me along the way. The first are my editor, Jack Heffron, and publisher, Richard Hunt. Both were patient and didn't pester me when I was running a month (or two) behind, and both were willing to give me a shot at writing a book when few, especially I, were sure that I could. Thank you.

I would also like to thank my immediate and extended family for not being too mad about me putting them in the book. That's a preemptive thank-you, to take the sting out of them realizing that I have put them in print.

I would also like to thank three men I have never met: Gerard Altoff, David Curtis Skaggs, and A. J. Langguth. Their books about Oliver Hazard Perry, the Battle of Lake Erie, and the War of 1812 are absolutely incredible. These men are real historians and made it possible for me to putz about pretending. I did my best not to plagiarize; if anything is too familiar, I apologize. Please know that you were the primary sources for information, and I consider it a pleasure to have read your work. If anyone is interested in learning the real story of the war, the man, or the battle, I highly recommend you check them out. Well worth the price.

I would also like to recognize my parents, Jim and Judy Heimbuch. My dad made a point of introducing me to history when I was young and instilled in me the idea that it is always, always, always more fulfilling and richer to do something than to have something. Without that lesson, that conviction, I might never have gotten off the couch. And for my mom, who has always believed in me—as a writer, as a father, and as a person. Thank you for making me learn those spelling words, and thank you for always showing an interest. It means the world.

Finally, I would like to recognize Commodore Oliver Hazard Perry for his bravery and dignity during his service to our nascent country. He embodied early on the same spirit that has protected this country and moved it forward through more than two centuries. But most of all, I would just like to thank him for not losing.

Table of Contents

Author's Note

I want to state for the record that I am not now, nor have I ever been, a historian. It's not that I don't have a tremendous amount of respect for the men and women who do that job—preserving and learning from the past, after all, can help us lay a true course for the future. It's just that I don't have the patience. I get antsy and irritable. I need tangibility, immediate human connection, and interaction.

I tried to be a historian when I was in college and chose American history as a minor. But, really, I was just looking for a minor. My alma mater, Miami University in southwest Ohio ("Miami was a university when Florida belonged to Spain" is still my favorite collegiate T-shirt), required that all English majors, despite concentration, have a minor in order to graduate. I had just come off a rough patch as a marketing major my freshman year—I was abused by calculus and tormented by macroeconomics—and I wanted to select something that I thought was in line with my course of study. As a journalism and creative-writing double major, I had to read a lot. Like, really a lot. And most of those books were by dead people, so I thought history would allow me to stay in my literary groove.

I was wrong. Being a history minor was hard. There were dates and names to memorize, court cases to learn the names and subheadlines of; there were quizzes and tests and multiple choice and true and false, and I wasn't very good at any of it. I wanted to write. I wanted to see and interpret. I wanted to have a visceral connection, and the way I was being taught history was about as personal as a night-drop at a bank. So I grew bored. I learned enough to get my head above water and remembered the things that piqued my interest: Jefferson and Sally Hemings, the Alien and Sedition Acts, *Brown v. Board of Education*, Elvis Presley, and Walker Evans. But my education in history was Swiss cheese at best, negligent (on my part) at worst.

It wasn't that I wasn't interested. It was that I didn't understand. I was more engaged by covering school-board subcommittee meetings for my hometown weekly, the *Avon Lake Press*, than I was by reading about Bunker Hill and Pearl Harbor. They just seemed like words on a page to me. I managed a respectable GPA in my history courses while throwing my heart into becoming a journalist and writer.

And then I met Professor Sherman Jackson, and he became the second person in my life to influence my view of and love for history. Jackson was a middle-aged (maybe on the back side of the middle) black man from rural Louisiana. He wore a salt-and-pepper soul patch and tweedy jackets, and spoke in the staccato cadences of bad Bill Cosby impersonations. But he was cool, very cool, like he just stepped away from playing a set with Miles Davis cool. Jackson was the best history professor I ever had for one simple reason—his stories. When we were learning about the Constitutional history of segregation, he told us stories about growing up poor in the segregated South. When we learned about *Brown v. Board of Education*, he painted a picture of a father who wanted nothing more than the right for his children to go to the same school as their white neighbors. He made me see history, a picture of it like a movie in my head, and he made me feel history like Coltrane blowing a love song. It's cliché for a writer to talk about a professor in such loving terms, such transformative terms, but it is true. Jackson helped me understand that history is about a lot more than facts and dates, and that the only way to understand it is to feel it.

In a lot of ways, Jackson's take on history was like my dad's. Though my father has nothing near the talent for storytelling that Jackson does—he tells stories like history is taught, just the facts— he practiced a sort of show-and-tell method of sharing history. You could bet that on any family road trip, there would be a stop at, or at least a passing mention of, a historic spot along the way. U. S. Grant's birthplace on the way to my grandmother's house in

Iowa, the battlefields at Antietam or Gettysburg on a college visit or when we took my sister Jill to a sports camp. Dad liked, and still likes, to stand in the very spots where history took place. Just like Jackson and his stories, my dad and his field trips made history personal, tangible. It was his gift, whether he knew it or not, to me.

Dad's a voracious learner. At an age when most of his peers are coming in on the final approach to retirement, he's taking classes at the community college in managerial accounting, something he has been practicing in his job for decades. And when I ask him why he does this, he says that it's good to keep learning. He got his degree in chemical engineering more than forty years ago and has, in the intervening decades unbeknownst to most of my family, taken enough correspondence courses to fill a wall with diplomas. But he has never been about accreditation or validation. For him, to live is to learn, and he's the same way with history. He immerses himself in it. Recently he wanted to learn about Dwight Eisenhower so he did what a lot of people do: he bought a biography. Only he bought three. And when he tells me about Ike, I can see the movie playing in my mind, the same one I saw in Jackson's classes.

After my sophomore year, I broke the news to my dad that I wasn't going to follow in his practical footsteps. I changed my major to journalism and creative writing. I would end up with a Bachelor of Arts degree, something alien to a man of science and fact. And at first, there was tension. But my dad, who walks in the footsteps of generals, respects action, and when he saw how hard I worked—devoting summers and breaks to working for the hometown weekly, taking on the writing and editing jobs at school over and beyond my class load—I think he realized I was more like him than he thought. I was immersed in my passion, doing it for real, just like he did, only on a different path. He gave me a notebook when I graduated, a linen-covered, college-ruled notebook, and in it he wrote that he was proud of me for working so hard and that he recognized I have a gift and a passion for the written word. "Go for it," he wrote. I have never written a single word in that notebook. It sits on a shelf in my living room empty, to remind me of the limitless potential he saw for me that day, but I have followed his advice. I've gone for it.

I knew I wanted to be a travel writer because it was, to me, an incredibly personal form of writing. A person can hide behind fiction, and they can pile facts up in front of their personality in nonfiction. Travel writing is innately about observation and translation, two personal endeavors. But it is very hard to break into, especially when you marry your high school sweetheart and put down roots. So for ten years, I have kept myself employed as a writer. First it was newspapers, then newsletters. Then I wrote advertising copy and flirted with the idea of law school. Finally, I find myself working in magazines, which suits me.

But in all that time I thought about my favorite books—*Blue Latitudes, Notes from a Small Island, Ghost Soldiers*—and about my burning desire to write a travel narrative. At a fateful lunch with an editor, in a perfect lightning-strike-me-now moment, I blurted out an idea about the Battle of Lake Erie. Within a month I had a contract.

So that's how I got here, to this point, to this book.

This story is personal to me, and not just because it is about something I did. It represents the fulfillment of that old resolve, of me at long last doing what I've always wanted to do. And I promise you that every word of it is true, even if it is not always factually accurate. I'm not a historian, after all, but I have tried to double-check dates and names as if studying for one of those old multiple-choice tests. If I miss something or get something wrong, I'm sorry. But understand that history, to me, is like travel writing, it's about observation and interpretation. It's about the present, the future, the place where you live, and, yes, you.

Thanks for reading.

–C. J. H.

One's destination is never a place
but a new way of seeing things.

—Henry Miller

CHASING
OLIVER
HAZARD
PERRY

Prologue

On the morning of September 10, 1813, a young naval commander received word that his enemy was amassing to the north of an island in Lake Erie's central basin. He had been waiting for that enemy to show his face, had been sent to this usually placid place for just that purpose—to wait. And when the enemy showed his sails, the young commander was supposed to kill him. Quickly elevated from lieutenant to commodore, the young officer sensed an opportunity he had long been waiting for—to strike his enemy's Lake Erie fleet and cut off supplies and reinforcements to a small but determined band of British, Canadian, and native warriors holding out against a siege on Fort Malden. The winds were against him, but he had the numbers—nine ships to six—even if he didn't have the guns. The enemy had chosen his moment well, a moment when he could no longer wait to leave his nest in the Detroit River corridor, a moment when he had the winds. But the young navy man had something his vastly more experienced enemy could not have known about—spirit. He had a burn for glory and an intrinsic heroism that few men could claim and fewer could replicate in the intervening years since that morning.

This was Commodore Oliver Hazard Perry's moment. And he seized it.

Later, on a muggy July afternoon in 1986, a young boy was doing his best to overcome a stifling case of vertigo as his history-loving, overanxious father tried to explain why the particular monolith they were now standing atop was built on this narrow strip of a Lake Erie island. It was built to commemorate the man and his moment and those famous words uttered in victory: "We have met the enemy and they are ours." Profound, poetic, and completely out of the realm of things the boy cared about at that moment—principally the feeling of nausea that was hatched on the ferry ride to Put-in-Bay and his general mistrust of large structures. Still, there he stood, absorbing subconsciously his dad's yen for history, if a bit too young to really understand.

Ten years later, that boy would graduate from high school with romantic dreams of far-flung adventures through the everyday world. He would dream of graduating from college and striking out to claim his piece-of-the-road legacy. Six years after that, the boy was married. Add another year and he would be a father with bills and responsibilities, joy and fulfillment, but in the deepest part of his mind—a place he let few if any into—the pull of the road would call him like an angel in his dreams, and it would echo until he could shove it back down again.

There's reason to believe that were it not for Oliver Hazard Perry's bravery and ability that day in 1813, we, as Americans, might now be worried about how many kilometers per liter our cars are getting, whether or not the Maple Leafs win the Stanley Cup, and whether or not Prince Harry will ever really settle down. And yet the Battle of Lake Erie and the War of 1812 are little more than footnotes in our history textbooks, facts that will not be on the test. It might be because the war was essentially a draw. It might be because Canada is not really that threatening anymore. But every time we stand up in our classroom at Perry High School, drive down the roads of Hazard County, Kentucky, or sing the national anthem, we pay tribute to this forgotten hero of that forgotten war.

For my part, the legacy of Oliver Hazard Perry was forged in the trip to Put-in-Bay when I was just a boy. We were new to Ohio, and Lake Erie seemed like an ocean, vast and mysterious. I remember little of that particular day, aside from the nausea and vertigo, but the legend and those words—"We have met the enemy and they are ours"—have resided in me in part because of the masculine stoicism of them, and in part because of the way in which my dad said them (awed and reverent).

In many ways Oliver Hazard Perry is an integral strand in the tapestry of my relationship to my dad, the relationship I have to where I have come from, and my relationship to history. History, heritage, plays an important role in our lives as Americans, even if it is an obscured role. The passage of time is often like a morning fog that obscures the events, people, and places that formed who we are today. It can be difficult to grasp from a textbook, difficult to understand in theory. Changing fashion and technology taken for granted often widen the chasm, making it harder to relate to what has come before us.

History can sometimes seem dead, sterile, nothing more than ink on a page. But history is anything but dead or ancient. History is a living chronicle of how we have come to be, an organic and meaningful testament to those who have come before us and a vibrant guide to those who shall later come. We can learn from history, and not just facts and dates. We can learn the true nature of place and gain in both perspective and appreciation of what we have, where we come from, and where we are going. But in order to truly understand and absorb history, you have to experience it, to see for yourself the difficulties and challenges, to feel what it was like.

❦

That is the true goal of this book: to immerse myself in the history, the mythology that has long lodged itself in the back of my mind. I hope to rouse the ghosts time has forgotten and remind readers just how close history was to changing, to creating an alternate world than that which we now occupy; it is meant to remind readers that history is everywhere, just waiting to be discovered, dusted off and learned from.

All you have to do is open your eyes and dive in.

≈1≈

My First Mistake

I should have rented a golf cart.

In hindsight the reasons are perfectly clear, but in the moment it seemed like a frivolous waste, a spoiler to the adventure I had in mind. My poor decision became particularly clear after the first mile, when my shirt was soaked with sweat and my wife, Rebecca, had stormed ahead pushing our youngest in a stroller. She had wanted to rent a golf cart, but my own inability to make such a decision, particularly in the presence of my mom, dad, brother, uncle, aunt, and two cousins—the extended family were visiting from Iowa—had set her off. It was probably something to do with the heat and the two-point-two-mile trek we now faced under an unforgiving Lake Erie sun and through the thick July air. It also had to do with the fact that our four-year-old and eight-month-old sons had to endure these conditions without so much as a water bottle. She had begged, and I had only meekly said, "Uh, maybe up the road." But she was clearly upset and more than that, it seemed to be getting worse.

She was mad.

I should point out that my wife is not an unreasonable person given to fits of rage. In all the years we have been together, starting from when we were seventeen years old, she has wanted nothing more for me than to be my own man and make my own decisions. I have struggled greatly with both. There was the time in college when she was all set to come on a spring-break trip with my parents and me to Calabash, North Carolina. We were leaving on a Sunday, and Dad, a man for whom schedules and timeliness are of utmost importance, wanted to leave early. She wanted to go to Mass. He didn't want to wait and so I did the thing I have done many times in my life: I deferred to him. We left her behind because I was unwilling to fight for another hour. There have been many occasions when my inability to stand up or speak out have caused tension—particularly when that standing up involved my father.

He's a good man, the best I have ever known. Not prone to anger or yelling, he always seems to keep his head about him, and more often than not he is right when he makes a statement. I had looked to him, his head covered in an army-green fishing hat, his eyes shaded by sunglasses, and beads of sweat dripping down his temple, when we stopped at the golf-cart-rental stand. I was seeking his approval before plopping down the cash for the cart that would have saved us from this punishing walk. It did not come, so I did nothing.

And now, as our eleven-person convoy meandered slowly along the side of the road that runs from east to west along the length of South Bass Island, it became evident that I was the leader, though I don't remember ever asking to be. I was in trouble for not renting the golf cart, a one-hundred-dollar expense that, when we stepped off the ferry, seemed like an extravagance but now, halfway through and facing the prospect of a long afternoon's silence from my beloved, now seemed a cheap necessity. And as I wondered how much farther it was to town exactly, and how much begging I would have to do for forgiveness, my dad and uncle lobbed questions at me. "Where was Perry sitting when he first saw the British?" "How long had the battle lasted?" "How many were killed?"

Good God, I thought, how the hell should I know? This was a research trip. And the whole point of a research trip is to find the answers, isn't it? You don't get a book from the library because you know how it ends. Still, we marched along—a beautiful and fit (if visibly peeved) woman marching ahead with an umbrella stroller carrying our youngest; me and our son Jack, my mom and aunt in the middle; and two middle-aged men and three teenaged boys bringing up the rear a quarter mile behind the leader—a golf cart full of weekend merrymakers passed us at what felt like race-car pace. As I tromped down the road I stared at the towering peak of Perry's Victory and International Peace Memorial, wondering if it was ever going to get any closer.

I can't remember how it came to be that all of us were here. I know I had planned on bringing Rebecca and the boys. I must have asked Dad if he wanted to come and by extension that meant Mom and my adopted brother, Kosta, who is a spitting image of the most recent actor to play James Bond. Mark and Linette and their two boys, Will and Tom, were in town visiting and are, like Dad, always keen to take a learning adventure. But I was the only one here on a mission.

A few months before, I had been having lunch with a friend of mine in book publishing. We had gotten to be friends because I had pitched several books to him that weren't worth writing. But he had seen my, I believe the word he used was "vim," and knew that there would be a time when I would come up with a good idea and be willing to work my ass off to write a book he could sell. Desperate to get something going—I was, after all, almost thirty and feeling like a failure for not having become a successful author by that point—I blurted out a topic without really knowing why.

"What about a book on Oliver Hazard Perry?" I had said. I was surprised when he leaned in and wanted to know what I had in mind. I spoke for the next half hour, gibberish to be sure because I didn't actually have anything in mind but felt desperate to sell him on an idea. I was stunned when a few weeks later I was signing a publishing contract to write the book you are now holding.

≈.≈

"It looks like something," said my delightfully happy Aunt Linette in her upper-Midwestern lilt. "I don't know what, though." In the distance above the trees, the three hundred-plus-foot monument—to Perry's victory and to the nearly two-century peace between the U.S. and Canada—rose like a mirage.

The way she speaks the words "I don't know what, though" sound more like "Eye dought knough watt, though." It really is the most pleasing sound, and I try to engage her in conversation. She is one of my most favorite relatives. Yet I find myself distracted by the damn golf carts and our complete lack of one. And the rucksack I carry, which holds my camera and a few books and notebooks related to the history of the Battle of Lake Erie, seems to be getting heavier as a greasy skin of sweat develops under the strap that crosses my body.

I'm not a small man. Heimbuchs rarely are. We are a large people, tall and fluffy and not built for these types of conditions where heat and humidity bear equal measurement in the mid-nineties. I am nearly six feet, four inches tall and have a BMI most doctors would agree is unhealthy. Yet I am neither the tallest nor the fattest in the family. But we are a happy bunch, by and large. Dad and Uncle Mark, both wine barrels of men, were awash in sweat but smiling. They grew up working fields in Iowa, and surely they could handle the sun and heat. Dad was slathered in sunscreen and enjoying the cover of his floppy fishing hat. Mom—who breaks the mold of Heimbuchs and shares Rebecca's slim build—and Linette were strolling along with red cheeks, but content. I may as well have not been there, but I felt a certain responsibility. This was my trip after all, and I was torn between my desires to entertain my relatives and to sprint ahead and do the right thing for my wife and children and rent a damn golf cart. Hell, I was ready to stand in the middle of the road and offer sexual favors to any passerby willing to part with theirs. But, as usual, I kept plodding along, hoping to keep my relatives happy and my children from succumbing to heatstroke.

Perry's Victory and International Peace Memorial stands like a 317-foot phone pole in the vast prairie of Lake Erie. As we approached on foot, Aunt Linette said it reminded her of something, but she couldn't quite figure out what.

When at last we reached the outskirts of the town of Put-in-Bay, we stopped at a roadside snack stand, where we got hot dogs with coleslaw and barbecue sauce, ice cream, and a bottle of water. Rebecca waited in the shade of a porch in front of a gift shop, giving sips of water to Dylan while the rest of the brood sat at a picnic table and devoured the meal, effectively replacing and perhaps doubling the calories we had just walked off on our two-mile trek from the ferry landing.

When you grow up in Cleveland, you come to expect that nothing good ever happens. Sports teams will always fall just a slight measure short, actors will become moderately famous, and, should the national press ever pick up a story from the area, it will have something to do with urban blight, corruption in city government, or Dennis Kucinich running once again for president. You come to accept that you will never be as notorious as Chicago, as glamorous as Los Angeles, or as, well, anything, as New York. There's little to grab on to in terms of history.

Cleveland does not evoke the same mental image as, say, Philadelphia or Boston or St. Augustine when it comes to famous things that happened long ago. So your reference points become a bit flimsy. As a sophomore in high school, I took a history class devoted almost exclusively to the Sam Sheppard murder case, which, unless you are from Cleveland's West Side, you probably don't know was the basis for the television series, and later the Harrison Ford movie, *The Fugitive*. The real plot—a doctor accused of killing his wife and blaming a mysterious one-armed man—was nowhere near as juicy as the movie. The real doctor never escaped from jail only to be chased by Tommy Lee Jones. In fact, he lost his medical license and eventually became an alcoholic professional wrestler, all the while maintaining his innocence. Cleveland's other big mystery turned out to be the greatest failure in the illustrious crime-solving career of Eliot Ness when he was the city's public-safety director. He was unable to solve a spate of gruesome murders in which little more than the torsos of the victims were found. These are small moments, but they are seemingly all Cleveland has to offer its residents in terms of local lore.

When you look at the role Cleveland, or the North Coast for that matter, plays in the theater of American history, it's easy to write it off in generalizations—an important shipping center, an important industrial center, the home of the great polka-squeezebox player Frankie Yankovic and bespectacled comedian Drew Carey. There are not great moments like the signing of the Declaration of Independence, the California Gold Rush, or the Battle of Antietam to point out, ones that define America and inform our national conscience. There have been few incidents that can be described as having lasting significance or notoriety.

But there is one.

Oliver Hazard Perry was a young naval officer—twenty-six years old and a lieutenant—who found himself building and commanding a squadron of ships on Lake Erie during the second year of the War of 1812. By and large this is a forgotten war, a footnote in most high school history classes. But its legacy remains for a couple of reasons.

The first is that it was during this war that Francis Scott Key penned the poem that would become "The Star-Spangled Banner." He was sitting on the deck of a British ship in Baltimore Harbor, trying to negotiate the return of a U.S. captive when the fort built in the mouth of the harbor survived an all-night bombardment by a British armada seeking a foothold in the Mid-Atlantic. The next morning, "by the dawn's early light," Key looked at the fort thinking he would find devastation from the "rockets' red glare, the bombs bursting in air," but instead saw a massive U.S. flag commissioned specifically for the fort still waving, "o'er the land of the free and the home of the brave."

The second reason involves the British burning the White House. This happened right after the siege at Baltimore, when the

British marched almost unmolested into Washington. They burned the public buildings—though they were almost gracious and civil in their respect for private homes—in retaliation for a raid into the Canadian capital at York (now Toronto) almost two years earlier. During that raid, U.S. forces had faced little resistance getting to York but were nearly decimated when they paused near an ammunition depot that exploded unexpectedly, burning, maiming, and killing dozens of men and setting the rest of the raiding party into a blind rage that ultimately ended up in the burning of the public buildings of York.

Commodore Oliver Hazard Perry. Apart from being a formidable naval tactician and war hero, he was an early adopter of the fauxhawk and proud owner of an enviable set of sideburns.

So those are the two things most people recall about the almost-five-year struggle. But it's actually a rich and intricate story. The war was brewing a long time before 1812. In many ways, it was almost as if the Revolution had never ended. Political infighting among early Americans was rampant, and the British, who had been tied up fighting Napoleon for supremacy in Europe, had acted with open disdain for the Americans. The British had made a habit of rounding out their naval ranks by plucking sailors from American merchant ships and had behaved aggressively in other ways. But this habit of impressing U.S. seamen seemed to be the breaking point. Early presidents saw the war coming but tried to avoid it. George Washington was too busy establishing a government and expanding a nation. John Adams wanted war but lacked the tools and the support from Congress. Thomas Jefferson, who was a better statesman and architect than chief executive, had the opportunity to go to war after an incident involving the HMS *Leopard*—more on that later—but chose instead to halt trading with Europe. The embargo crippled the northeastern shipping economy and enraged the South because it hurt their relations with the North and with France. Fearing the possibility of a coup, Jefferson had pared down the military, leaving him no option to fight. He left office having lifted the embargo, but when James Madison took office, he faced a nation on the verge of civil war and an economy that had ground to a halt. It might have been a *Wag the Dog* scenario, but Madison, long respected for his intellect and subtle persuasive powers but not known for strength, decided that the fate of the nation rested on the possibility of another war for independence from the English. Small, slight, shy, and brainy, Madison did not fit the mold of a wartime commander in chief. It was almost like the geeky kid was losing friends after scoring a date with the cheerleader, so he needed to find his self-respect by kicking the bully's ass and declaring geekiness cool—a 1980s Patrick Dempsey movie.

Perry's role in the war was equal measures blind luck and pure tenacity. After a relatively unremarkable early career in the navy, he decided to stay on when Jefferson fired nearly all of the officers at sea, including his father—a Revolutionary War hero with a lot of guts and a less-than-healthy dislike of being told what to do. Some early fumbles—he crashed the first ship he commanded—combined with his genetic link to his dad made advancement in the ocean fleet nearly impossible for Perry. So in late 1812, he wrangled some political and military connections for an assignment building the first fleet of American warships to sail on Lake Erie.

In today's mind-set, Lake Erie seems like a pretty important piece of real estate. But in 1812, it may as well have been on Mars. It was way out there, in the old Northwest Territories of Michigan, Ohio, Indiana, and Wisconsin. Perry took the job as a way to build a name for himself. The British had controlled Lake Erie and all of Michigan early in the war. They had sparred with U.S. forces on Lake Ontario, but they had built momentum after marching from the tip of Michigan's middle finger to Detroit with hardly a shot fired. They had stepped onto America's back porch and were ready to let themselves in. To say that the early days of the war were unsuccessful for the Americans is like saying that New Coke did not quite meet expectations. We were getting our collective butt kicked, and the planning efforts in Washington were like a rerun of the Keystone Cowboys.

So Perry's mission to build a fleet that could challenge the British squadron's dominance of Lake Erie was strategically important but sort of like putting the star on top of a dead Christmas tree. Still, over the winter of 1812 to 1813, he threw himself into it, constructing several gunboats, outfitting merchant ships with armament, and building two twin-sailed brigs—the *Lawrence* and the *Niagara*—in the shallow waters near Erie, Pennsylvania. He did all of this under the watchful eyes of Captain Robert Barclay, a seasoned, one-armed British sailor who had fought at Trafalgar. Perry was like the rookie pitcher sent in to strike out Babe Ruth. Only the thing was, he thought he could do it. For several weeks during the summer of 1813, he played a cat-and-mouse game with Barclay, waiting for the British captain to leave his safe haven on the Detroit River near modern-day Amherstburg, Ontario, when suddenly, on the morning of September 10, Barclay decided to come out and fight.

Barclay's men and a contingent of British ground forces and native warriors were being starved out of their base at Fort Malden. Perry had cut off resupply lines from the eastern end of Lake Erie, and army General William Henry Harrison had put an end to ground advancement by building a fort near Toledo called Fort Meigs and stationing his forces there. A harsh summer had led to poor crops, and the British were starving. Barclay had to make a move, and Perry, who had moored his ships off South Bass Island, was ready.

At first the battle was all Barclay. For three hours, Perry and eight of his nine ships battled unfavorable winds and the experienced British forces, taking heavy casualties. Then, with his flagship, the brig *Lawrence*, beaten to tatters and 80 percent of his crew fallen to casualty, Perry made a move that made him a legend. The other brig, *Niagara*, was captained by Jesse Elliot, an officer superior to Perry who had achieved a great deal of success on Lake Ontario. Elliot had failed to engage in the battle, blaming the wind. But Perry thought Elliot was being a coward, and so, with British guns blaring and his ship a ragged hulk, Perry climbed aboard a rowboat with three other men (one of them his younger brother) and rowed across a half mile of open water through enemy fire to take command of the *Niagara*. He quickly relieved Elliot of duty and engaged the ship in the battle.

Many of the British officers, including Barclay, had been wounded during the pitched fighting, and two of the British ships had become entangled. The winds shifted, and Perry sensed the opportunity to win. In fifteen minutes of maneuvering and firing, he put a decided end to the battle, becoming the first captain—American or otherwise—to take an entire British squadron. When he was finished, he penned a note on the back of an envelope to Harrison. "We have met the enemy and they are ours," he wrote, and overnight became a national hero for quite literally changing the tide of an ugly war.

The siege on Baltimore and the burning of Washington would happen later, but America had found, in Oliver Hazard Perry, its first American-born hero. I think the reason I blurted out his name in that meeting with the publisher was that Perry is very much the kind of person I am attracted to and equally the kind of person I am not. He was bold and daring. I couldn't make up my mind to rent a golf cart. He was a romantic figure, like Hemingway or Kerouac or my high school friend Kevin and college friend Gene. He was bigger than himself. I have always wanted to be bigger than myself, to drink in the world and let out a loud belch. But apart from changing my major from marketing to English in college and telling my wife I loved her for the first time, there have been few moments when I have ever been bold. I used to read books like Kerouac's On the Road, or Bill Bryson's Notes from a Small Island, or Tony Horwitz's Blue Latitudes with a sense of awe and wonder and no small amount of jealousy. Those authors threw caution to the wind in pursuit of something. For Kerouac, it was Neal Cassidy and the American West. For Bryson, it was an extended ramble to say good-bye to his adopted homeland. For Horwitz, it was a round-the-world trip with a drunken Englishman in pursuit of Captain Cook. These were men I admired for their ability to live out loud, to pursue their bliss.

As I mentioned earlier, I first heard the story of Perry and the Battle of Lake Erie when I was something like ten years old. We were still relatively new to Ohio, having moved there from north-central Wisconsin during my early elementary years, and my dad took us to the monument on a summer weekend outing. I suppose he is like many dads, particularly those of the generations born before interstate highways linked the nation, in that he likes to stop and read the roadside signs. Nearly every family trip from my youth involved at least one stop at a place of historical significance. So it should be no surprise that, when establishing ourselves in our new home, he would want to visit the most historic spot around, Perry's Victory and International Peace Memorial.

The memorial, which is built like an oversize Greek column, stands tall and proud from the narrowest point of the hourglass-shaped South Bass Island. If you have ever boated on the central part of Lake Erie, near Sandusky, you have probably seen it, standing like a telephone pole in a cornfield, as if it were pointing to something really important in the sky. I love the monument. In fact it is among my favorite in all the collection of the National Park Service, if for no other reason than its peculiar placement.

⊰ ⋅ ⊱

As we finished our hot dogs on the picnic table and decide to split up—my wife and our children, my brother, and my two cousins opting to explore the gift shops and general kitsch of Put-in-Bay proper, while my mom, dad, aunt, uncle, and I headed over toward Perry's Victory and International Peace Memorial Information Center—I found myself looking up at it and remembering that first visit when I was a boy. It's the same thing, the same granite and height, but for some reason it felt grander and more important than it did in my youth. And it made me wonder how many other roadside attractions I needed to revisit to gain a proper perspective on their enormity.

In part, that's what this project was about—finding the lasting legacy of something I discovered in my youth. I wanted to understand better what it was like to be a sailor on Perry's flagship, the *Lawrence*, and get to know more about the man himself. I wanted to understand more clearly that history is everywhere and that this particular history is always there, waiting for me to discover it. The project also was about me putting my toe in the water. It was about me, at least for a little while, trying to see if I could call upon Perry's and Kerouac's spirit and do something brave.

⁕

"I've got it," Linette said as we cut through the back alleys of town on our way to the visitors and information center. "I know what it looks like."

"What?" I asked, my attention suddenly drawn from the complex tableau of thoughts running through my head. History? Whether or not Rebecca would forgive me for the golf cart fiasco? The fact that a nearby island is known as Rattlesnake Island for obvious reasons and my almost paralyzing fear of snakes?

I didn't ask those questions. Instead, I said, "What does it look like?"

"A bottle of dish detergent."

She was right. Atop the column is an odd-shaped parapet that bears a striking resemblance to the retractable top of a bottle of dish soap. And all at once the grandeur of the moment, my awe of the size of the thing and the history it protects, were snapped up in a television commercial for lemon-scented Joy.

This is what I love most about my Iowa relatives—their ability to knock the pretense and magnitude of any situation down to an appropriate size. They are the kind of people who would stare from the rim of the Grand Canyon and say something like, "Man, that sure is a big hole. I wonder how long it would take to for my pee to hit the bottom." Or, looking at St. Peter's Basilica, might utter, "I'd hate to have to clean all that." They are innately practical and fun-loving, and while I had doubted whether or not it would be a good idea for me to undertake my first research trip for my first book with such a large crowd, I suddenly knew that having them along was exactly as it was supposed to be.

Golf carts be damned.

We spent the better part of an hour in the air-conditioned information center, perusing the artifacts of the battle, including one of the largest miniaturizations I had ever seen. It depicted various stages of the battle, with model ships that emulated the movement of both sides on that day. It was the kind of setup a grown man who never got over his childhood hobby of building model trains might have, encased in glass and detailed to the smallest degree. I struck up a conversation with a ranger—decked out in green National Park Service sweater and Smokey Bear hat—who seemed completely unimpressed that I was researching a book, though he did dig into a plastic file container for additional pamphlets to aid my research. These weren't the abbreviated pamphlets that just any tourist could get to, mind you; these were special, and he handed them to me with the same zest one might have when handing a toll ticket to a truck driver in the middle of the night in nowhere Nebraska.

"You ought to watch the movie," he said, looking over my shoulder to another visitor who might need help and pointing to a door that looked like it could lead to a conference room. "Everything you need to know is in the movie."

And the movie *was* good. It explained the mechanics of the battle, where the ships entered, how they maneuvered. In a sense, it was a moving version of the big display out in the lobby, only better because it had a soundtrack. I feigned taking notes, if for no other reason than to show Uncle Mark that I knew how to, and afterward went back to the lobby to have a closer look at the ten-foot-high statue of Perry that dominated the room. His pose was awkwardly heroic, as if he had just made a gesture beckoning his men forward into the throes of the battle, and even in marble he looked young. Indeed, when he made his famous stand, he was four years younger than I was on that day and the bearer of more responsibility than I will probably ever know. In that moment, the one in which he is now forever frozen in stone, he looks every bit the American hero—the uniform, the determined gaze, and the hair, perfectly windblown and askew.

In a way, the statue was almost cartoonish. I couldn't help but wonder if he ever actually stood that way—half-twisted like he was wringing himself out after a dip in the pool. But the longer I stared, the more I felt like I was looking at someone, something I could never be. The hair alone—swept forward across his brow and curled from wind with the kind of sideburns any facially follicularly challenged man like myself would envy—was enough to make me almost swoon. I thought, "Damn, he looks cool." Really cool. Miles Davis cool. What I wouldn't give to look that cool, if only for one day. I imagined myself traipsing down the aisle of my suburban grocery when someone stops me to ask directions. And I turn and point the way to the frozen peas, striking an indelible and terrifically manly image that would last through time.

Just as I was considering whether or not to change hair products, I noticed that my traveling companions had made their way toward the exit onto the east lawn that leads to the memorial itself. So much for my superhero ways.

The cost to ride the elevator to the observation deck of the memorial was three dollars, which Dad said seemed excessive as the afternoon had turned hazy and the television screens in the information center with live feeds from cameras on the top had shown that we wouldn't have been able to see much anyway. So we decided to take in the lecture being given by two young rangers—interns on summer break from college—in full period costume.

One was dressed in a sailor's uniform; the other wore the coat, bandoliers, and tight pants of a soldier. They took turns lecturing, like some sort of cut-rate Laurel and Hardy, playing off one another. At one point while the sailor was speaking, the soldier reached into his off-white cotton haversack and pulled out a bright blue Nalgene bottle to sneak a few sips of water before his next spiel. There really is nothing like the national-park system when it comes

The statue of Perry inside the visitors center, with Perry's Victory and International Victory Memorial in the background. I wonder if I could strike such a manly pose reaching for some frozen peas.

to authenticity. They carried muskets and, during their talk, asked questions of the audience of about forty people who had gathered on the stone steps at the base of the memorial. I don't mean to sound like a show-off or anything, but the questions were easy, and it seems that between my dad, a history buff, my uncle, an expert in anything involving black powder and a projectile, and me, a person who had actually watched the film inside and taken more than one whole page of notes, we answered them all.

"Can anyone tell me who won the War of 1812?" asked one of the rangers.

"Um, no one," I said, rather sheepishly.

"That's right," he said, ready to move on. But I wasn't quite done.

"It was concluded by the Treaty of Ghent without either side gaining or losing any territory or power." He seemed pleased that someone had taken the initiative to answer fully.

"There are two things that every navy needs," said the other. "The first is ships. Can anyone tell me what the other is?"

"People," said my dad, rather confidently and, I thought, obviously. Still the ranger looked surprised, as if he had asked that question all summer long and no one had gotten it right. But he had just finished talking about the British forcing American merchant sailors into conscription to fight the Napoleonic wars, so it didn't seem a terrible stretch to think maybe people had something to do with his answer.

Later in the talk the first ranger, whom I found out was studying to be a teacher at my alma mater and getting college credit for his role in the National Park Service, was discussing firearms of the day. "Muskets were notoriously inaccurate. Can anyone tell me why?"

Earlier in the presentation a man in the audience identified himself as a lieutenant colonel in the army. I figured he would answer this one, but Uncle Mark, who has an impressive gun collection locked away in his basement armory, spoke up.

"Because the barrels aren't rifled," he said. "The bullets come out flat, like a knuckleball."

Heimbuch boys 3, Rangers 0. It was like we were playing the kindergarten version of *Jeopardy!* and the rest of the crowd eyed us as if we were ringers sent in to spoil their good time.

After a brief and somewhat entertaining demonstration of the unreliability of period field weaponry—the soldier Marcus (the one who was studying to be a teacher) had made an off-handed comment about how the muskets of the age would only reliably fire twice in a row before requiring cleaning. Sure enough, two shots and then the other intern went to fire a third, only to have the musket misfire. He spent nearly five minutes clearing the powder pan and cleaning other parts of the firing mechanism before it finally did go bang. "That would have happened a lot," said Marcus. "Only try to imagine having to do that with a bunch of British soldiers shooting at you." Indeed, I thought, that would have sucked.

Our visit to the memorial was finished. I spoke with Marcus about campus life for a few minutes before catching up with Dad and Uncle Mark, who were looking at the signs spread around the base of the memorial. We rejoined the rest of our group for ice cream and discovered a bus that would take us back to the ferry launch. This made Rebecca very happy—the combination of shopping in the tourist stores, eating some mint-chocolate-chip ice cream, and not having to walk back the way we came—and I could suddenly foresee the end of my punishment for the golf cart episode.

We were on the island only three or four hours, and my first big research trip had yielded little more than a twelve-minute film, some single-spaced pamphlets tucked away in my rucksack, five photos, and one of the tastiest hot dogs I have ever eaten. I realized straightaway that finding the lasting legacy of the North Coast's most important historical moment might be more difficult than I had thought, especially given the seeming lack of interest from the population at large. Still, as the sun began to set and the ferry carried us back to the mainland at a lumbering pace, I realized that this was exactly what I was looking for—a bit of adventure and fun tracking down a history I had long lived with. I had just begun to scratch the surface of what I was after, but the groundwork was laid for the rest of this project. If nothing else, that was enough to fuel my enthusiasm and continue on.

≈ 2 ≈

Notes on the Battle

A week or two after returning home to Cincinnati from the lake, I started to feel a bit anxious. I liked Perry, or what I knew about him, but not just for his victory. It was his swagger that drew me. But I wondered if it was a mistake to try to write about history. I'm not a historian. I lack the patience to do the research. I also worried about writing about this particular kind of history, the history of a battle. My dad would know the story, and I worried about letting him down. Someone may read the book and shoot it full of holes. Plus, was it really what I wanted to do? The Battle of Lake Erie does rank among the pinnacle battles of American history. It's certainly no Gettysburg or Bull Run. Nor is it as famous as the Battle of the Bulge, or Lexington and Concord. But this lack of notoriety should not be mistaken for a lack of importance. Any event in which people, mostly men, lost their lives in armed conflict can only be described as important. While motives and goals and accomplishments of particular battles vary in degree of historical significance, there has never, and I mean never, been a person killed in conflict whose mother was not brought to tears. All battles and all casualties of battles are important.

But the Battle of Lake Erie, in terms of historical importance, has two things working against it. Number one is that it was a naval battle and, Trafalgar aside, naval battles seldom get the popular attention terrestrial battles get. Naval battles—and I'm speaking in generalities here, so please no angry letters—seem to have smaller body counts than those fought on land, particularly if they were fought prior to the Second World War, and they are usually shorter in duration. It's not often that a naval battle is waged over the course of months for obvious reasons of supplies and the ability to dig in. There are no trenches on the surface of the water, so targets tend to be engaged quickly and sunk, captured, or lost in a series of evasive maneuvers. There's also something less naked, less relatable, about naval battles. If you are interested in, say, Civil War infantry battles, you can go to a place like Antietam and walk the grounds where it was fought. You can put yourself in the shoes of the Yankees and Johnnys Reb and easily transport yourself to that day.

If a battle was fought on a square-rigged ship in the middle of a lake, it's awfully difficult to re-create those circumstances as a casual traveler. Naval history requires a good deal more imagination and research. Understanding these types of battles is more an academic exercise and thus more work. And who wants to do that kind of work? So there will always be a certain mystery to battles fought on the sea, a mystery that's difficult to nail down.

The other big thing working against the Battle of Lake Erie is that it was fought during the War of 1812. In the pantheon of American wars, the War of 1812 ranks just below the Spanish-American War and the war between Michigan and Ohio over the land rights to Toledo in terms of popular intrigue. It lacks the polished masculinity of Teddy Roosevelt's Rough Riders and the trivial kitsch of the Toledo engagement. No, the big wars in American history—and you can ask any seventh-grade student this question—are the Revolutionary War, Civil War, World War II, and Vietnam. But surely these aren't the only wars the country has fought. I mean, the very name World War II suggests that it was a sequel of something.

The trip to Put-in-Bay had been informative, and the pamphlets secreted to me by the park ranger added to my knowledge of the battle. But I needed to know more. As a product of my information-glutted and inherently lazy generation, I began my research the new old-fashioned way—with Google. The search engine gained traction as a bastion of information when I was in college, and I think seldom a day has gone by since my graduation when I have not Googled something. Recipes for Cornish hens that I will never prepare, the proper maintenance of disposable razors, the proper calculations for converting inches to meters, and, I must sadly admit, my own name. There's something exhilarating about punching up your name in the thin Google search bar and having it return results. I have a fairly unusual name, so I rarely find a Google doppelganger. The results generally have something to do with old newspaper articles I have written that are now stored on a basement server in a newspaper morgue. I read some of these stories and think *Good God, what were you thinking writing a lead like that?* Or *How do I go about deleting this to make sure no one ever, ever reads this pathetic attempt at writing?* No doubt I will one day Google myself only to find an electronic version of this chapter and once again be shamed by my complete lack of writing ability.

The search for "Battle of Lake Erie" turned up only a few results, mostly having to do with books written by a man named Gerard Altoff who, for the better part of three decades, served as the head ranger and historical master of the Perry Memorial. By all accounts, he is among the greatest living experts on the battle and on Oliver Hazard Perry. I make a note to reach out to him and continue my scroll through search results.

The Wikipedia entry on the battle is surprisingly stark, but the poignant facts are there. Early on the morning of September 10, 1813, Commodore Oliver Hazard Perry and his fleet of nine ships advanced on a British column north of Rattlesnake Island. A bloody battle ensued in which Perry's flagship, the brig *Lawrence*, was almost completely destroyed. More than a hundred men died or were injured on the decks before Perry lowered his colors and left the ship aboard a small rowboat, transferring his flag to the other brig—the largest ship in his fleet—the *Niagara*. Ironically, Perry's battle flag bore the famous (at the time) last words of American Navy Captain John Lawrence—"Don't Give Up the Ship." The *Niagara* had failed to engage in the three-hour battle and was unscathed, seaworthy and armed. Perry took control of the brig and within fifteen minutes managed to end the battle by overtaking the two biggest British gunships, the *Queen Charlotte* and the *Detroit*, the masts of which had become entangled in shifting winds and the thrum of battle. Alas, for the British, who had come looking for Perry in order to open resupply lines from the eastern end of Lake Erie for the starving soldiers at the embattled Fort Detroit, there was no joy in the end. Perry was victorious and all ships returned to the nearby islands to bury their dead and make repairs before being transported to Erie, Pennsylvania, for a long winter of captivity and repairs.

Perry's famous transfer from the Lawrence *to the* Niagara *during the Battle of Lake Erie. While the facts of the transfer vary, the truth of his heroism is incontrovertible.*

The battle proved an important victory for the Americans, who had lost most of what is now Michigan with hardly a struggle in the early days of the war and who, with almost shocking alacrity, had failed every attempt to make inroads into the British Canadian territories. In short, the good ol' U.S. of A. had been getting its butt handed to it for more than a year by a superior force, and the prospects of the war were dim. Perry's victory represented a sea change in the war, taking it from a losing proposition of maniacal avarice to a stalwart standoff. Go America!

Still, even in this brief description of the battle and its context to the rest of the war, several aspects of Perry's actions that day struck me as not only incredibly heroic but sumptuously lucky. How, after all, does a ship's commander lose more than a hundred men in close combat with a superior enemy and not receive so much as a scratch? Or how about that row from the *Lawrence* to the *Niagara*? Historical accounts claim the distance between the two ships was roughly a half mile. And yet he managed to ride a rowboat over that distance in the midst of fierce battle, carrying his battle flag, and remained untouched. Not even a splinter. It was mind-boggling. This man belongs in the pantheon of American heroism right next to Davy Crockett and Daniel Boone. I wanted to see the movie, starring someone like John Wayne or Steve McQueen calmly taking a stroll across the bloody, pitted deck of his ship, stepping over the bodies of sailors and lowering himself into a rowboat. John Williams could write the soundtrack to play as Perry assesses the situation from wave level then clambers aboard the *Niagara*, wresting control from its captain, Jesse Elliot, and putting a violent period on the end of the story.

But this wasn't a movie. This was a real person. The plot reads like a script, but here he was, twenty-six years old and hundreds of miles from his home in Newport, Rhode Island, acting with equal parts bravery and foolishness and, in the moment, creating for himself a legend that would keep at least you and I interested two hundred years later.

"Perry was kind of a hothead, a glory seeker," Gerard Altoff tells me over the phone from his home near Williamsburg, Virginia. "In those days seeking glory was like seeking fortune. You could live the rest of your life off glory."

Altoff is retired now, living near the epicenter of early-American history. I read both of his books about the battle, *Oliver Hazard Perry and the Battle of Lake Erie* and *A Signal Victory: The Lake Erie Campaign 1812–1813*. Both provide the mechanical descriptions of the battle—what ships moved where and when—and outline the incidents that reflect Perry's remarkable good luck. Both seem to laud Perry's actions, but neither reflects a particular admiration for Perry the man.

My noodling Googling also turned up a poem about the battle, written by poet Philip Freneau, on the James Madison Institute's Web site.

"Battle of Lake Erie," by Philip Freneau
September 10, 1813

"To clear the lake of Perry's fleet
And make his flag his winding sheet
This is my object—I repeat—"
Said Barclay, flush'd with native pride,

To some who serve the british crown:—
But they, who dwell beyond the moon,
Heard this bold menace with a frown,
Nor the rash sentence ratified.

Ambition so bewitch'd his mind,
And royal smiles had so combined
With skill, to act the part assign'd
He for no contest cared, a straw;

The ocean was too narrow far
To be the seat of naval war;
He wanted lakes, and room to spare,
And all to yield to Britain's law.

And thus he made a sad mistake;
Forsooth he must possess the lake,
As merely made for England's sake
To play her pranks and rule the roast;

Where she might govern, uncontrol'd,
An unmolested emprire hold,
And keep a fleet to fish up gold,
To pay the troops of George Provost.

The ships approach'd, of either side,
And Erie, on his bosom wide
Beheld two hostile natives ride,
Each for the combat well prepared:

The lake was smooth, the sky was clear,
The martial drum had banish'd fear,
And death and danger hover'd near,
Though both were held in disregard.

From lofty heights their colors flew,
And Britain's standard all in view,
With frantic valor fired the crew
That mann'd the guns of queen Charlotte.

"And we must Perry's squadron take,
And England shall command the lake;—
And you must fight for Britain's sake,
(Said Barclay) sailors, will you not?"

Assent they gave with heart and hand;
For never yet a braver band
To fight a ship, forsook the land,
Than Barclay had on board that day;—

The guns were loosed the games to win,
Their muzzles gaped a dismal grin,
And out they pull'd their tompion pin,
The bloody game of war to play.

But Perry soon, with flowing sail,
Advanced, determined to prevail,

When from his bull-dogs flew the hail
Directed full at queen Charlotte.

His wadded guns were aim'd so true,
And such a weight of ball they threw,
As, Barclay said, he never knew
To come, before, so scalding hot!

But still, to animate his men
From gun to gun the warrior ran
And blazed away and blazed again—
Till Perry's ship was half a wreck:

They tore away both tack and sheet,—
Their victory might have been complete,
Had Perry not, to shun defeat
In Lucky moment left his deck.

Repairing to another post,
From another ship he fought their host
And soon regain'd the fortune lost,
And down, his flag the briton tore:

With loss of arm and loss of blood
Indignant, on his decks he stood
To witness Erie's crimson flood
For miles around him, stain'd with gore!

Thus, for dominion of the lake
These captains did each other rake,
And many a widow did they make;—
Whose is the fault, or who to blame?—

The briton challenged with his sword,
The yankee took him at his word,
With spirit laid him close on board—
They're ours—he said—and closed the game.

Not exactly "The Raven" or "O Captain! My Captain!," but still
pretty compelling stuff. Always count on an epic poet to add a touch
of drama to any situation. Barclay had a tough task that day. Just the

day before, supplies at Fort Malden had dwindled to a single day's ration of flour for bread. The British, who had stormed through Michigan from the north, at Fort Michilimackinac, all the way down to Detroit, had relied heavily on Lake Erie as a means of transporting goods and equipment to the western forts. That dominance of the lower Great Lakes was challenged by the construction of the Lake Erie fleet and, ultimately, destroyed by Perry and his noble band of sailors.

As I read, I imagined myself on board the *Lawrence* with heavy artillery zipping past my head. I wondered if I would have the courage to see 80 percent of my crew dead or injured and decide to risk my hide to win at all costs. Probably not, since I have never had the courage to do something as daring as join the military, let alone command a fleet in battle. I was always scared of basic training. Do you have any idea how much they make you run? I try to avoid running, unless being chased by a rabid squirrel or in pursuit of the last box of Cinnamon Life on the store shelf. It doesn't suit me. When I run, I look like a polar bear in need of a bathroom. It's not pretty. Plus, with the military, there's always a risk of, you know, death. And I'd kind of like to take a long time to die. Seventy-five, eighty-five years if possible. My dad was in the army. Right out of college, an engineering degree from Iowa State and an officer's commission. I have always had a lot of respect for him for that. Every time I meet a soldier—and I have met several covering military affairs as part of a few newspaper beats—I feel a sense of inferiority. It's not that they are better people than I am, just that they did what I was unwilling to do. At the same age my dad was wearing a uniform and serving death notices to new widows on the South Side of Chicago, I was married and working as a reporter. But whenever he talks about the army, I am all ears. Whenever an opportunity to cover something military-related has cropped up, I have volunteered.

After reading all I could find online, two books by Altoff, and a biography of Perry titled *Oliver Hazard Perry: Honor Courage and*

Patriotism in the Early US Navy, by Bowling Green State University Professor David Curtis Skaggs, I felt I had enough of a handle on the mechanics of the battle to continue my journey. But I needed to get out, to hit the road. And the next place I wanted to go had nothing to do with the battle or even Perry, except that it bears his name. The next step of my chase after the commodore involved a trip north to Perry, Ohio.

I have never had what you might call the fighting spirit, but I do have a wandering soul. My wanderlust, however, has never led to much. I tend to wander mentally, taking imagined trips between work tasks and home. I picture myself, lottery winnings in the bank, a new Volvo in the garage. I'd drive to Maine and stock up on gear at L.L.Bean. I'd follow the Trans-Canada Highway from Atlantic to Pacific or just meander around the Midwest for a while. Even in my fantasies, I'm not too adventurous. I've never dreamed of climbing a mountain—good God, that sounds like a lot of work—or scuba diving in the Great Barrier Reef. In my mind, travel should include no more than two nights in a row in the outdoors. I love being outside, but I love a Continental breakfast a bit too much to settle for twigs and berries over an open fire. No, a dream trip for me would be two weeks of somewhat familiar territory, taking time to make it more familiar. I was born too mild, though I do possess the wanderer's wonder. If Kerouac is 51 Flavors, I'm vanilla with the potential for becoming French vanilla. But at least I want to be out there, right? I want to chase something, even if it means not going too far from home.

And that's why I found myself sneaking away from a family reunion later that summer to a speck on the map—to chase Perry in the Ohio town named after him. I still didn't know much about him, but I understood enough to know that I would never be capable of doing the things that he did. That doesn't mean I'm not curious by association. It just means I might not sail against the greatest naval force on earth, might reconsider my choice of vocations and take up farming or weaving. I was already envious of Perry and his swagger, the same way I was envious of Kerouac or my high school friend Kevin. They put themselves ahead of others' expectations for them. They were brave and a little arrogant; I apologize for asking the waitress for more ice water at Perkins. So in a lot of ways, I realized then, I wasn't just chasing Perry or a piece of history, I was chasing a piece of me—the piece that throws caution to the wind and chases his dreams. You know, within reason.

~3~

Perry, Ohio

I took a left off the main highway right in front of the small, squat windowless building with the enormous Hell's Angels insignia bolted to the side and then followed the long access road toward the unfinished hourglass shape of the massive cooling tower. It was a lot bigger than I had imagined it. *They* were, actually. There were twin towers, but only one had ever been used, and on this summer afternoon it was puffing a plume of steam over the lake. The access road was empty, and as I got closer to the gate I saw the sign: PERRY NUCLEAR POWER PLANT. NO TRESPASSING.

Was that what I was doing? Trespassing? On the grounds of a nuclear power plant? This is crazy, I thought. Images of men clad in black cargo pants and serious-looking boots swinging from the trees and popping out of the sewer in front of my car made my palms a little moist, despite the James Bond mystery and excitement of it all. As I approached the gated driveway, I expected Homeland Security commandos to put a hood over my head and whisk me off on a Learjet to some country I've never heard of and throw me in a prison cell putrid with the scent of human waste. "They are going to waterboard me," I said out loud, "and President Bush would have absolutely no problem with that."

The facility drew nearer. I couldn't explain it, but for some rea-son I felt I had to inspect it. There was something duplicitous about it—a nuclear power plant bearing the name of a man who never saw the illumination cast by a lightbulb or felt the pallid breeze of central heating. Of course, that it is named the Perry Nuclear Power Plant is a matter of circumstance. It happens to be located in Perry, Ohio. The name was not a homage to the Oliver Hazard Perry I am interested in. But the name of the town was, or so I thought before speaking to Mary, the curator of the Perry Historical Society's small but lovely museum. She's what drew me to the farthest reaches of Cleveland's eastern suburbs this day, and just before I got to the unmanned gate, I turned the wheel hard and followed the same access road back out. I really am the biggest wussy ever.

Just before I buried the accelerator of my small car, I paused to look into the guardhouse adjacent to the front gates of the facility. It was empty. And, as near as I could tell, it had been for some time. I wasn't quite sure how to feel about that. On one hand, I probably wouldn't be arrested or swept off to a foreign country with no extra-dition treaty. On the other hand, I thought maybe it was sending the wrong signal in this post-9/11 world to leave the front door of a nuclear power plant unguarded—unless you count the Hell's Angels clubhouse at the end of the drive as security. In that case, everything is fine.

❧⸳❦

I found Mary by the purest of accidents. Her name was listed on a Web site somewhere, and I e-mailed her asking if there was anything in Perry that might be of use in my adventure. I was thinking a statue or a bell cast from the iron of one of the *Niagara's* cannons. Perhaps a historical marker. Those were always good for a quick read and a picture. Mary encouraged me by writing that a portion of the Perry Historical Society's museum was dedicated to the commodore and the Battle of Lake Erie. This was good news.

Mary e-mailed directions, and we arranged to meet on a Saturday afternoon in July. If the definition of a small town is a cross-roads, then Perry is a three-way intersection. Far from the myth of golden streets paid for by the nuclear facility, the town—if you could call it that, as there was no discernible central business district—is sleepy and quiet. It's the type of place I've always dreamed of retiring to, and an exact replica—down to the lack of sidewalks and the plethora of plywood yard ornamentation depicting a fat woman bent over—of the type of place that makes my wife's skin crawl.

The museum, as it turned out, was once the town hall, and it had been donated—or near-donated—to the historical society when a new, better one was built. It was small, maybe thirty by fifty feet, with a tall ceiling and the vestiges of a choir loft, so it was no real surprise to learn that it had once been a church. Mary was nothing like I imagined her. From her e-mail, I imagined a silver-haired, lithe woman in her sixties, like Bea Arthur when she was on *The Golden Girls*. But I was greeted by a shortish woman with mostly pepper hair and the broad ethnic features that always scream to me: Pennsylvania. Coal-mining town. Italian. And I was right on all counts.

Mary was surprised by my relative youth—I do have a youngish face for a thirty-year-old—and she was almost painfully polite and sweet. Touring the one-room museum with her, I felt like a child prodigy for having any knowledge about Oliver Hazard Perry. I half-expected to be rewarded with a gold star and an extra cookie just before nap time.

I was here to do a job. Indeed, I had driven all the way from our home in Cincinnati, a distance of 250 miles or so, to see what the magical Oliver Hazard Perry wing would hold, what insights I could find to help me understand him. When I had stepped into the small entryway and had not been immediately blown over by a multimedia display of the battle, I had assumed that what I came to find was in a basement or back building or something. This museum, this room, really held nothing but a bunch of old stuff.

I know that sounds moronic. It is a museum after all, but these were not artifacts of historical importance. They were articles of personal importance. There were wedding dresses and soldiers' uniforms donated by local residents, or by their families after they died. Bits of newspapers and scraps of metal brought back from distant wars.

When at last Mary led me to the OHP wing, it was nothing more than an alcove to an emergency exit with two lithographs of the battle, a sketch of Oliver Hazard Perry, a print of an ancient photo made at the unveiling of the statue of the commodore that once graced Cleveland's Public Square, and a description of the events of September 10, 1813, that made the Wikipedia listing look like the Library of Congress.

It was all very neat to see, but after the drive up and my near-encounter with both the Hell's Angels and Homeland Security, I had hoped for quite a bit more about the town's namesake—at least I had assumed it was named for him.

"There was some controversy about that," said Mary, whose sweet nature (equal measures librarian and Red Cross aid worker) made me feel a bit like I was interviewing my own grandmother, albeit a shorter, Pennsylvania Italian version. "A few years back a teacher at the junior high tried to prove that the town was not named for Oliver Hazard Perry but for his brother who settled here some time after the war."

"Really?" I said, thinking, Why not? This place might as well have been named for someone else. It's not as if the legacy of the presumed namesake—who it turns out never actually set foot in Perry—was thoroughly preserved.

"But I did some research," Mary said. "And the town of Perry was founded in 1815, just two years after the battle. That other Perry the teacher was talking about didn't come here until 1820, so there's no way it could be named after him."

What a relief, I thought. And thank goodness for Mary. I was seething, feeling like I had just paid seventy-five dollars for a movie that didn't even play, like I had been somehow ripped off. But when Mary offered to show me around the rest of the museum, I graciously accepted, as men who grew up boys in the Midwest with their grandmothers around were obliged to do. But I was basically 0 for 2. The visit to Put-in-Bay had been more trouble—what with the golf cart fiasco and all—than it had been worth. I hadn't learned all that much I hadn't found on Wikipedia. I hadn't been to the top of the monument, I hadn't been stumped in the Q&A with the college interns. And now this place, which I had such high hopes for, was letting me down. I had probably built up Perry and Mary and the tiny museum a bit too much in my head. I had expected to find the unfound, to uncover a treasure trove of insight and artifact. What I found were copies of lithographs in store-bought frames behind Aunt Edna's famous pie tin and Great Uncle Earl's spare set of false teeth.

I couldn't be mad at Mary or at the museum. They both were doing exactly what they were supposed to be doing—preserving a bit of the village's past. Only nothing much had happened here in the 190 years of its existence. That wasn't Mary's fault. I was mad at

The "Perry Wing" of the village's museum. For some reason I doubt the fire extinguisher was period-authentic.

myself for not vetting things, for not planning, for not being willing to accept things the way they were. I am a dreamer. And the problem with dreaming is that reality rarely syncs up with expectation. But since I was already here, I figured the least I could do would be to take Mary's tour. Had I not been so distracted by the feeling that I was wasting time, I probably would have seen the beauty of the Perry Museum. It was extraordinary for being ordinary, for guarding the history of the everyday past. It was exactly what I had always believed was great about history—that everyone and everything can be remembered, and should be by those willing to do so. Mary was more than a curator; she was the keeper of the town's past. I respect and admire that, which is why I still feel a little bad for what happened next.

We were halfway through the exhibit of World War I–era pens when I suddenly felt a terrible pressure in my stomach. Here in this cavernously quiet room I felt the need—that familiar and troubling sensation of pressure needing to be released. It must have been the McDonald's breakfast I ate on my way to the museum, or maybe it was just that time of day that I would take for granted under noisier circumstances, but as Mary spoke about how the little boys just love to see the unexploded artillery shells, the sensation grew unbearable. I felt I could burst, and Mary's voice, so gentle and unaware of the anguish I was feeling over what I had to do, trailed off into the darker recesses of my brain while an image began to form of my jellylike entrails splattered all over the antique piano—the prize of the collection—and old photos of Mildred So-and-So on her family's farm outside of town in 1928.

I was getting seriously uncomfortable here and had to think fast to find relief, and yet I didn't want to do anything that might be construed as rude to Mary.

Then, like divine gastric intervention, it hit me. I walked around to the other side of the chest-high display case in search of a creaky place in the floor I had remembered stepping on earlier.

When at last I did find the spot, I stood squarely on it and sort of rocked back and forth while at the same time relieving myself of the terrible pressure. I must have made a grimace, which one is apt to do when trying to control the release of a notably powerful fart, because Mary asked if I was all right.

"Oh yes, I'm fine," I said. And she commenced rounding the display case where I was sure she would discover the odor that had boiled over from inside of me. "Say, Mary," I said, "I was wondering if you could tell me about the painting in the vestibule."

Luckily, she fell for my diversionary question and led the way out of the big main room toward the entry hall, which had formerly been the church's narthex. We left my contribution to the historical-society museum, and Mary explained the true source of the town's fame. It seems that Perry, this bucolic hamlet of questionable lineage, had a pseudo-famous resident. Or it once did.

Hugh Mosher, who was born in Perry some time in the mid-nineteenth century, was a world-class fife player. Something probably akin to being a first-rate juggler or mime today. But he was well known, particularly in Ohio, where fife playing was evidently premium entertainment in those days. It turns out that Mosher's passion for the dwarf flute earned him an opportunity to take his place in American history long after shuffling from this mortal coil. In 1875 he posed for painter Archibald MacNeal Willard's work titled *The Spirit of '76*, a print of which hangs even now on the wall just inside the door to the museum. Willard, it would seem, was a stickler for details, bringing in an actual fife player to pose for the role of fife player in his famous composition. Annie Leibovitz could do with such devotion to detail.

Mary was kind enough to tell me everything she knew about Mosher and the local fire department and the local school district, which had, since the 1970s, received huge annual tithing from the power plant, to the tune of some twenty million dollars in free annual money. This abundance was legendary in the greater Cleveland of my youth. In fact, there were rumors that the source of Perry High School's boys' tennis teams' great success was annual summer trips to Europe to play tournaments, all on the school's dime. The money was so overwhelming that, according to Mary, the school board seriously considered gold-plated doorknobs when drawing up plans for a new middle school. Imagine that. I remember longing for toilet paper that didn't rip at the slightest touch when I was in junior high, let alone hardware crafted from precious metals.

Toward the end of our conversation, Mary said she hoped she had helped with my book and asked that I send a copy along once it was finished. She would be sure it ended up in the museum archives, which I presumed to mean some shoe boxes in the attic. I thanked her profusely and stepped out into the midday sun, hoping she had a poor sense of smell from her childhood in coal country and desperately wanting a beer.

≈.≈

Before I reached the railroad tracks on my way out of town, I noticed a restaurant on the side of the road. The Pirate's Cove. Slim, high windows, a blackened door, and one of those hand-painted signs lit from the inside beaconed me near. I knew that, despite my disappointments at the museum, this place would have beer, and it would be cold and good.

It took a moment or two for my eyes to adjust to the darkness. The barroom was dark and lovely and almost empty, save for a woman tending bar and a man sitting in the far corner, flirting with her over empty glasses. There was something deliciously seedy and small-townish about the Pirate's Cove. For starters, the name is one you might find only in a town like this, with its modest appeal to tourists from as far away as Cleveland Heights or Chagrin Falls. And despite being well maintained and relatively clean, every wooden surface in the bar seemed to have a sticky sheen on it that was both amusing and disgusting. And even on a sunny afternoon, the place was dark with a slight reddish pallor cast about everywhere and the sick blue glow of a television mounted behind the bar.

Yes, this place would have beer. Lots of it.

The bar maiden, whose name I couldn't hear over the television, which was blaring a Ben Stiller comedy so loudly I thought I felt the bar quake, was stunningly pretty, but not in a magazine-model sort of way. She looked like that girl in high school who sent tingles down the back of your neck and into your loins just by being near you. I surmised she had been a capricious, possibly even wild youth because she seemed so comfortable handling the tipsy man at the end of the bar. She seemed like she would be comfortable handling anyone. I liked her before she said anything and immediately, as I so often do, began formulating a back story in my head that explained what a beautiful woman would be doing in a place like this on such a perfect sunny day. She was probably popular in high school, but not a cheerleader. No, she was popular with the local guys, farmers or auto mechanics. She was smarter than anyone gave her credit for but did not go to college after graduation. Maybe she didn't have the money, maybe she made the error in judgment of sleeping with her boyfriend without a condom—you know, just once because he really needed to. Maybe she had family issues, but any way you sliced it, she never left Perry except for a trip with a friend that still brings a smile to her face. And now she was tending bar because she had inherited the place from an uncle or an old man who fancied her. And she was happy—happy with beer-league softball and tailgating at Browns games and spending Christmas at her mom's place.

I was forming the image of her boyfriend—a cell phone salesman in my mind—when she brought me back to the present by asking what I would like to drink. "Oh, uh, I don't know," I stammered, trying to figure out where the hell I was. "What do you recommend?"

"This your first time here?" It was a question, but the way she said it, it sounded like a statement.

"Uh-huh."

"Then you need to have the Pirate's Booty. It's a mystery beer."

"Sounds good," I said. "I'll have that." Though I was suspicious of what mystery beer in a place like the Pirate's Cove entailed. Probably fermented urine and fish tails or something like that. She brought me the biggest, coldest beer I have ever seen, and when I drank it I was a bit surprised, let down really, to learn that it was just Budweiser, but it was the best Budweiser I had ever tasted. I took her up on her offer of a second, and her recommendation of the Pirate Burger for lunch. She promised that it was not made from pirates.

Maybe it was the buzz from the first beer or just an inherent belief that two men drinking alone at a bar should speak to one another, but I soon found myself talking to Dave, a long-haul trucker who had just stopped in for a bag of chips, a couple cold ones, and a couple shots of Yukon Jack before he took his wife to a wedding later that afternoon. I told Dave that I had just met Mary at the historical society and asked if he knew her.

"Mary? Everybody knows Mary," he said. "And Mary knows everybody. Hell of a lady. What were you meeting her for?"

I told him about my book and my presently fruitless quest to learn everything I could possibly learn about Oliver Hazard Perry and the Battle of Lake Erie.

"Oliver Perry?" The way Dave said it, I had an inkling that the good commodore might be a subject of interest for him. "Never heard of him, who is he?"

"He's the guy this town is named for," I said, astounded and trying my best not to sound that way.

"Sumbitch," he said, like it was one word. "Had no idea."

I could see that Dave was not going to be of much use in terms of historical research, but he just might be a fine lunchtime companion. Dave had lived in Perry for going on eighteen years and had never had an inkling to leave. Indeed, living in this place made him feel centered as his career took him all over the country. Perry was the perfect place to come home to, he said. It was quiet and nice and pleasant, unlike a lot of other places.

"Well, you seem like you know this area pretty well," I said, leading up to the most curious thing I had seen all day.

"Yup," he said, taking down a two-ounce shot of Yukon Jack in a quick tip of the chin.

"What about the Hell's Angels?"

"Nicest guys you ever met in your entire life," he said, without hesitation and with more than a touch of warmth, though that might have had something to do with his friend Jack from up north. "My property butts up to the back of that little place they got over off the highway, and I'll tell you, once you get to know them, there is nothing they wouldn't do for you."

"Really?" I said, feeling a pang of disappointment, since the most exciting moment of my day had been my imagined brush with danger near their clubhouse. Next he would probably tell me that the bikers were just a bunch of dentists and accountants out for Sunday rides. Or that there was no Homeland Security assault team stalking my every move.

"Yup, nice, nice guys. Helped me get my car out of the snow once." I bought Dave a drink, his fourth since I sat down, paid for my deliciously greasy Pirate Burger, fries, and two mystery beers, and headed out into the harsh light of afternoon.

My research would have to continue on another day. But I had learned a few things. First, I was going about this all wrong. I would never be able to sneak away for enough weekends to cover all the ground I wanted to cover. And even if I could, I wouldn't feel satisfied. This was my big thing, the thing I had hoped to do for most of my conscious life. Ever since I began reading travel and adventure books, since I realized my dad had given me a gift dragging me to those historic signposts along the way, since I realized that Oliver

Hazard Perry represented the zesty yin to my chicken-stock yang, I had wanted to do something like this. I needed a bold gesture. I needed to step out, to immerse myself in the journey. My first two forays—to Put-in-Bay and to Perry—were mere toes in the water. I needed to get out there and see what there was to see, to give my-self a shot at finding what was left of Perry around Lake Erie and challenge myself to be away—from work, from my family, and from my own self-restrictions. I needed to spend time walking in Perry's footsteps, reading the signs like my dad, and traveling the unknown road like my literary idols. I needed a road trip. A R-O-A-D trip. A chance to spread my unused wings.

The idea warmed me on the ride back to Cincinnati as I planned the places I would go. By myself. An open mind and an open road. I got excited. I thought about going to new places just because I was interested—not for a family trip, not for a work assignment, but because I wanted to. It would be the first step toward a bolder life. I just needed to ask my wife if it would be okay and try to get some time off of work. And make sure the kids would be okay. And figure out how to pay for it. And exactly where I would go and how I would get there and . . . oh, screw it. Kerouac never thought about that stuff. Why should I? I was no longer Craig the wannabe dreamer. I was Craig the doer, whatever needed to be done. I was going to chase Oliver Hazard Perry to the ends of the earth—or all the way around Lake Erie, whichever worked better with my schedule.

Look out, world. Here comes Craig Heimbuch—man of action, man of adventure, man with no clue what he's doing.

≈ 4 ≈

Setting the Scene

Oliver Hazard Perry had one job and one job only when he was given the commission as commodore of the Lake Erie fleet: build some boats, find the British fleet led by Commander Robert Barclay, and kill them. It was that simple. Or that direct, because when it came to facing even a frontier outpost of the most successful fighting unit in history, nothing is simple. And that is where Perry's luck came in.

As I mentioned earlier, the American war effort in 1812 and early 1813 had not been going well. The three-headed military leadership—the Secretary of War, the Secretary of the Army, and the Secretary of the Navy—differed greatly on strategy and approach. It was commonly thought that the best way to best the Brits would be to start with a full-frontal attack on the Eastern Canadian strongholds of Quebec and Montreal. But this plan never came to fruition, in part because of a dangerously fractured military structure and in part because of the reluctance of militiamen to cross borders. The militia was like a disorganized National Guard, and members of individual militias saw themselves as freedom fighters, defenders of their land, liberty, and families. They were meant to act as a deterrent in the case of invasion, not as an invading army.

The regular army and navy had been pared to bare minimum under the Jefferson administration. Immediately following the conclusion of the Revolutionary War, the founding fathers divided into factions. Those from the northeastern states preferred a strong federal government that helped boost their trade- and shipping-driven economies. The southern states preferred a loose confederation of relatively autonomous states, giving power to each state to govern as it saw fit—especially in the area of slavery. These differences made divining a structure of government difficult to say the least, and even after the ratification of the Constitution and Bill of Rights, there were those who feared for the stability of the nascent country. Jefferson, it seems, was one of those.

Apart from the overwhelming expense of maintaining a regular army and navy—which was considerable and put pressures on the already indebted federal coffers (Jefferson once made arrangements to pay back France for its Revolutionary-era loans in grain instead of cash)—there was a significant fear of an armed uprising. Fear of a coup and the opportunity to shed payroll (by releasing enlisted men and officers) and generate cash flow (by selling equipment and ships to the private sector) motivated the third president to trim the military to its barest bones so that by the time the War of 1812 was declared, a hybrid system of regular military and volunteer militiamen was the best President Madison could muster.

But militiamen were undisciplined, untrained, unreliable, and hesitant to march a single step into Canadian territory. There were several reasons for this attitude, including a sort of unionesque "that's not my job" stance as well as doubts about the necessity of the war—this was largely a conflict that would benefit northern traders who had been denied access to the British market and had lost sailors to impressments. The attitude also sprang from the fact that many of the nonnatives living in Canada (some estimates put it as high as 80 percent) were American born. Put yourself in the shoes of a militiaman from, say, Kentucky. Your unit is called into service and you walk all the way from the rolling hills of the Bluegrass State, across Ohio and Pennsylvania on nonexistent roads through harsh terrain, constantly concerned about the presence of native tribes you have been told would gladly eat you. You arrive in upstate New York. It's lovely, but when you get there an army officer barks orders at you and tells you to get yourself across the Hudson River to attack the people living there. Never mind that some of those people may be just like you and that this war was started by a president and congressmen you more than likely had no role in electing to benefit New Englanders with whom you share no common interests. You can start to see their hesitation. Militiamen were under no obligation to follow the army's orders; indeed, there was no real benefit for them to do so. Couple all this with the fact that your home is left undefended and the British Indian agents have been feeding tribes Scotch and firearms, and you can get a pretty clear picture of why these farmers and craftsmen might want nothing to do with an invasion of Canada.

So indecision and poor planning were hurting the efforts to make a big push into Canada in the east, and the English were making headway in the Old Northwest. Starting at Fort Michilimackinac in Northern Michigan—which is around the tip of the middle finger on that handy diagram many Michiganders use for a map—the English made their way down to Detroit with little resistance. The Americans had pushed into Canada near Fort Malden, but having no support from an inland navy, they were left dangerously exposed and were pushed back. Meanwhile Virginia-born future president General William Henry Harrison, who had served as governor of the Indiana Territory and liaison to native warrior-statesman Tecumseh, had amassed troops and marched from what is now Cincinnati to northwest Ohio. The march, particularly the part from what is now Tiffin to Perrysburg, was an arduous trudge across the boggy, sticky mire known as the Black Swamp—an appropriate and menacing name if there ever was one. It was here that he established a base called Fort Meigs.

If you can imagine Lake Erie as being roughly the size and shape of a slightly deflated football, then Fort Meigs is located on the bottom of the left-side tip of the ball. Fort Malden, the English stronghold situated near where the Detroit River meets Lake Erie, is at the top of the left-side tip. They are shockingly close together. With today's military technology, we have grown accustomed to hearing about shipboard missiles that can be launched from Boston Harbor to strike within ten feet of a target in Washington, D.C., and of those that can be fired from a Kansas wheat field and hit a target orbiting the earth. We have learned to kill each other from great distances, so it strikes us today as preposterous to be able to drive from Fort Meigs to Fort Malden—if border crossings weren't such a pain—in about the time it takes to finish a cup of coffee. The venti cup, to be sure, but a cup of coffee nonetheless. A modern fighter jet could take off from Fort Meigs, drop its destructive payload on Fort Malden, and be back before the kettle boils.

But William Henry Harrison did not have modern jet fighters or surface-to-air missiles. He had men with feet and the occasional horse and wagon, miles of swampy goo, and a significant river to cross in order to make a full-frontal attack on Fort Malden. Doing this would be impractical. From its position on the bank of the Detroit River, Fort Malden was all but impenetrable. Earthwork mounds as high as twelve feet were topped with cannon capable of creating a deadly crossfire. Below the mounds sat strategically built trenches that required an invading force to climb a steep grade into the waiting, and one would assume downwardly aimed, barrels of twelve-pound, long-barrel cannon. With no way to storm the fort, Harrison decided the best tactic would be to wait the British out in a land-based siege. Within the earthen walls of Fort Malden lived twelve hundred men who required food and ammunition. They would have to come out sometime.

And that was where Perry fit into the plan.

In a letter dated July 5, 1813, Harrison expressed his optimism to the young commodore. This was "a more favorable moment for fighting them than any other that will occur," wrote the future president. Harrison knew that a British retreat from Fort Malden would mean trooping more than a thousand men loaded down with equipment across the flat, barren land on the north side of Lake Erie, essentially leaving open all of the territory around the lake for the Americans. The British had to stay, they had to fight, but first they had to eat. As mentioned earlier, the summer of 1813 was harsh in southwestern Ontario, and the land yielded few crops. The British had been using unfettered access to Lake Erie like a drive to the supermarket. Commander Robert Barclay and the British Provincial Marine had no competition for the lake and were able to ferry supplies back and forth from the Niagara region—the right side of the deflated football near what is now Fort Niagara and Buffalo—to the other end of the lake. And Harrison, lacking any sort of naval support, was powerless to stop it.

So Perry was given an important assignment and one with long-lasting and far-reaching consequences. He had been stationed in New York and was told to go to what is now Erie, Pennsylvania, raise a crew, recruit soldiers and sailors, convert a few small ships for battle, and build two two-masted brigs. Quality was of relatively little consequence in this instance, but this was not the general trend. The War of 1812, you'll remember, was the conflict that turned the USS *Constitution*—a frigate built in 1797—into "Old Ironsides," so named because the construction and materials were of such high quality that British shot was said to have bounced off its sides. But Perry's orders were for speed and efficiency, not quality. The brigs *Niagara* and *Lawrence* were never intended for longevity. Historians commonly state that both ships were built for a single battle—the one that would either force Barclay and the British off the waters of Lake Erie or end American hope of retaining a stronghold in the Old Northwest.

To that end, and following the completion of construction, Perry followed the instructions Harrison had laid out for him in that letter from July 5, 1813. "You have no doubt been informed of the great adventures to be desired from occupying the harbour . . . [of] the Bass Islands. Your float stationed there with a detachment of the army would effectively cover most of the weak posts and a large part of the frontier of this State," wrote Harrison. The Bass Islands, on our convenient football model, are located right about where the seams begin on the left side. There are three Bass Islands—South, Middle and North—and a collection of smaller islands including Gibraltar, Rattlesnake, Pelee, Kelleys (actually this is the biggest of them on the American side), and others. Positioning his flotilla of nine ships in the harbor of South Bass Island, Perry had effectively cut off the British route to reinforcements. For Barclay to make his grocery run, he would have to get past the commodore, so it became a waiting game.

On more than one occasion, Perry sailed the thirty or so miles to the mouth of the Detroit and tried to tempt Barclay into a fight. But the captain could not be tempted. It was his fight to start; he alone was in the position to initiate contact. So Perry waited. He met with Harrison near what is now Sandusky, Ohio—home of the Cedar Point amusement park—to discuss contingencies. There were no radios, no text messages, nothing to provide instantaneous communication; so all military planning had to be done cooperatively. Contingencies had to be worked out ahead of time. Returning to the football analogy, it's like the coach and the quarterback sitting down on Tuesday and planning out an entire game to take place on Saturday. Perry and Harrison had to consider all possibilities. If Perry were able to stop Barclay, then Harrison would be in a position to attack Fort Malden. If Perry lost, then Barclay would have the run of the lake and could replenish his supplies at Fort Malden. Harrison's siege would be extended or, worse, for naught.

Unable to bait Barclay into a fight, Perry and his men—a combination of sailors, merchant marines, volunteer soldiers, and militiamen from as far away as Kentucky—waited for more than a month. Imagine waiting a month to face the possibility of your death, knowing that on any given day, if the winds were right, it just might show. The waiting must have been anxiety—and tedium—exemplified. And yet that's what they did: wait. And wait. And wait some more until early on the morning of September 10, 1813, a call came from a lookout that sails were spotted to the northwest. Barclay had picked his moment, and the waiting was about to end. Perry assembled his men and set out northwest toward Barclay's distant sails. He sailed into the wind, tacking back and forth, fighting for every inch of distance. Barclay, meanwhile, had the wind to his back. The breeze was light—a ranger at Perry's Victory and International Peace Memorial told me four to five miles an hour—but consistent. He sailed straight toward Perry, a slow and measured approach to conflict.

The British fired first. They didn't have the resources to cast new cannon for the battle, so they used recycled ones taken during the seizure of Fort Detroit. These were long guns—they fired smaller projectiles over a greater distance. Perry's ships were outfitted with carronades. Named for Carron, the town in Scotland where they were developed, Perry's guns had a reputation as ship killers. They were short range—a half mile or under—but packed a wallop with a thirty-pound projectile that would do a hell of a lot of damage to a wooden hull. But he had to get in close to use them.

Barclay's initial shots fell short, but the distance was closing between the two squadrons. At around 11 A.M. the first shots started connecting with their targets, and the battle began in earnest. Naval warfare in the early nineteenth century was a far cry from the technological smorgasbord of today. Whereas now a ship can fire a missile from three hundred miles away or a submarine can attack from under water with deadly result, warfare in the Age of Fighting Sail was a lot more personal. Opposing ships moved in close enough for

An artist's rendition of the Battle of Lake Erie. Even now it's hard to imagine the point-blank violence and confusion of war in the Age of Fighting Sail.

their crews to identify the enemy's facial expressions as they put a lit fuse to black powder and sent them to their death. As cannon roared their evil charm on and below decks, sharpshooters armed with muskets were cached in the rigging, attempting to pick off opposing officers. The scene was deafening, the pounding concussion of cannon sending ripples across the water and through the men on either side. Screams of agony as sailors were pelted with barely subsonic shards of wood and torn to ribbons by grapeshot.

Perry and his Lake Erie Squadron fought the unfriendly winds and sailed through a maelstrom of lead and smoke for three hours before he made his famous row from the *Lawrence* to the *Niagara*. They fought hard and managed to inflict a good deal of damage on their British foes, wounding Barclay and other senior officers and forcing them from the battle to seek medical attention. Junior officers in the British fleet took charge of the two largest ships, the HMS *Detroit* and HMS *Queen Charlotte*. They fought with vigor and did their best, but when Perry assessed the extreme damage to his *Lawrence* and decided to engage the *Niagara* on Elliot's behalf, the winds shifted. In the confusion of shifting winds and drifting gunsmoke—and while Perry was making his immortal row—the spars of the *Detroit* and *Queen Charlotte* entangled, making it nearly impossible for either ship to steer successfully. Unable to maneuver and draw an advantage, the big ships were sitting ducks. By the time Perry engaged the unscathed *Niagara*, he had the wind and used it to fire a full broadside down the keels of the two big warships. The changing wind, the tangled ships, the injured enemy officers—providence was in Perry's favor that day. And when, after fifteen minutes of Perry commanding the *Niagara*, the British struck their colors and surrendered, and the young commodore cemented his reputation as "Lucky Perry."

The dead were buried—some at sea, some in graves near what is now Put-in-Bay. Six sailors, three British and three American, were buried under what is now the public square at Put-in-Bay. They were dug up a hundred years later and reburied under the base of Perry's

Another version of Perry's transfer from the Lawrence *to the* Niagara, *the singular moment that solidified his fame. According to historians, his younger brother was one of the men in the boat.*

Victory and International Peace Memorial. The ships were repaired as well as possible and transferred back to Erie, where the American sailors spent a long, harsh winter aboard. Their captured British enemies were sent to POW facilities in New York.

Perry, meanwhile, joined Harrison, sailing a small ship with a contingent of marines up the Detroit River to the Thames River. He sailed as far up as he could, then mounted a borrowed horse and joined Harrison's pursuit of the British and native warriors who had fled Fort Malden following the battle—Indian forces under the command of the famous Tecumseh had watched the battle from canoes and reported the results to their leaders. Harrison and Perry chased the British before running into an ambush of native soldiers. They managed to overwhelm their surprise attackers. It was here, during the Battle of the River Thames (also known as the land battle of Lake Erie), that Tecumseh, the greatest leader of indigenous peoples of the age, was killed under uncertain circumstances.

The tide of a losing war had been turned. Perry went on to serve in other capacities and pressed for the court-martial of Captain Jesse Elliot for not engaging the *Niagara* earlier in the battle. Elliot was cleared of charges, but the two feuded for a lifetime.

Perry's luck finally ran out when he died of yellow fever after being bitten by a mosquito during a military exploratory expedition to South America in 1819. He was only thirty-four years old—to the day. He was buried in Trinidad, then reburied in Newport, Rhode Island, at the Old Common Burial Ground, before being dug up a second time and reburied in that city's Island Cemetery.

＊．＊

And that's the long and the short of it. I spent a year dissecting the story, looking for little plot twists and areas I could explore. I looked for clues to what I hoped to find when I at last set out on the road. I made meticulous plans for routes and schedules, hotels and campgrounds. I estimated costs and squirreled away bits of extra money that came in from ghostwriting and freelance projects. The budget would be tight—most of the monthly income my wife brought in as a teacher and an editor was accounted for—but I figured I would make it. I just had to stick to my plan. It was July 2008 when I made my first trip for the book to Put-in-Bay. It was September 2009 when the plan I dreamed up on my way home from Perry was set to take flight. I would be gone five days. First I'd drive to Cleveland, where I would leave Jack and Dylan with my mom. Then I would go west along the lake, turn north into Michigan, and head east across Canada. I'd round back west at Buffalo and stop in Erie on my way back to Put-in-Bay. I would double back to Cleveland, pick up the boys, and be back at my desk in Cincinnati bright and early Monday morning.

When I was packing, my wife, Rebecca, stopped me mid-fold and told me how proud she was that I was finally doing it, finally becoming the person she had always known I could be.

"It's just a week, it's not that big of a deal," I said. But she wasn't buying it.

"It doesn't matter if it's a week or a year," she said. "The point is that you're doing something you've always wanted to do. I'm proud of that."

"What about the boys?" I asked. They would stay with my mom so that we didn't have to pay a babysitter in Cincinnati while Rebecca went to work. "Will they be okay?"

"They'll be fine," she said. "They'll be with Gigi." (Which is what they call my mom.)

"What about you? What about work?" I asked.

"We'll both be here when you get back."

"Are you sure?"

"Craig, you want to take care of us, and I love you for that," she said. "But stop it. Don't look for an excuse not to go. I'm sad you'll be gone, but I would be sadder if you didn't go."

I choked up a little, zipped up my bag, and thought, "Well, here goes nothing."

5

Lighting Out

It was raining when I left my parents' house early on a Tuesday morning. I hadn't been able to sleep the night before, giddy as I was with excitement. For a relatively young father of two young boys, someone who had married right out of college but still dreamed of an adventurous life, the prospect of five days on the road alone was almost too much to handle. I had driven to my parents' house from Cincinnati the day before and left my sons with my mom. Now I was on my own. I could hardly believe I was doing this. Was it possible I would finally have an adventure?

Adventure was sort of a strong word for it, I suppose. The plan was to spend four days circumnavigating Lake Erie, staying one night in a hotel and spending the remaining nights camping in Canada and Pennsylvania. I would stop back to see the kids for a few hours and then head back out to Put-in-Bay for the annual historic weekend marking the anniversary of the battle. Held the second weekend in September, the historically themed event marked not only the 196th anniversary of the Battle of Lake Erie but also the unofficial end of the summer party season on the Lake Erie islands. (More on that later.) First, I had a lake to drive around.

My first destination was Vermilion, Ohio, and the Inland Seas Maritime Museum. I have known the museum existed for most of my life, since it is situated at the mouth of the Vermilion River, where it and roughly nine million boats, including my dad's twenty-two-foot inboard-outboard Pro-Line, dump into the lake. Having grown up holding back seasickness while my dad patiently waited for the acclaimed Lake Erie walleye to take his line, I would guess I had gone past the museum a hundred or more times without ever venturing inside, though I always made a silent promise to stop in the next time I was out that way. Well, after more than two decades of making the promise, it was time for me to keep it.

There are plenty of easier ways to get to Vermilion from the West Side of Cleveland, including the freeway and turnpike, but as I backed out of the driveway in the drizzling rain falling from the purple pre-dawn sky, I was feeling nothing if not romantic. If I was going to drive around the lake, then I was going to stay as close to it as possible. I chose Lake Road, aptly named because it runs along the lakeshore, not only because it is my favorite road in all of Ohio—I sometimes find myself meandering down it by car when I'm visiting the folks for the holidays—but also because it is Route 6.

What, pray tell, is so special about Route 6? Well, as any hyper-literate college sophomore with a wandering heart and a penchant for the open road can tell you, Route 6 is the road chosen by the hermit king of the road warriors, Jack Kerouac, in the beginning of *On the Road*. City boy Jack, who would later be memorialized in a Pete Droge song as having written words "for the young and ramble-hearted," dreamed of an America of heft and proportion, of the places that existed outside the city, where the roads meandered through forest and prairie and over mountains. He dreamed of a great adventure with his friend Neal Cassidy, a psychotic, if not sociopathic wannabe philosopher who encouraged his bookish and brainy college-boy protégé to join him in Denver for the time of their lives. After a long winter hemmed up inside a stuffy apartment writing a book and living with his mother—a winter in which his fantasies of the wide-open West grew more vivid and lurid—Kerouac hatched a plan to take a bus from New York up into rural Massachusetts, where he would find the headwaters of Route 6, toss his pack over his shoulder, and stick out his thumb, destined for Denver and California, three and a half thousand miles down that long stretch of two-lane.

So that's just what Jack did. He saved up his pennies and borrowed the rest from his mom, and, with a ticket and fifty bucks in his pocket, he headed north out of the city, along the Hudson to Route 6. Of course, when he got there it was raining and cold, as spring in the Berkshires tends to be. And he arrived in the middle of the night. He stood at a lonely crossroads, waiting, shivering, and slowly witnessing his Route 6 dream die. He eventually settled for a ride back to New York and a series of bus rides to Chicago, never setting foot along the road that runs a half mile from the house I grew up in, but that's beside the point. The point is that he considered it. He even attempted it. And that was worth something to a seventeen-year-old kid who was bored to death with his life, itchy to do something big, and impressed by the thought that his favorite writer very nearly walked through what would become, forty years later, his hometown.

I first read *On the Road* between high school and college, and I remember thinking how amazing that such an adventure—not only a physical journey, but a journey of friendship and art and discovery—could even be possible. Do people really just pack up some stuff and go? Fifteen years later I still had my doubts, but there I found myself, faced with the ultimately meaningless decision of whether to take the easy way (the interstate) or the interesting way (Route 6), as I began this latest leg of my great adventure. What the hell, I thought, if I'm going to do this thing and write a book about it, I might as well do it right. So Lake Road, Route 6, it was. After all, you only live once.

The modern history of northern Ohio can be witnessed pretty clearly as you drive west out of Cleveland in the form of the houses that line the road. And Avon Lake, where I grew up, exists as a microcosm of this history. Lakeshore property is a premium draw for the few nouveau riche of Cleveland. I say nouveau riche because the old money lives on the east side of town, and because Avon Lake and other suburbs on the West Side once existed as affordable land for the upwardly mobile, socially striving blue-collar workers from the steel plants of Cleveland and, thirty miles to the west, Lorain. It helps to think of Cleveland and Lorain in terms of concentric circles of the Industrial Golden Age. Imagine two rocks being dropped into a pond a couple dozen miles away. In the epicenter of the waves are heavy industry—steel, shipping, and salt mining. The first ring is soot-blackened neighborhoods that looked sad when brand-new and look downright depressing today. This is the Near West Side—Ohio City and Tremont. In Lorain there are the rows of pillbox houses now overgrown by weeds and rife with crime. The next set of rings is a little nicer, lower-management stuff mixed with upper-management and blue-blood stock—Lakewood, Rocky River, and the parts of Lorain close to Sheffield Lake. Then there is the space between. Like the creamy center of an Oreo cookie, Avon Lake is sandwiched between Bay Village to the east and Sheffield Lake to the west.

These were good, hard-working, commuter-class people. If they had a little more money, they lived in Bay Village. If they had a vision for a better life for their families, they lived in Avon Lake. If they lived in Sheffield Lake, they had equal, but lesser, measurements of both. There's a neighborhood in Avon Lake known as "The 45s." The name isn't some veiled reference to violence. It's a geographical reference. "The 45s" were named because they are located where the forty-fifth stop of the electric railroad connecting Cleveland proper to the suburbs once stood. I tried to think about this as I passed the roads leading back to the streets filled with charming Cape Cod cottages; to imagine the will it took for steelworkers and laborers to suffer through forty-five stops in the morning and forty-five stops at night just to get to work and offer their families something other than the coke-smoke air of industrial Cleveland. It's a Billy Joel song, really.

Evidence of that proud blue-collar history still exists in Avon Lake, but for the most part it has become, like so many other suburbs since the advent of the interstate and white flight, a place for chain restaurants and grocery stores, Mercedes and McMansions. Along the lake, huge stone-and-brick monstrosities have choked out the view for those who happen to live on the south side of the road. Often two or three small, charming cottages are bought up and donated to the local fire department for a practice burn so that lots can be cleared and charmless castles thrown up to hog the views for one or two people who will live there until, like all things trendy, they decide they need to be someplace else. Build and destroy, build and destroy. Destroy.

Leaving Avon Lake, I saw evidence that gentrification has begun in Sheffield Lake and rears its ugly head in the form of signs reading NEW MODEL OPEN and LAND AVAILABLE FOR DEMOLITION AND CONSTRUCTION on either side of the road. I sipped the coffee my dad had poured into a travel tumbler for me and tried to remind myself that at the time of the Battle of Lake Erie, none of this was here. This was all woods and farmland, native country. And as I crossed the Black River in downtown Lorain—a waterway so choked with the poisonous by-products of steel production upstream that all fish caught in the river are presumed toxic and thus banned from consumption—I felt a little jealous of Oliver Hazard Perry and his men and even the British for that matter, because they got to see this area while the seeing was still good.

This area, this landmass and body of water formed by the slow-moving and destructive force of glaciers, is still pretty. In the giant oaks and elms and maples that shade lawns and provide protection for the few old cottages along the shore, and in the picturesque cliffs just tall enough to provide perspective over the water, I saw enough beauty to inspire a better writer to pen an ode or a sonnet. It is my idea of heaven, and yet I wonder what it must have been like before the lots were divvied up and roads were cut, before houses stood shoulder-to-shoulder like the wall around a hockey rink. And I can't. I can't begin to imagine what it must have been like to sail along the shore in one of Perry's square-rigged ships in the summer of 1813.

⤳⸱⤶

Having assembled his flotilla in Erie, roughly one hundred miles east of Cleveland in the tiny section of Pennsylvania that borders Lake Erie, Perry sailed west toward a chain of islands that demarcate the westernmost of the lake's three distinct basins, another sixty or so miles to the other side of Cleveland. Setting out in the same direction in the early-morning hours, I try to imagine what it must have been like to stand aboard those ships, facing into the wind and knowing that the only things that lie ahead are waiting and war. Perry's mission of drawing out Barclay's British ships from the westernmost point on the lake for a pitched battle to determine inland sea primacy meant that there could be little doubt of any other conclusion. Guns would be fired. Blood would be shed and men would die. And when the smoke cleared, there would emerge a victor.

The Battle of Lake Erie was a last stand of sorts, for both sides. The clock was ticking for the Americans, who had been so roundly defeated in the western theater up to that point. Infighting and political derision were eroding support for Mr. Madison's war, and the United States badly needed a victory. For the British, the stakes were equally high. Though successful in their bid to take much of the Old Northwest—thanks in large part to support from natives led by Tecumseh—the British military was stretched thin. An arduous campaign against Napoleon had sapped resources, and the scale of the North American continent required a constant and free-flowing supply line to maintain strength.

For much of 1813, American ships under the command of Captain Jesse Elliot had caused problems for the British fleet on Lake Ontario, though Erie remained open and free. Admiral Barclay could move with ease from either Fort Malden in the west or Fort Erie in the east, but now, suddenly though probably not unexpectedly, the Americans were making a stand. And that stand meant war.

I tried to put myself in the place of one of the sailors on Perry's flagship, the brig *Lawrence.* Having spent a good deal of time on the lake when I was younger, I could almost feel the sting of the wind on my face as I made my way through the rain-soaked streets of Lorain toward Vermilion. I could feel the subtle undulations of the waves, which, unlike those on other great bodies of water, are consistent in neither size nor direction. That's one of the qualities that make Erie unique among the Great Lakes and have inspired a bit of lore since the earliest mariners took to the waters. The French, who used the lake as part of their massive trapping and trading business in the Old Northwest, called it Lac du Chat—Lake of the Cat—to suggest its temperamental personality.

Consisting of three main basins—the deepest to the east, then the central next to Cleveland, and the shallow west famous for its late-summer run of perch—the lake combines below-water topography with a location at the confluence of winds from Canada and from the south, making Erie very unpredictable for sailors. It can sneak up on you quickly and without warning. Just like a cat. Though the smallest of the Great Lakes and barely reaching a maximum depth of 210 feet (compared with Superior's 1,332 feet, Michigan's 925 feet, Ontario's 802 feet, and Huron's 750 feet), Erie is home to more than fifteen hundred shipwrecks. Going back to 1679, there have been just 4,262 ships lost on the whole of the Great Lakes, according to the Great Lakes Shipwreck File Web site, so Erie's proportion for loss is disproportionate to its relative size.

Gordon Lightfoot may have made Lake Superior famous for the *Edmund Fitzgerald*, but Lake Erie has created more paperwork for insurance companies.

The lore of Lake Erie surely would have been known to Perry and his men. Trained in the open water of the Atlantic and Caribbean, Perry must have found Lake Erie strange and foreign, even given his task and its potential for the highest currency in the early U.S. military—glory. No saltwater spray, no vast and open sea. It must have felt like sailing in a bathtub during an earthquake.

Just before I reached the town of Vermilion, I pulled into the parking lot of a bait shop-grocery store—or what might have once been a bait shop-grocery store—that looked forlorn in the shadow of a massive and strangely quiet Ford plant. I climbed a slight hill and over a railroad track. Looking out to the water, I saw an ore carrier in the shipping lanes five or six miles offshore. It was massive, even from such a distance, and very similar to one my dad rode on the summer before, from Detroit to Duluth, Minnesota, and then back to Gary, Indiana. The ship, which was easily two hundred yards long, was probably crewed by twenty or so able seamen and a team of officers who lived in the relative luxury of private cabins.

The modern fleets of Lake Erie ships are like this one, big and sturdy, or like the fishing boat my dad had always wanted. I tried to blink out the ore ship and replace it in my mind with Perry's nine ships sailing west past this point of land, their total length shorter than the single boat on the horizon. And then I looked to the left and right and saw the smokestacks of power plants, the masts of telephone poles and the rivers of blacktop, the train tracks. None of this was here, I told myself, none of it. Sure, this was the same land—well, except maybe the hill, which I am certain was built to accommodate the train tracks. There may have been someone—a farmer, a native, a soldier, a volunteer—standing where I now stood when Perry sailed by. That person may have seen Barclay's sails on the horizon, transporting food, soldiers, and munitions from east to west. That person may even have stood and watched in the after-math of the battle as Perry—who was to become the most famous person in America for a time—moved his tattered ships and those he had captured back toward Erie.

I tried to make a connection, to imagine that person or any of the men on the ships. I tried to rationalize that it is the same lake, the same depths, and the same random smattering of waves, the same shore, exposed to erosion and serene views. I tried, but I failed. The world Oliver Hazard Perry existed in, the waters he sailed and the shore he passed, seemed too distant. Another time, sure, but also another place altogether. Maybe, I thought, it would come to me. Maybe I just had to drive a little farther.

⁓ 6 ⁓

Vermilion

An hour after I headed out, the sun was up and the rain had cleared off—as they say, you don't like weather in northern Ohio, wait forty-five minutes. I pulled into Vermilion as the town was waking up. Sleepy and quaint, situated along the Vermilion River, which has the highest per capita concentration of recreational boats on the Great Lakes, the town makes you want to buy property. Charming streets nestled by cottages and Victorians simply beg for a walk, while the main thoroughfare offers independent restaurants and cafés, old buildings housing other commercial interests, and pocket parks meant for doing nothing but sitting for a while and watching the traffic on the river near where it empties into the lake.

For someone born and bred into the homogeny of the suburbs, Vermilion is a world apart: you can feel your pace slow down when you get out of the car. And though there are plenty of visitors—most related to the river and some coming for the out-of-this-world authenticity of the French restaurant Chez François—it doesn't feel touristy. There's no pandering, only a couple T-shirt shops, and absolutely nothing that feels plastic or contrived. It is, in short, my version of heaven.

Having lived in southwest Ohio for more than a decade, my wife and I have talked a lot about moving back north. Our families live near each other, and being parents to the only grandchildren not in Cleveland, we feel a certain subtle pressure to move back. But we resist. In part because we like where we live and in part because the pressure would not necessarily be eased by our return. But also because we would want to be in different places. My wife would want to be near the family, in Avon Lake or another nearby suburb. I would want to live in Vermilion.

A suburb of nothing, it stands apart from the world I inhabited growing up, though my exposure to the town came young and relatively often. It was on this river, slow moving and brown, that my dad kept (and still keeps) his boat. My mom used to live to shop at Buyer's Fair, a small department store with shockingly good prices on name-brand designer clothes, and my sisters and I used to love getting ice cream at Etta Mae's, a small parlor and restaurant in the heart of downtown.

Of all the places in Vermilion I had visited—I once, in high school, drove all the way to the public library to get a copy of Ernest Hemingway's *Islands in the Stream* on tape so I could listen to it before an English test—I had never been to the Great Lakes Historical Society's Inland Seas Maritime Museum. Situated about two hundred yards west of the mouth of the Vermilion, the museum combines a stately old home with a concrete building that leads to a two-story model of an ore boat's pilothouse, which faces the water. Standing to the replica's right is a small lighthouse. Both are visible when you round the break wall at the mouth of the river, and I remember asking my dad and being told by him on several occasions that we should take a trip to see what was inside. For more than twenty years we made the same promise, that next time we'd go. We never did.

But a small newspaper item I had found the summer before finally gave me enough reason to visit. Apparently the Great Lakes

Historical Society had been given a grant by the National Park Service's American Battlefield Protection Program to explore with ground-penetrating radar the lake bed near where the Battle of Lake Erie was fought. The grant provided two years' worth of funding for equipment and staff to explore the site in hope of finding wreckage, carnage, or artifacts left by Oliver Hazard Perry, Barclay, and the rest of the warriors on that day. I had clipped the article and hung it on a bulletin board in my home office to remind myself to stop at the Inland Seas Museum—where the effort was to be based—during my trip.

I pulled off the main road and up a side street toward the museum and the lake. I parked and climbed the stairs to the museum's front door, which was locked. The sign said it would open at ten, so I had forty-five minutes to kill. I decided to go for a walk, first up the side streets past the perfect cottages and a bed-and-breakfast that was calling out my name, and then up the street where I had parked. The street was lined with quaint shops, one of which was open and sold coffee. I needed coffee in a bad way. The excitement of setting out had worn off, and I could feel the numb buzz of sleepiness clouding the peripheries of my mind.

To say that Vermilion is charming is like saying Barack Obama talks pretty good. This town has everything you could want, including a Hungarian restaurant, a hippie sandwich shop that made the local paper for playing host to Garth Brooks and Trisha Yearwood despite being only about eight feet wide and ten feet deep, and myriad other eateries and curiosity shops. Vermilion is built for tourism but isn't touristy. In fact, it's always seemed like a local secret. Just over halfway between the Rock and Roll Hall of Fame in Cleveland and the greatest roller coaster park in the world, Cedar Point, Vermilion is a place you wouldn't pass through unless you were looking for it. There are plenty of other towns with better beach access, plenty with a more vibrant nightlife, but no town on Lake Erie has that quaint New England feeling of Vermilion. It's like

Cape Cod without the crowds or coastal Maine without the ten and a half months of winter. If this writing thing works out for me, I think I'd like to try to convince my wife that we should find a little place on one of these side streets, a cottage or an old Victorian, and never again leave the house. It's that great.

Unfortunately, given the size of the town, it didn't take long to walk the central business district, and the coffee, a powerful and acidic blend that threw open my eyes but was tearing streaks in my stomach, needed to be absorbed. So I looked for a place to get some eggs and found it in a little yellow cottage with a wrought-iron fence and a wide front porch. When I was a kid the place was called Etta Mae's, an ice-cream shop with homemade waffle cones that could take five sweet and blissful years off your life. It was still the same place but with a different name that I can't quite remember. They still served ice cream, but now they served breakfast too. It was too perfect—a small independent café in a perfect little town.

I asked for a table by the window and grabbed a copy of the *Lake Front News*, a small weekly newspaper serving the tourists and

Vermilion, with its perfect little streets of perfect little houses, is the kind of place that makes me want to buy property. It is, in my idealized view of the world, a perfect place.

realtors of the entire North Shore. The cover story was about a Boy Scout who had renovated an alleyway in Sandusky to earn his Eagle Scout badge, and the centerfold story was a first-person exposé asking, ARE THERE LARGEMOUTH BASS IN LAKE ERIE? Thank God, there are, according to the author, and if you can find them it might just save your angler's soul during the three weeks between walleye and perch seasons.

The eggs were excellent, the home fries superb, and the toast arid. It was nice that the server, a girl who looked fresh out of high school and maybe waiting for school to start at Ohio State, had listened when I asked for it dry. Just try getting service like that from Perkins. I had another cup of coffee and checked my watch. It was 10:05, so I paid my bill and collected my stuff.

"Mind if I take this?" I asked the server, holding up my copy of the *Lake Front News*.

"If you really want to," she said in the tone locals use when they can't believe someone might actually find where they live interesting or, God forbid, enjoyable. I tucked it into my bag and made a vow to one day buy property in this town and eat breakfast at this place and read this rag every Tuesday for the rest of my life.

I strolled back down to the museum and tried the door again but was surprised when I tugged and it didn't budge. I double-checked the sign, and sure enough it said the place opened at 10 and then I checked my watch, which now read 10:15. How quaint was this place? They didn't even pay attention to their own business hours. I strolled onto the lawn next to the museum, past the small lighthouse and toward the beach, when I heard a voice call from behind.

"You trying to get in here?" the man asked. The way he said it, I wondered if he thought I was some kind of burglar instead of a patron.

"Yes, yes I am," I said, turning back toward the door, which I hoped he was unlocking for the day.

The Inland Seas Maritime Museum is owned and operated by the Great Lakes Historical Society. A grant from the federal government is helping researchers here study the site of the Battle of Lake Erie.

"We don't open for another hour. Budget cuts."

"But the sign," I said.

"Don't have the budget to change the sign."

"I see," I said. "So eleven then?"

"Yup. And you can thank the assholes down in Columbus for that little inconvenience." The Inland Seas Maritime Museum was apparently receiving state funding, and Ohio's recent economic woes had tightened the hours they could keep. Still, I wondered why the doors would be closed if he was inside. I mean, what cost is there to allowing me to enter when the employees are already at work? I chalked it up to a subtle form of protest, a way for the scientists and curators to stick it to the statehouse man, thanked him, and went down to the beach for a stroll.

For the next hour I walked up and down the small beach and upriver, watching the slow movements of an out-of-season town as it awakened. I've always loved looking at the boats, which are segmented unofficially by size. About a half mile from the mouth of the Vermilion River, a bridge prevents larger boats from entering the marinas beyond. In fact, once when the river was running high, a former neighbor of my parents' tried to get a thirty-foot Wellcraft past the bridge to his dock, but the raised level meant he needed everyone on board to push against the bottom of the bridge to maintain clearance. Tolerances are pretty tight on the Vermilion, pretty tight indeed.

Downstream from the Route 6 bridge, the larger boats vary from lake-borne yachts to sailing vessels with masts too tall to clear underneath. The sailboats vary from small family boats to the kind that are passed down through generations and crewed by professional sailors. It always seemed a bit incongruous to me that someone would keep such a large boat on Lake Erie, a relatively small body of water. I spent some time just looking at the big ones, the ones docked near the Vermilion Yacht Club in a tony residential neighborhood that I've always known as the Lagoons. The houses here are all white, all takeoffs on the Cape Cod and saltbox formats, and all expensive. This is a place for well-heeled retirees or litigators from Cleveland who need a place to relax, and in many ways it's set up like a suburban development, only instead of streets, canals form the frontages of property. This too is a world apart—private beach, private supper club, and the yacht club. And all of it directly across the river from the Vermilion Public Works Department. Ah, sweet irony.

Among the ways to kill an hour along the Vermilion River is to read the names people give to boats. Perry's brigs were named for Captain James Lawrence, who famously uttered the slogan "Don't Give Up the Ship" emblazoned on Perry's battle flag, and for Fort Niagara, which Perry had been instrumental in storming in the months leading up to his Lake Erie campaign. But it seems there was no such meaning or heroism in the naming of most of the boats on the Vermilion. They ranged from the romantic *Lady of the Lake*, an aging sailboat, to the indignant and lowbrow fishing boat called

Kiss My Bass. But my favorite that morning was the name of a fifty-five-foot, three-deck yacht from New York called *Big Old Bitch.* It instantly brought to mind the image of a middle-aged divorcee who took her corporate-baron husband to the cleaners after she caught him schtupping his secretary and took the boat just for good measure. Or maybe it was just the opposite. Maybe it was a man who had escaped an oppressive female in his life—an overbearing mother? a controlling wife?—and was now living his dream of sailing the seven seas and a few big lakes. Maybe it was a jocular redneck who'd hit the lottery or a rap star avoiding an assault charge by never setting foot on land. Freud could have a field day with boat names, and I wouldn't mind sitting in on the session when he confronts the owner of *Big Old Bitch.* I would probably even bring popcorn. If I ever hit the lottery or topped the bestseller list and bought a boat, I wonder what I would name it. Probably nothing you could safely or easily print on vinyl and attach to the hull. Maybe something to exorcise my demons like "Yeah, I was an English major and you said I'd never amount to anything. Well how do you like me now, Uncle John? I've got a boat." What do you think? Too long?

The hour passed quickly, and I returned to the Inland Seas Maritime Museum to find the doors open and an elderly woman sitting behind a desk in the gift shop–entry. Her white hair was fleecy and looked like it might have been held on with Elmer's white glue. She was hunched behind a tall desk and seemed ready—hell, content—to spend the afternoon waiting for a visitor. But she wasn't really excited to see me. Instead, she looked at me like I was a new brand of stool softener—interested, but ready to stick with the kind she knew. She asked if I had ever visited before and had me fill out a short questionnaire, the answers to which I was certain would go into the next request for state funding: Is this your first time visiting? Would you come again? Do you think the Great Lakes Inland Seas Maritime Museum is a worthwhile use of public funds?

I asked her about the grant the researchers had received to study the battle site, and she claimed to have no idea what I was talking about.

"Well, are there artifacts from the battle on display?" I asked.

"Should be, if what you say is true," she said, "but I haven't been through in a while."

Okay, maybe that wasn't exactly what she said, but the general tone, if not the exact words, was correct. So I paid my three bucks and headed in.

The museum is relatively small and quaint in that do-it-yourself kind of way that small museums have. The displays were rudimentary compared with the big-budget productions of the Rock and Roll Hall of Fame or the Smithsonian. But here they were perfect, with blinking lights on display maps and VHS movies running on continuous loops. A majority of the museum is devoted to shipping and related industries like salvage and towing. As it should be. Shipping is a big deal on the Great Lakes. Shipping built the steel industry as large quantities of iron ore were mined in Minnesota and brought to Cleveland (and eventually Pittsburgh) to be turned into steel. All kinds of things have been and continue to be shipped out there. Spend any time along the shore of any Great Lake and you're bound to see the huge ore ships and container boats seven or eight miles offshore like tiny giants, huge among peers but lost in a universe of water and wind. I scanned a lot of the displays, which were a bit anachronistic, and stopped only to take a couple pictures in the model pilothouse, which jutted like a porch from the museum toward the lake. The display, which was probably half or quarter scale but still big enough to walk through, was a faithful representation of the helm of one of those big ships, and the windows provided a panoramic view from west to east and all points north. It was cool—but not the reason I was here. I wanted to see if the ground-penetrating sonar equipment purchased and used with the federal grant money had brought up anything from the battle that was now on display.

So much for that.

Downstairs from the main level, a mural of Perry crossing from the *Lawrence* to the *Niagara* mid-battle greeted me, along with models of his ships and a diagram showing the location and maneuvers of the battle. Under a large glass box at the foot of the mural—which struck me as rather comic book-like (as if Batman might have been pulling an oar and Aquaman swimming alongside)—was a near-rotten piece of what I assumed to be driftwood. It turned out to be a section of wooden anchor from one of the American ships that had fought in the battle.

At last! Contact! I should have been elated but found myself only moderately whelmed. For one thing, it didn't look like an anchor. For another, it just didn't seem important. I had hoped for shards of exploded cannonballs or torn and bloody uniforms. A piece of something real would have been great. I was hoping for the *Mona Lisa* when, in fact, most of the small area devoted to the battle was finger paint—representative of history, but not actually historic. I was disheartened until I saw a glass case tucked beneath the stairs with some fairly old-looking objects inside. I went over to investigate and saw some things that were relatively menial but important for their age. A cup, some tools, some medical instruments, and a case to hold them. I got excited, thinking I had just laid eyes on actual battle artifacts until I read the small typewritten signs detailing each one. Everything in the case was period-accurate, meaning it had come from the time of the Battle of Lake Erie, but none of it had actually been there. All this time, all the excitement and . . . nothing.

I had struck out again, the victim of my own overinflated expectations. Even when I asked if I could speak with some of the researchers working on the Battle of Lake Erie project, I was told they were out on the water and not available. And if I would leave a number or, better yet, an e-mail, they would surely get in touch. They never did. So, almost two and a half hours after getting to

Vermilion and fifteen minutes after getting inside the museum, I decided it was time to move on. I was heading to Fort Meigs, the base that served as the staging area for the ground offensive that followed the Battle of Lake Erie.

⁂

I was frustrated, to be sure. It seemed like things never quite work out for a guy like me in the way they worked out for guys like Oliver Hazard Perry. I got in to the college I wanted to attend, but only after I was wait-listed; I played on the championship tennis team but was the only one to lose in the big tournament. I got the girl, but, well, there is nothing wrong with the girl. It's just that when all of our friends were building houses and spending a week every year in the Caribbean, we were renting while scraping together money for Christmas gifts and groceries. I really can't complain about my life. I've never been homeless, I've never really missed a meal, but it seems like I am always improvising and justifying. I compare myself to my dad, who is meticulous and for whom everything seems to work out. And to Perry, who flew by the seat of his pants most of the time and things not only worked out, he managed to survive pitched battles on boats without a scratch.

The problem had to be my expectations. I had been looking forward to this trip for so long—not just this one, but any trip like this—that I had overinflated things. Perry probably could have turned a morning like this into a swashbuckling adventure. Dad would have found contentment in learning about the history of container shipping on the Great Lakes. Me, with my romantic delusion and high expectations? I got a mural of Perry, a rotten piece of wood, and a case full of things that might have belonged to the crews of the *Lawrence* and *Niagara* had they shopped elsewhere. If you had handed the three of us a lemon, Perry would have sucked it down with a shot of tequila, Dad would have made lemonade, and I would have stood there with sticky hands and a rotten peel.

Still, it wasn't a complete waste. The part of me that thirsts for adventure may have been disappointed, but the part of me that likes a nice sweater got to spend a morning in the town where I would love to spend the rest of my life. I had a nice breakfast and a nice stroll, and I now know the answer to a question that has long nagged me—yes, there are largemouth bass in Lake Erie.

~7~

Fort Meigs

Determined to stay off the interstate highways, I left Vermilion on the same Route 6 I entered it on. I was still excited despite the lackluster results of my big circle tour's first stop and was bouncing along the lakeshore on empty blacktop, past quaint cottage communities and beach shack-themed bars and, of all things, surf shops. In all my time living along the shores of Lake Erie, surfing was one thing I had never seen. I witnessed the putrefied algae wash of water along the beaches, survived the medical waste epidemic—of which I am reminded every time I hear Billy Joel sing "hypodermics on the shores, China's under martial law / Rock and Roller cola wars, I can't take it anymore"—and saw the radical turnaround of water quality following the infestation of a tiny bivalved mollusk called the zebra mussel.

This shellfish, which looks a lot like a clam but is roughly the size of a dime, has done more to clean up the waters of the lake than any clause of the Clean Water Act by essentially acting as tiny water filters. These little buggers actually eat the stuff that gave Lake Erie its reputation for stench and the occasional fire. Individually, they don't move a whole lot of waste, but it's kind of a lucky thing they reproduce more prodigiously than a pack of rabbits on Spanish fly in the Grotto at the Playboy Mansion. And when they first arrived in Lake Erie, the party line was to bitch about them. The shipping companies were to blame, everyone griped. They brought the beasties in from the Atlantic in the ballast water tanks of massive ocean-going ships that found their way up the St. Lawrence, across Lake Ontario, up the Niagara, and finally into the rarefied waters off Buffalo, Erie, Cleveland, Lorain, Sandusky, and Toledo. They were going to kill off the walleye population, the lake's only saving grace, and the perch. What will happen to the perch? The sky is falling! There will be no more fish fries at the American Legion! How will we survive?

The fever has broken in the decade since the zebra mussel started eating through the postindustrial, possibly radioactive shitcloud we were so eager to defend. And what happened? The lake has gotten cleaner—a lot cleaner, like so much so you can no longer give directions to your buddies from Chicago as "east until you smell it and north until you step in it" when they want to know how to find the lake. And the walleye are still there, and the perch still run, and because the water is cooler when it's not full of cyanide and runoff, Lake Erie's long-forgotten populations of salmon and steelhead have started to come back. Oh shucks, guess we might have overreacted about the whole end-of-the-world-is-nigh thing.

But for all the recovery of the lake's fisheries and the return of people to the water as swimmers and kayakers and canoeists and sailors, I can honestly say I have never seen anyone try to surf Lake Erie. Boogie board, maybe, but a surf shop? I'm all for playing up the waterborne-playground part of the lake's personality, but this seemed like a stretch.

I continued on Route 6 through Huron and Sandusky and over toward Port Clinton before veering south toward Perrysburg, a smallish city on the southeast side of Toledo and home of Fort Meigs, every northern-Ohio eighth-grader's second favorite—behind the Cedar Point amusement park—field trip destination. Perrysburg is named, conveniently enough and in a similar spirit as Perry, for Oliver Hazard Perry. But unlike its name-cousin on the other end of the state, Perrysburg seems to embrace the heritage of the good commodore a lot more than the complete strikeout of a town I had visited the summer before.

I followed a sign on the outskirts of town directing me toward Fort Meigs, the installation built by General William Henry Harrison as a place to wait out the winter of 1812–1813, along wooded streets and the kind of Americana neighborhoods that might give Norman Rockwell red, white, and blue wet dreams. To say Perrysburg is quaint is probably a stretch. *Quaint,* when used as a general descriptor of a small municipality, is usually reserved in my mind for the white-steeples-and-maple-syrup towns of Vermont and New Hampshire. Vermilion is quaint. But there is another kind of quaint that might be appropriate, a more distinctly Midwestern version of the word. Midwest quaint is a notch above poverty and two notches below ostentatious wealth. Midwest quaint describes a town of Carhartt jackets and pickup trucks, a town where folksy crafts are sold in storefronts and where everyone still turns out for the Fourth of July parade, despite the fact that nothing new has been added in thirty years. Midwest quaint isn't postcard perfect; rather, it's the places John Cougar Mellencamp sings about where the quarterback dates the cheerleader and gets her pregnant and they live in a little pink house and he works down at the mill. Sure, once or twice she might call the cops because he tied one on with his buddies and took out his frustration at not having become Tom Brady on her. But she'll forgive him, like she always does, and when they get old they won't talk to each other anyway. That's Midwest quaint. I like Midwest quaint.

Apparently one of the unfortunate side effects of living in a Midwest-quaint town must be a certain blasé attitude toward directional signage, because after that first sign pointing me in the general direction of Fort Meigs I drove for what felt like an hour without seeing another one. Usually in these situations, I just stay on the main road. Things usually work themselves out when you stay on the main road, but I found myself past the big shade trees and the central business district, past the charming old houses and the less charming new ones and the charmless apartments and the almost stultifying trailer parks, wondering where the hell was Fort Meigs.

I found my way back to the downtown and parked near one of the shops on the main drag and turned around to find, a blessing to my eyes, a monolith in a public park near the Maumee River and topped by a statue of Oliver Hazard Perry. Set in bronze, it is the same heroic pose—like a matador who just tricked the bull into going for his cape—he holds in the statue in the atrium of the visitors center on Put-in-Bay, but outside in the afternoon sun, it appeared somehow more epic, more romantic in the glinting metal. I strolled over to take a few pictures when an old man—probably in his mid-eighties—sauntered up to me and asked what a young fella like myself was doing shooting pictures of a statue of some long-dead and nearly forgotten ship captain.

"I'm working on a book about him," I said.

"That's good to hear," he said. "Most people your age don't seem to care about history. It's all just facts and stuff you have to learn in school. But you can learn a lot from those people, a lot of things that have been forgotten."

The man told me his name was Russell. He wore khaki pants just below his nipples and a floppy bucket hat, but he looked like he still took a measure of pride in his appearance. I thought he probably shaved every day and had his shirts pressed. He was not large, maybe five-seven, and a little thick through the middle, but I could tell he'd earned it. He grew up near Perrysburg and had lived there most of his life. He was retired from the insurance industry and a widower—his wife had been gone eight years. I asked him about his interest in history. Was it a hobby? Was it something he took pretty seriously?

The bronze statue of Perry in Perrysburg is the twin of the one at Put-in-Bay in all things except material. It was near the base where I met Russell. Again, note the hair.

"I *lived* history, Craig," he said with a sort of far-off gaze that would have seemed cliché had it been given by an actor in a movie but which was powerful in person. It wasn't Charlton Heston in *The Ten Commandments*; it was more genuine than that, more matter-of-fact. "I witnessed history firsthand in Europe, France, Belgium. I watched my friends become gifts of history against the Nazis and almost became one myself. But that was a long time ago." *Gifts of history*–he actually said that. I knew then that this was a special encounter.

I wanted to ask him for details about his service, but he had that distinct quality of humility I have found common among veterans of the Second World War. It seems universal that their experience in the war was among the most profound of their lives, but like a sinner who finds God on a mountaintop and spends the rest of his life in quiet reflection, they usually seem hesitant to share it. The idea of a war hero wearing his medals on his coat lapel and telling his tale to anyone who will listen is contrary to reality. Russell and the other men like him whom I have met through my career as a journalist tend not to seek glory or affirmation from others. Remembering their personal experience of war is enough for them or perhaps too much for them to share. Rather, they just want the war itself to be remembered.

Things must have changed a great deal in the 130-odd years between Perry's time and Russell's. Men like Perry and his contemporary Stephen Decatur did what they did in the pursuit of glory, because glory was capital that could be spent in the advancement of their aspirations. A man needed to be a hero in order to be more than a simple man. But talking to Russell, I got the feeling that the most a man like him could aspire to be was simple. To do your duty, to serve your country, to do so with dignity and, yes, pride, but not bravado. It's from meeting people like Russell, icebergs who only expose the very tip of their truth, that I have become suspicious of any soldier, sailor, or marine who wants me to tell their story to the world. Russell and men and women of his ilk seem more genuine. They have proved themselves when it mattered most and can leave acclaim for those who fell short, for those who regret the things they have or have not done, for those who need a singular moment to justify a lifetime. I wanted to hear Russell's story, I wanted to know every detail, but I also knew that he would never tell me and by somehow coaxing him into giving up his ghosts, I would have done him a disservice.

So I settled for talking to him about Oliver Hazard Perry. Russell had been more of a William Henry Harrison man. It was probably because he had grown up in the shadow of Harrison's great fort, he said, but even from a young age he was fascinated by Harrison. A Virginia boy, the son of an officer with longings to become a doctor, Harrison found himself in the service of the country as governor of the Indiana territory. He was the white world's conduit to arguably one of the greatest Native American leaders to ever live—Tecumseh. And white settlers met with Harrison on several occasions, constantly pleading with Tecumseh to abandon his hopes of uniting the North American tribes, to stop taking whiskey and weapons from the English, to stay and fight alongside the Americans when the time for fighting came, or, at very least, to stay neutral. Harrison, who won at Tippecanoe, who ascended to the presidency and who built Fort Meigs as a shelter from the coming onslaught of British and Indian forces on their march south from Michigan and as a place to avoid the cold and disease of the Black Swamp, was someone Russell could identify with. He admired the man who was willing to be the stopgap, the man who stepped up to face the British and prevent His Majesty's forces from taking all of Ohio and the lands beyond.

Russell and I spoke for the better part of an hour, neither of us taking a seat, just two friends visiting on the street. And when he said he needed to be moving on, to go home and take a nap, I asked him for directions to the fort, and he happily obliged.

"The signs are terrible," he said. "I don't know how they expect anyone to find the place."

Russell began shuffling down the sidewalk, walking upright but with the measured gait of time. He was no Abe Vigoda, hunched over and weak, but his posture had lost the snap it must have had when he was fresh out of basic. Instead, walking away, he looked like he might have been off to make some iced tea and sit for a spell. I was compelled by an urge I had experienced before after meeting a veteran, but had never acted upon. I stepped alongside of him. "Russell," I said. "Thank you for your service."

And he looked at me with those faraway eyes and said, "Thanks for remembering." A tear formed in my eye as I watched him go. Russell could have been a liar, he could have been taking me for a ride. He could have been a convict or a tax cheat. He could have been a wife-beater or a deadbeat dad, but none of those things crossed my mind in that moment. The only thing I thought as I glanced over my shoulder to see him disappear down the sidewalk was, "There goes a real-life, honest-to-God hero."

Russell's directions were perfect, but he had neglected to tell me that the fort was not open on Tuesdays. When I pulled in, the parking lot was empty and the visitors center dark. A footpath led from the visitors center to the spike-topped log fence sticking out of an outer earthen embankment. I followed the path to a door that was set below the incline on either side like the drawbridge of a medieval castle. The heavy wooden door was closed and locked, so I decided to climb up the embankment to peer over the fence and see what was inside. Sticking my head between two hewn tree trunks, I looked in to see an empty scene right out of *Dances with Wolves*. Log buildings were set along an interior dirt path. Earthen ramparts rose like the spine of a mangy dog, and the whole place seemed like some abandoned Hollywood back lot. I was half-surprised a group of extras from a movie didn't walk by.

I could have just walked away, maybe promised myself I would come back another time when the visitors center was open, but I had struck out in Vermilion and didn't have another stop planned for the rest of the day, so screw it. I was going to find a way in. My first attempt was rudimentary and a bit naïve. I followed the earthworks around the wall until I found a place where I thought I might be able to swing my leg over and drop down into the fort. Finding it, I hiked up a leg and swung it over the timber fence post but quickly abandoned this strategy for a couple of reasons: a) the sharpened post posed a rather nasty threat to the possibility of my wife and I ever having a third child and b) the drop to the ground on the other side was every bit of eight or nine feet, and I didn't have much confidence in my ability to land without breaking an ankle. Like a lot of men, I like my private parts intact and my legs free of fracture, so I pulled my leg back over the fence and, with the weight of my bag and camera hanging off my back at a precarious angle (and having the natural balance of a wet noodle), I deftly fell flat on my ass and slid halfway down the grass-covered bank. From that prone position, I looked left and right and noticed a worn path of grass descending down around the fort into some woods that looked like a property divider between the fort and whatever was on the other side. What the hell? I planned on visiting Fort Meigs only once.

I should interrupt this story here to mention that for all my bravado and bravery, I have a five-year-old's fear of ghosts. It's not that I necessarily think they are real; it's just that I tend to give myself the creeps when the situation I am in seems even the slightest bit ghosty. When I was studying for my confirmation in junior high, my class had an overnight in the church—an all-night God-a-thon led by our pastor, who was trained as an archaeologist and had the air of a philosophy professor. Sometime after dinner, Pastor Stilsky was explaining the Holy Trinity, the three beings in one God—Father, Son, and Holy Ghost. I don't know if I had never heard the Holy Ghost part before or what, but all of a sudden I became Shaggy from *Scooby-Doo*, paranoid and afraid to turn any dark corner for fear of being confronted by an actual ghost. For the next two

The view of Fort Meigs from the side by the river. This was what I saw when I emerged from my Mystery, Inc., walk in the woods. "Like, zoinks, I wonder if it's haunted, Scoob!"

decades, I avoided being in churches alone because there was always this part of me that knew, just knew, that I would be sitting in a pew and look up to see an actual Holy Ghost coming right for me.

When I took my first real job out of college in rural Virginia—a place so rife with battlefields and the attendant ghost stories it makes Stephen King's mind seem like an episode of *Teletubbies*—I could never be alone without getting the creeps. I slept with the television on for nearly a year because I somehow thought it might prevent visitation from a spirit of one kind or another. So, yeah, I'm afraid of ghosts, but only when I am alone. It doesn't matter if it's day or night, outdoors or indoors, if the place could be haunted I assume that it is, and I break out in, like, *zoinks,* goose bumps.

So I should have known that following a trodden path into the woods adjacent to a place where very real people had died and were buried, a place intended—no, actually built—to allow the occupants to kill those who dared get near would set off my ghost tickles, the skin-crawling feeling I get down the back of my neck and spine. This is a feeling I have grown to dread, a feeling that makes me want to run as far as possible, as fast as my legs will take my fat ass to a place like Starbucks or Target or some other homogenized, impossible-to-possess locale where I can get a grip on myself and calm the hell down. I wasn't ten steps into those woods, down the slanting path that fell along a small creek deep into a shallow ravine, when the alarm went off. The day was sunny, perfect in most any regard, but in the trees it was darker. To the right, up a sharp incline, was dense vegetation; to the left stood tall trees; and, visible through the leaves that were just starting to turn, was the high wall of the fort that seemed so much bigger, so much more imposing, from this angle. It was supposed to seem that way—impenetrable. That was part of the design aesthetic. My footfalls on the slightly crunchy trail seemed to echo, and a small breeze blew some leaves off the trees, which sounded like firecrackers to me. I nearly wet my pants when I heard some movement in the scrub. Soldiers, I thought, dead British soldiers coming back to take their revenge on the first American they find!

⁕⁖⁕

Nerves frayed and muscles tense, I thought of turning around and running right then, but that would mean turning my back to the unknown. If I continued the way I was going I might run into something, but at least it would be frontal. So I marched on down the path until it opened onto a grassy hillside, and I felt like I had just been reborn. I paused to turn around and peer into the trees I had just come through and saw a rabbit on the path—undoubtedly the source of the noise in the underbrush. Smiling at having survived and at my incredible cowardice, I looked around from the hill and saw the Maumee River flowing about a hundred yards off and down in the distance. Turning back to the fort, I saw a break in the fence line and walked over to it. Turns out it was a former gun emplacement, a sort of cannon deck that was nearly flush with the hill and provided easy access into the fort. Just a quick step down and I was in.

The creepy Scooby-Doo-meets-Edgar Allan Poe feeling that had nearly made my heart stop in the trees seemed to come in waves once I was in the fort. I followed the gravel trail around the interior, pausing to read the signs detailing the history of the fort and how Harrison and his men and those they protected survived British assaults from locations across the river, and how Tecumseh and his warriors laid siege to the fort, itching to burn it and everyone inside before being pulled away by their British allies.

A little arty, I know, but the view up one of Fort Meigs's cannon was too cool to pass up. This one was directed toward a sight on the other side of the Maumee River, from which the British shelled Harrison and his men inside the fort.

I stood at the gun emplacements and tried to imagine redcoats charging up from the river with murder in their eyes. I tried to imagine hiding behind the earthworks Harrison had built for protection from cannon fire as I read the headstones, scattered throughout the grounds, of men who had been buried where they lay following a battle. It was heady stuff and in the most unusual location. Growing up in Ohio, you are conditioned to believe stuff like this happened in other places—the South, Europe, out west—but here I was just minutes from a sleepy Ohio town, standing on the graves of men who died trying to protect this place and others like it. When I thought that way, it didn't feel like I was surrounded by ghosts at all, but by heroes. I felt haunted only when I neared the buildings that had been re-created by historians and park rangers—places like the path through the woods that, looking back, was probably nothing more than a way for landscaping trucks to get their mowers through to cut the lawn on the hillside. And I began thinking that maybe it wasn't the death or destruction that scared me; maybe it was the intrusion.

Strolling around the empty fort, I remembered the last time I had visited. It had been on a school field trip. The ground I was now walking was abuzz with reenactors in period costumes performing military cadences, blacksmithing, sewing cloth that could be purchased in the gift shop. It was entertainment. It was vaudeville. Maybe that's what was so disturbing to me: the first time I had visited I was there to be distracted. I never noticed the headstones, never stood and imagined the view from the gun emplacements and what it would be like to cling to a small earthen hill for cover, praying to God that one of the rounds fired from across the river doesn't make contact.

This time I was not at Fort Meigs to be entertained but to discover, to learn, to pay homage to those whose lives I could never really understand, but whose sacrifice benefited me still today. That's what men like Russell want—appreciation, not attention. I don't want to argue the merits of historic places like Fort Meigs putting on a show to bring back visitors. It's how they pay for the serious history that goes on in places like that. But I think a person reaches a point in life when they need to stop feeling like they need to be entertained and start feeling like they need to listen. I strolled the grounds for the next forty-five minutes or so thinking that history is important not as a means of entertainment but as a means of acknowledging that the world, the whole of your life, is only a small part of something much larger, something much more profound.

Feeling a little smug about my new philosophy, I found an exit from the fort and made my way back toward my car, certain I would never again be afraid of a ghost. In fact, I would welcome the opportunity to witness the past reaching out to me. I still wasn't sure I believed in ghosts, but if I did I hoped they would be like Russell, someone who did something extraordinary and went on to live an ordinary life. And if I ever did come across that kind of apparition, I hoped to have the opportunity to chat. No, I thought, nothing is going to scare me now.

And at that moment, a trash can not ten feet away began shaking and fell over, and I had an out-of-body experience—watching myself, legs pumping, heart racing, bag and camera trailing behind as I sprinted fifty or so yards to my car. And when I got there, when my hands touched metal and I snapped back to the first-person perspective, I looked back to the overturned trash, afraid and knowing I was going to see the ghost of a British soldier or a Kentucky volunteer standing there or, by God worse, coming toward me. What I did see reinforced in my mind was that you can take the boy out of the ghost story, but you can't take the ghost story out of the boy. A large raccoon climbed out of the blue plastic bin and walked slowly toward the woods.

I really am the biggest wimp.

~8~

The Unlucky Traveler: Part One

I left Fort Meigs in the late afternoon under cerulean skies, and the feeling that arose when I got on the open road was what I had been hoping for all along—I felt free, boundless, like I was on an adventure. The morning had been less productive than expected, but there's something about being alone in the car with a destination in mind but no schedule to keep. It's difficult to describe, even harder to force.

I've always been a driver. When I was old enough to get my learner's permit, I insisted on driving everywhere my mom or dad had to go. For about ten days after passing the learner's-permit test, I was insufferable, a hanger-on. I must have driven my parents and sisters crazy by pleading, begging, smooth-talking, and cajoling my way into the driver's seat while they were forced to ride shotgun. Once, my mom, dad, a family friend named Mindy, and I piled into my dad's Buick for a twenty-four-hour drive to Crested Butte, Colorado, where my sister was spending a summer interning at the Rocky Mountain Biological Laboratory. That trip to the Rockies presented the perfect opportunity for any inexperienced driver with a yen for the road: Nebraska. If you have never traveled across Nebraska from east to west, let me tell you that everything there is to see can be seen within five miles of the state line. There's massive expanses of prairie and the occasional truck stop boasting the world's largest something—twenty-four-hour video arcade, cup of coffee, shower stall, or Port-o-Let—and not much else. For what felt like days, I sat erect behind the steering wheel with hands at ten and two, smoothly switching lanes to overtake a sleep-deprived trucker. I thought of little other than the fact that I was driving. My God, but I was in heaven. My instinct for the road—what my troll of a driver's-ed instructor would call "The Seat," as in "No need to do all thirty of your required instructional hours, Craig, you have The Seat"—was awakened into a full-blown passion, one that has yet to waver fifteen years later.

It was only a few moments after leaving Fort Meigs that it hit me: I was on a road trip. There were snacks in a bag on the floor of the passenger seat, books on tape, and mix CDs scattered about the cabin. I had nothing to do other than what I chose to do, freedom to decide my next destination. A smile, like that of the Grinch when he finally understood the true meaning of Christmas, unfurled across my lips, and I felt somehow lighter, as if I could really and truly breathe. It was elation, well, not elation like I felt when my sons were born or elation like the moment Rebecca agreed to marry me, but elation as self-actualization. I felt as if I was in the place—behind the wheel—that I had always meant to be. And my life came into focus, if only for a fleeting moment. I had crossed over from youth to adulthood. I had gone from the carefree life of a student to having real-world responsibilities of job, wife, and children without a whole lot of reflection. Mind you, it wasn't regret that accompanied these thoughts, but appreciation. I appreciated my wife and kids, appreciated my dad, who must have realized I had made the switch long before I did. But appreciating my life was not the same as living it. I realized that I had not been living it, and that was perhaps why I felt so drawn to stories of adventure, to characters who damned all hell with tomorrow in the pursuit of heaven today. I read travel magazines and books about hitting the road, I learned about people like Perry who didn't wait for permission to do the things they wanted. I escaped in my own head, figuring there would always be time to do what I wanted, to live a life lived only in dreams.

And yet here I was. In the car. On a trip. Writing a book. I was doing the things I had always wanted but had lacked the guts or had waited for permission to do. I pulled onto Interstate 75, heading north. Home was now behind me, more than 150 miles in the other direction. And I wore that Cheshire Cat grin because I was doing it, damn it, even if I hadn't realized it that morning when I left my children in bed and struck out in the pre-dawn darkness; even if I hadn't realized it when I planned my route; even if I hadn't known what I was doing the entire time. Something had brought me to this moment, this adventure, this enterprise, and by God I was glad it had. Because in that moment, I was as close to the person I have always wanted to be as I ever will be, and there was no turning back. There was nothing that could stop me.

And so it was that I merged onto 23 North and crossed from Ohio to Michigan, a border that is marked by both a sign and a rapid acceleration of all cars in all lanes. The speed limit might only be five miles per hour faster in Michigan, but entering the state is like the moment when the flag drops at the Indianapolis 500. Cars were suddenly all American and all traveling at great speed. I tried to keep pace in my small-engine road warrior of a Volkswagen, at first by bumping the acceleration in the cruise control and then with the pedal, but I couldn't seem to catch up. The power was not there. Something was wrong and I mentally went through the three things I know about cars, hoping to find a simple solution to my acceleration problem. I knew the car could go—I had certainly had it past seventy in the past—but something was preventing me from keeping pace with the upper tier of velocity on the road.

The outfitter Cabela's has a megastore in Dundee, Michigan, roughly halfway between the Ohio line and Ann Arbor, my destination for the evening, and I pulled in to give my car a rest and try to figure out what was causing its loss of power. Cabela's is kind of like Disney World for people who spend their free time killing things—hunters, fishermen, people who consider décor tasteful only if it includes furniture hewn from driftwood, blaze orange and Realtree fabric, and plenty of stuffed carcasses. I had been to the store several times with my dad, a farm boy raised with a rifle in his hands. For him a trip to Cabela's is akin to a Catholic visiting a holy site—it emphasizes his beliefs and offers him opportunities to buy plastic rosaries—figuratively speaking, of course.

I fancy myself to be a bit of an outdoorsman. I like going on weekend backpacking trips with my father-in-law, taking the family canoeing on a nice summer afternoon, and casting a fly-line for trout. I have always enjoyed camping, but I'm not necessarily a Cabela's kind of guy. Though I have shotguns, I'm not a hunter. My body count is limited to two pheasant shot at a hunting club near my parents' home and a squirrel I shot with a BB gun while visiting my cousin Kevin in middle school. I believe I cried myself to sleep that night.

I have nothing against hunters, but in the world of outfitters I am an L.L.Bean kind of guy, and the difference between L.L.Bean and Cabela's is akin to the difference between a Crip and a Blood, East Coast and West Coast. It is perhaps most clearly illustrated in a head-to-head comparison of catalogs. The L.L.Bean catalog is filled with pictures of WASPy-looking people going to farmers' markets in Subaru Outbacks or taking a spin around Bar Harbor on a mountain bike. The Cabela's catalog features somewhat lurid images of high-powered rifles and men and women in top-to-tails camo stalking wild boar. One can imagine the models in an L.L.Bean catalog unpacking their car on Cape Cod, sipping white wine, and enjoying a lobster bake before setting off on a family hike. Cabela's models, by contrast, one has to assume, walk off the set to gut a deer and cure their own jerky. To the uninitiated, the difference is subtle. But for me, they are worlds apart.

In any regard, Cabela's seemed like an okay place to stop and figure out what was wrong with my car, which was not presenting any symptoms other than a hesitation to go really fast. I knew what was happening the second I pulled off the highway and navigated with an open window to the massive Cabela's parking lot—easily the largest parking lot I had seen all day, complete with massive statues of white-tailed deer in mid-leap and a bear rearing back on its hind legs like porn for the trigger-happy. I heard a grinding coming from the back right side of my beloved Jetta, a cross between the sound of tin cans bouncing along behind a matrimonial limousine and those same tin cans being worked over in a food processor. As I searched for a parking spot—the place was surprisingly busy for a weekday—I could feel my cheeks redden in embarrassment at the sound of my car. I felt like white trash, but a survey of the tanklike crewcabs filling the parking lot might lead one to believe that such a person would be right at home in this place. My brake pads were obviously shot, brake pads I had personally installed in a magnificent, though misguided, attempt to be a manly man capable of fixing things and comfortable with a good deal of dirt under his fingernails.

My embarrassment lasted only a few moments, though, because a soup can of a man with a windblown goatee in a leather outfit that vaguely smacked of dominatrix pulled up beside me on a ferociously belching Harley-Davidson that more than drowned out the crunch emanating from the stern of my vehicle. The noise, which had felt like a spotlight directing the Second Amendment army of shoppers to the suburban sissy boy in the kraut-burning VW, was, for a moment, shut off, and I followed the Harley to an open spot roughly six miles from the front doors of the store.

As a rule, bikers scare me. Not only am I horrified at the prospect of riding a motorcycle, but I have seen way too many documentaries on The History Channel about how brutal biker gangs have been and continue to be. But I was rattled. My road bliss had been shattered when I first heard the sound coming from my car. What began as a perfect drive on the early leg of a multiday road trip had quickly become something more sinister and terrifying. And I was at a place where men gathered—and even the women have a way of being men at Cabela's—men who know how to fix things, men who drive huge pickups and kill clawed and fanged animals for sport.

As he dismounted, the biker pulled off his sunglasses, revealing a sun- and windburn combination that resembled the face of a raccoon in a photo negative. He had clearly been on the road for a while. Thankful for his noisy distraction and being a nervous talker, I asked him where he had come from.

"Hell," he said, without the slightest hint of irony. The tone in his voice was flat and serious. I almost immediately regretted my need to speak.

"Really?" I said. "How was the weather?" Heh-heh. I nearly pissed myself when he had said that he had come from Hell, and I could not believe I was cracking wise to this man, who had surely killed more than his fair share of suburban sissies. Stop talking, I thought, and yet there I was nervously chatting him up. Gomer Pyle, you are a brighter man than I.

"Oh, not bad," he said. "I thought it was going to rain, but it's held off pretty good." Wait, shit, was he kidding? Oh no, he's playing games with me, I thought; now I will definitely turn up in a ravine somewhere, just bones and sneakers and brake pads among the fetid water of some southern-Michigan industrial spillway. It turned out, as he smiled and continued to talk, I didn't have much to worry about. Go figure. Nancy-boy was 0 for 2 in that department this fine day. The biker, Dave, worked for a marketing firm in Dayton, Ohio, and had been in Hell, Michigan, as part of an annual six-day solo bike trip. "My wife lets me take a week every year and just go ride," he told me. "It gets me out of her hair and afterward I'm better with the kids."

Dave, as fate (and the odds) would have it, was not a maniacal killer bent on spilling my intestines on the ground for being a smartass but a fellow road warrior. He had been making these annual asphalt assaults for years, and I could tell by talking to him that they were therapy. It wasn't that he didn't love his family; it was that he also knew that to love other people, to be a husband and father, sometimes you have to do things for yourself—things to make yourself happy. This is something I have always wrestled with. By nature, I am a pleaser. When I was young, I tried to please my parents. When I got married, I wanted to please my wife. I am more than willing to stay home with the boys while my wife goes out with her friends. Five nights a week if that's what she wants. It's not that I want her gone; it's that I admire her ability to do those things. Most times, when I leave the house for anything other than chores, errands, or work, a sense of guilt fills me up and leaves a trail back toward home like a slug on a garden path. I get fidgety. I get nervous. I keep thinking I should be someplace else, even if I have just gone to see a movie with a friend. I'm just naturally this way.

But something had changed, if only for a moment, when I got on the road leaving Fort Meigs. I felt okay with doing something for myself. Yes, I could rationalize that it was for work since I would be writing about it, but I also couldn't, since the whole idea of writing books was something I had dreamed up. I hoped that when I got home I would understand what Dave's wife understood, that doing something for me made me better for those who need me. Then again, with the sound coming from the back of my car, I just hoped I would make it home at all.

We chatted on our hike to the store entrance, and when he asked what brought me to south-central Michigan on a Tuesday afternoon, I began telling him about Oliver Hazard Perry and the Battle of Lake Erie.

"Really?" he asked. "That happened around Put-in-Bay? I thought the only thing that ever happened there was people getting drunk and puking in the harbor."

"Well," I said, "that pretty much sums it up now, but a couple hundred years ago things were a little different."

We stood outside the entrance, and I told him about Perry and his heroism during the battle. It felt a little strange, talking history to a complete stranger, but also soothing. I worried that replacing my brake pads would be difficult without any tools, and it was too late in the day to go to a garage. I worried about the effort and whether or not it would throw me off my schedule. I wanted to eat well in Ann Arbor that night, not spend an hour and a half changing brake pads. Part of me was probably trying to put the whole thing off. In my mind the task at hand was a relatively simple one, but a pain nonetheless. Plus, the awful groaning grind of the naked pad against the disc had sort of ruined my road buzz. Talking to Dave was a way for me to hold on to it or at least put off its funeral for another couple minutes.

"So why are you here instead of on Put-in-Bay?" Dave asked and I realized I had not really told him what brought me to Michigan.

"I'm going to Ann Arbor," I said. "The University of Michigan has a collection of Perry's papers that I'm hoping to take a look at."

"Sounds cool," he said. "Good luck with that. And whatever you do," he paused and looked around, "don't come back to Ohio as a goddamn Wolverines fan."

I promised that I wouldn't, and we parted ways once we were inside.

If Cabela's is Disney World for hunters and sportsmen, then the towering edifice in the central atrium of the store is Magic Mountain. Standing probably forty feet high is a fake rock edifice covered, and I do mean covered, with hundreds of post-op taxidermy specimens. Anything from mountain goats to grizzlies, African antelopes to quail, all dutifully stuffed, all replete with plastic eyes that seem to follow you wherever you go. I tried not to stare at the death hill, but everywhere I went in the store—from the shooting section that has pallets of ammunition stacked in the aisles like yogurt on special at Costco, to the camping section that seems to make inordinate accommodation for firearms if not campers—I could feel them watching me.

After a half hour or so of perusing shotgun shells and bottles of deer urine (which promises to ward off the smell of the hunter and attract a huge buck intent on mating), I realized I had no reason to be there other than to figure out what was going on with my car and, with luck, to get a few tools that might help in the repair. My hotel—the only one I had booked for my trip—was a scant seventeen miles up the road, and my time might be better spent going there instead of wandering around the palace of death.

I found a couple hand tools and some extra batteries that I thought I might need for the flashlight I hoped I had remembered to pack. I wanted to find an automotive tool set but was surprised when I didn't see one. Then again, you'd think something like that would be basic to packing for a road trip, but I was still new to this and couldn't beat myself up too badly for that.

After trekking six miles back across the parking lot, I did a quick inspection of my rear tires, getting low to the ground and trying to assume the posture of someone who might know what the hell they were looking for, and decided that if I had made it this far, surely my little vehicle could make it to the hotel just up the road. I formulated a plan to check in and then find an auto parts store to buy new brake pads and then find a Target or Walmart to buy a cheap set of tools to install them. Once done, I would wash up and head into Ann Arbor for an overpriced meal at a hip café, preferably something that featured a tapenade or rémoulade or some other thing that I don't really understand but is surely not to be found in the culinary section of Cabela's.

I was feeling strangely optimistic that I would be able to fix the problem myself. Just pop over to a shop, pick up some parts, and remedy the situation with relative ease. I might have to give up the stroll around the University of Michigan campus I had planned, but oh well, I thought, such is life. Though my chase of Oliver Hazard Perry—and his gifts for bravery, resourcefulness, and luck—had been pretty well blocked at every turn, I felt as if maybe I really was making progress, that some of those gifts had begun to rub off on me. Maybe I too was evolving into a dashing hero, graceful under pressure.

There was even a bit of pluck in my gait as I reached my ailing car. I had no idea that my grand dreams for the freedom of the open road had only begun being crushed, and that missing an evening walk would be chief among the least of my problems.

❦ 9 ❦

The Unlucky Traveler: Part Two

The hotel was on the outskirts of Ann Arbor, home to the University of Michigan, and near Ypsilanti, the home of Eastern Michigan University. It was just off a four-lane road that was probably called "Pedestrians Beware Boulevard" or something like that. Having located it, I decided that, with evening pressing, I should find brake pads and tools before checking in, so I followed my instinct for urban planning in a direction that I thought might lead to a big-box store and auto parts retailer.

It's uncanny to me how similarly all suburbs and small cities are laid out. Just look around and you can probably tell where you are, even if you have never been there before. Zoning laws are like a universal language. Malls and big-box stores are always on the outskirts of town near a main road. Auto parts stores, ethnic grocers, and plumbers are usually near older, working-class neighborhoods, and fine dining and boutique shopping are reserved for central business districts. I felt like a Kalahari Bushman reading animal tracks as I turned from the main artery to a smaller one and watched for small houses and Indian grocery stores. Within five minutes of beginning my measured hunt and without asking directions, I found a place that sold brake pads. The man behind the counter, who introduced himself as Matt, a name that did not match the embroidered patch on his shirt, was tall and thin and friendly. He seemed eager to help, like maybe he was bucking for a promotion to assistant night manager. I felt privileged to be a part of him chasing his dreams.

"I need rear brake pads for a 2003 Volkswagen Jetta GL," I said.

"I hope we've got 'em," Matt said as he began punching a perplexing number of keys on the inventory computer. As Matt typed for what seemed like whole minutes, I began to wonder if he was searching for the part or writing a novel.

"Those things are supposed to make your life easier," I joked, pointing to the computer.

"I'm just trying to be thorough, sir," Matt said. Forget assistant night manager, this kid had day-shift supervisor written all over him.

Matt jotted a few numbers on a piece of paper and disappeared into the back with the purposeful stride of a man on a mission. He returned a few minutes later with an armful of boxes and set them down on the counter with a pronounced thud. It turned out I had options when it came to brake pads, and Matt was prepared to discuss them all in the finest of detail. But given that it was now raining and the daylight was fading and I still had to find tools and a place to eat, I decided to let this eager young man off the hook and buy the cheapest ones, without further consideration of viscosity, wear, or warranties. Matt looked simultaneously pleased with the sale and saddened at my indifference to his years of accumulated brake pad knowledge, and I felt a little guilty for this last part, so on the way out the door I made sure to offer a "You've been a big help, Matt" loud enough that his manager and the manager of the Indian deli three doors down could hear me.

And so, with a now badly grinding back wheel and a slightly lighter wallet, I set out into the rain to find a big-box store and a cheap set of tools. I made my way back to the Target I had seen earlier, and in the parking lot once again felt self-conscious about the noises emanating from my beleaguered VW. Nestled on the precipice of two major college towns, Ann Arbor and Ypsilanti, the store was everything you might expect—large, busy, and oddly dorm-scented. I love places like this. I have since the first time I managed—after two bus rides and a long walk—to get from my freshman dorm to the Walmart on the outskirts of town. And everywhere I looked I saw versions of myself from those first heady days of college. Part of me wanted to grab a freshman by the scruff of the neck and make them promise not to be an English major, and part of me wanted to ingratiate myself into an invite to a party. By God, I did love college. I loved it for all the reasons most people did—the parties, the freedom, the drinking and bar food—but also because in college I would have just sent my car to a garage and gotten it fixed, instead of trying to do it myself . . . in the dark and the rain in an unfamiliar place.

Tools purchased and brake pads secured, I made my way to the hotel. I hadn't wanted to spend a lot money on this trip because a) I would have felt guilty leaving my wife and kids at home while I traipsed off down the road unknown, spending cash that could have been used for groceries and tuition for my son's preschool and b) because I usually don't have that much. Unlike a lot of my friends, I was an English major in college—a double English major, in fact—with a history minor. So while my buddies were trapped in the tedium of learning thermodynamics and economics, I was immersed in full-blown studies of Kerouac and James Joyce. And while my friends drearily studied for and sweated exams, I was writing term papers about Hemingway's use of the unreliable narrative in *Hills Like White Elephants* and how it related to the movie *The Usual Suspects*. I used to think having no math and no exams in college was a wonderful thing, but my paycheck for the last decade has proved otherwise.

So the hotel was cheap, but not too cheap. It was the kind of place where road-warrior traveling salesmen would stay, and people in town for the big game—regular people like plumbers and family men with mouths to feed just looking for a quick getaway without many frills, but not biblically austere either. When I walked into the lobby, I was soaked from rain and frustrated and losing my sense of adventure. A man was in line ahead of me checking in, and he seemed like a guy who had maybe been in this place before. His name, which I could see embossed on the oversize sample case resting at his feet, was Darryl. Like my biker friend Dave, Darryl was a road warrior. He was a salesmen from the oldest of schools. His briefcase was shabby and so was his hundred-dollar suit, but it was worn with pride and a sense of joie de vivre. Darryl didn't do anything quickly, including checking into moderately priced hotel rooms. I stood dripping behind him for nearly ten minutes as he dazzled the kid behind the counter—whom I assumed was working to help pay tuition—with magic tricks and challenging him to figure out how he had done them. At one point, I half-expected Darryl to turn to me with his worn but friendly smile and say, "Hey, you wouldn't mind letting me cut you in half, now would you?" To which I could only reply, "I really wish you would."

My patience had grown facial tissue–thin, and thanks in large part to the deluge outside, even that was becoming tattered. So when Darryl finally finished his grand finale, I stepped up to the counter and was surprised to hear, "You must be Craig. I have your key right here for you." I was a little stunned. And wondering how the kid knew my name without me uttering so much as a mumble. He handed over the information and the key and a map of the place and bid me on my way. All without me saying a word. This I could get used to.

Without wondering what would have happened had I not been me and had just accepted the room key of a total stranger, I found my room, which was thankfully on the first floor and featured a nifty, not-seen-since-the-1960s walk-out balcony that was separated from the parking lot by a strip of grass about fifteen feet wide. I moved my car into the space outside the door and brought my bags inside. The rain was clearing off slowly, leaving the sky a menacing purple and the air just slightly thinner than motor oil. But I had made it to the hotel and I had the tools I needed, including a flashlight and, relatively speaking, all the time in the world to make my simple repair. I was tired and frustrated and had lost the edge of adventure and excitement I had set out with, but I figured all I needed was a hot shower, a good meal, and a good night's sleep. In the morning, the car would be fixed and I would be on my way, having met the enemy and making it mine.

This assumption kept me calm as I loosened the lug nuts and got my car up on the jack and loosened the bolts holding the brakes onto the rotor. True, I had to spend a day's worth of my allotted traveling money on parts and tools, and true, I was technically behind schedule, but things could be a whole lot worse. *Things could always be worse.* I kept telling myself that as I pulled and yanked, yanked and pulled, and twisted and levered and grunted, trying to get the brake caliper to come off the rotor. When my friend John and I had done this the first time, the thing had popped right off—a testament to German manufacturing foresight that a couple idiots could, without an instruction manual, so easily navigate the mechanics of the thing. But this time was different. This time, rather than a fluid motion of seamless precision, there was a series of grunts and hunks and chucks with very, very little movement on the part of the supposedly moving parts.

Finally, after more than an hour of sweaty, dirty effort, I managed to remove the caliper from the rotor. For anyone who doesn't know the mechanics of brakes and the changing of pads, it goes something like this:

Step 1: Remove caliper from brake rotor.
Step 2: Remove old pads and replace with new ones.
Step 3: Replace caliper.
Step 4: Have a nice salad, 'cause you're done, baby.

This is, of course, assuming that things go well. If they don't, there are several additional steps that involve a lot of swearing and banging on things and questioning your religious values. This was the direction my adventure was going in, especially once I had the whole thing apart and realized I had forgotten to buy a C-clamp. Why is this so important, you might ask? Well, a C-clamp is important because one cannot put the brakes back together without one. After wrestling with the caliper for an hour and spending another trying to get the thing back together with new pads on it and without the requisite C-clamp, I was sweaty, filthy—covered from head to toe in grease and lubricant and the general mélange of grime and shit that washes down the blacktop parking lot of a cheap hotel in the rain—and completely broken. I needed another tool and I knew exactly where to get it. All I had to do was get there. I was going to be damned to the lowest, hot-test point in hell before I called a cab and let this little repair cost me even a single nickel more than was absolutely necessary, so I did what any red-blooded American man would do—I decided to get the thing back together again the best I could, pack up my tools and drive, without a rear brake, to the Home Depot I had seen from Target across Dead Pedestrian Boulevard earlier.

I went back into the hotel to grab my wallet and wash my hands and face, which looked like I had been auditioning for a part in a minstrel show, only when I went into the bathroom—and this is just my luck—and turned on the faucet, nothing came out. Nothing. Not a damn drop. Great, I thought, just fucking great.

I'm usually a pretty positive person. I can always see the upside of things and can usually keep my cool in a tense or emergency situation. But when I was driving on a four-lane highway without any brakes, covered in quickly hardening, pore-clogging grime, hungry, tired, spent, and being honked at by unfriendly locals who didn't like my emergency-flasher-and-ten-miles-per-hour pace on a dark, stormy night, my hopes had splintered and, just a day into my big adventure, I wanted to go home.

~10~
The Unlucky Traveler: Part Three

A lot has been made of Oliver Hazard Perry's incredible luck. As I would learn later on in my journey, it was one of the things his contemporaries found so completely and utterly endearing about him (that and, one has to assume, really awesome sideburns). He was lucky that he was able to get the ships of the Lake Erie fleet built, lucky he could get them launched. He was lucky when he managed to row from the *Lawrence* to the *Niagara* without being killed, lucky, in fact, to not be hurt at all during the battle. He was lucky when the winds shifted and he was able to capture the British squadron.

He had been lucky in so many ways, from his marriage to his greatest adventures. But it turned out the commodore and I had a similar lack of luck when it came to vehicles. While his was temporary, mine was seemingly a more permanent kind of problem. The Jetta is the first car I have ever purchased myself, my first new car, and has been cherished for years of relatively problem-free service, despite a sometimes forgetful owner. I have little doubt that Perry felt the same way about the first ship he ever commanded, the schooner *Revenge*. But first, I'm going to drop a little history on you.

Perry's father, Christopher Raymond Perry, gained acclaim or at least notoriety for his service in the navy during the Revolutionary

War. Having grown up in a pacifist Quaker family, Christopher was nevertheless a bit of a hothead. Seeing revolution brewing in colonial America, he enlisted in the local Rhode Island militia at thirteen, and by fourteen—the age when I began longing for the freedom of a driver's license—he enlisted in the regular army in anticipation of fighting the redcoats. He was captured and put on board the infamous prison ship *Jersey* in New York Harbor. Not one to be held, he escaped and joined the Continental navy and eventually found his way on board a ship heading toward England to launch an attack against the British home soil. He was, almost fatefully, once again captured and imprisoned in Ireland. While in prison, he met Raymond Wallace, the cousin of the woman who would eventually become his wife, Sarah.

Christopher escaped again and made his way to a ship. The only problem, of course, was that it was a British ship, and at the time the English were none too keen on the idea of letting an escaped American prisoner tag along on a journey back toward his homeland. But Christopher was more than likely pretty smart and definitely ballsy as hell. Seeing no other way home, he impersonated a British officer so convincingly that he managed a ride all the way back to the United States, undetected. The elder Perry returned to find the war over and, having learned so many skills as a sailor, he joined a merchant crew sailing for Ireland. On board that ship was his former prison-mate's cousin, Sarah. They courted, were married, and moved to South Kingston, Rhode Island, to start their family.

In August 1785, Sarah gave birth to their first child, Oliver Hazard Perry, and soon Christopher was father to a brood of three. But Sarah was the bigger influence on young Oliver, according to biographer David Curtis Skaggs. A direct descendant of the infamous—thanks in large part to the historically iffy portrayal by Mel Gibson in the film *Braveheart*—William Wallace, Sarah was headstrong. At one point, Skaggs writes, Sarah packed up their three children and moved from the country house owned by a grandfather to a neighborhood closer to town. It was not known if she did this on her own without consent from Christopher or whether he was at sea, but either way it was a gutsy thing for an eighteenth-century woman to do.

But if Oliver Perry got his chutzpah from his mother, he got his career from his father. Early Americans were in large part suspicious of a standing federal military. The first president and war hero George Washington put off the creation of a strong army and navy on the grounds that he too—even he—was concerned about the high cost and the threat a standing military could pose to a nascent and free country. But if Washington chose to focus on policies of neutrality and paying down the considerable national debt incurred by the revolution, then the second man in the job, John Adams, was the era's equivalent of a neo-con war hawk.

In his book *Union 1812: The Americans Who Fought and Won the Second War of Independence*, A. J. Langguth describes Adams as being Washington's opposite when it came to military outlays. He commissioned forty-four warships built to support a standing navy and went on a recruiting binge. Adams drew criticism from southern gentlemen like James Madison and Thomas Jefferson but managed to push through the Sedition Act, which basically made editorializing ill will toward the president a crime punishable by fines and prison time. So much for Jefferson's First Amendment.

With naysayers silenced and strong support from the northern states that looked forward to the protection a navy could provide for the largely trade- and shipping-based New England economy, Adams set about building the military. Among those called to action was Christopher Perry, who was commissioned a navy captain and given the order to construct, crew, and launch the ship *General Greene* in 1798.

The elder Perry's problems with the navy began almost right away. Construction ran late, stirring admonishment from the top brass, but when the *General Greene* finally did launch in June 1799 it carried the thirteen-year-old Oliver, who had joined the ship with his father's approval. While its first mission was to Cuba to protect American shipping interests from French pirates, Christopher Perry would continually have run-ins with authority. By the time the Jefferson administration took over, his time had come.

Jefferson saw two reasons to reverse Adams's military buildup. First, he was mistrustful of a standing army, and second, it was expensive. Jefferson took over a federal government in debt greater than the gross national product. He scrapped all but thirteen of Adams's forty-four warships and culled the army and navy of expensive officers. Christopher Perry was gone, but his son was offered one of 150 midshipman positions—the other 3,350 were being eliminated in a preview of American corporate downsizing. Oliver decided to roll the dice with the navy, thinking it would present career opportunities he could not get working a trade back in Rhode Island.

Only a couple of decades after the Revolution, the drumbeats of war with England or France were echoing with every step Jefferson took. There were those who thought the Revolution would not be complete without a second war with England and those who wanted to wage war against France, fresh from its own revolution, for what was considered despotism. A particular incident above all others raised the volume of those voices calling for war. An abbreviated version:

Early in 1807, the USS *Chesapeake* set sail from Hampton Roads, Virginia, carrying a full crew and civilians bound for the Mediterranean. Commodore James Baron, the captain of the *Chesapeake*, expected an uneventful voyage, so he was surprised when, only five miles into open ocean, he encountered the British HMS *Leopard*. So surprised was Baron that he had allowed luggage to be stored around the ship's guns, making firing them nearly impossible without some serious effort.

Impressment had been a problem since the days immediately following the Revolution. The British Navy, which in those years was composed of nearly seven hundred ships, needed men to fight its war against Napoleon. British laws considered all those born under British rule to be British nationals, despite country of residence or citizenship. So it was not uncommon for British forces, flush with ships but short on men, to stop American merchant and military ships in search of those the Crown considered deserters. This was exactly the intent Captain Salisbury Pryce Humphreys had in mind when he sent a request to Baron to search the *Chesapeake* for four men suspected of desertion. Baron refused the request after a half hour of negotiation by Humphreys' representative aboard the *Chesapeake*. Things went badly from there. Baron was essentially caught with his pants down when the *Leopard* hauled off and fired a warning across the *Chesapeake*'s bow. Guns stowed, he issued an order to his men to silently prepare the cannon for a fight. The order was received, save for the silent part, and soon it became obvious to Humphreys that the Americans intended to fight. The *Leopard*, on full alert, laid into the *Chesapeake* with a barrage of fire. Baron was able to fire a single shot from his badly damaged ship before surrendering and giving up the men. It was a humiliating defeat, especially since it occurred so close to soil. It was cause enough, many argued, for war.

But Jefferson didn't want war with England. Fighting the English would be costly in dollars and lives, and there was little reason to believe it would be possible to win. Still, Jefferson was being openly challenged—thanks to the repeal of the Sedition Act—and he needed to do something to win back confidence, so he turned his sights to the Barbary Coast in North Africa.

The nations along the Barbary Coast had quite a racket going in those days, and racketeering it was. They demanded protection money for European and American merchant ships hoping to do business in the Mediterranean. The U.S. had been paying this tribute, though not as much in terms of amount as European countries. But Jefferson decided enough was, well, slightly more than he was comfortable with. He refused payment and began sending his nascent navy to deflect threats and, if need be, to battle the pirates. Oliver Perry was part of this effort, though not as heroically as his contemporary—and eventual best friend—Stephen Decatur.

Decatur became a hero when he led a raid to destroy the captured ship USS *Philadelphia*. The *Philadelphia* had become stranded in a low tide and its crew of 250 was taken captive in Tripoli. Not wanting the ship to fall into the wrong hands, Decatur was chosen to lead what might have been a preview of a Navy SEALs-style raid in which he and a small group of men boarded a small boat and hired a local to tell the pirates they had lost their anchor and would they mind if they tied up to the *Philadelphia* for the evening? Once attached to the much larger ship, Decatur and his men snuck aboard and, using knives and swords, silently took out the crew. Silently, except for one sailor, who, having broken his cutlass, grabbed the pistol of the pirate he was fighting and killed the man, alerting those on shore. Before leaving the *Philadelphia* and hightailing it back to the naval ships outside the harbor, Decatur and his men used sperm candles to set the ship ablaze. (For more on this, I highly recommend reading *A Rage for Glory: The Life of Commodore Stephen Decatur, USN*, by James Tertius de Kay.)

Overnight, or as closely to overnight as word could spread from the other side of the world in those days, Decatur became a hero. Perry, on the other hand, saw no action other than the signing of a treaty to end the conflict during his time along the Barbary Coast. Instead, he used his time to buddy up to the man who would change his fate forever, Commodore John Rodgers. Rodgers was a powerful figure in the early U.S. Navy and, ever the type-A person, Perry saw value in getting on his good side.

After returning from the Barbary conflict, Perry was assigned to oversee ship construction in New York, but he maintained communication with Rodgers, who would prove more advisor than commander to Perry. Eventually, and with Rodgers' help, Perry was given his first command, of the schooner *Revenge*, in April 1809.

Relatively speaking, the *Revenge* was a small ship. It was too narrow to carry the stores necessary for service on the open ocean, so Perry was relegated to duties similar to those of the modern Coast Guard. After sailing with the New York squadron in the summer and fall of 1809, he received orders in the spring of 1810 to report to Charleston, South Carolina. There, he was given the order to patrol the line between Georgia and Spanish Florida to enforce American neutrality and customs laws and be on the lookout for smugglers. Perry took these orders very seriously and saw in them the opportunity to prove his mettle as an officer. He got that chance in July 1810 while cruising near Cumberland Island, Georgia.

Perry had taken on board a deputy U.S. Marshal, according to Skaggs, with a warrant for the seizure of the merchant ship *Diana*. Sailing from Wiscasset, Maine—and they certainly know how to name towns in Maine—the privately owned *Diana* had been commandeered by its hired British sailing master, a guy by the name of Tibbets. Tibbets had disguised the *Diana*, calling it the *Angel*, and was using it for illicit activities. The owners in Maine wanted it back.

When Perry found the *Diana*, it was operating under British colors and resting under the battery—read: big-ass guns—of the British brig *Plumper* and schooner *Jupiter* near Amelia Island. Perry sailed the *Revenge* and three other U.S. Navy ships right up to the *Diana* and took it back, despite being highly outgunned and overmatched. He had guts, there was no doubting that, especially when, on the return trip north, with the *Diana* in tow, he was confronted by the British sloop-of-war *Goree*. Again highly outgunned, Perry played a game of chicken with the *Goree*, refusing to yield, refusing to back down. He stayed cool and remained calm, doing nothing rash and not allowing the British ship to get in the way of his mission. He stared the *Goree* down and was able to bring the *Diana* back to its owner.

With a bit of accomplishment under his belt and having proved his worth as an officer, Perry asked to be reassigned to a position closer to home so that he could be near his wife, Elizabeth Chaplin Mason. Rodgers was proud of his young protégé and made the request happen, giving Perry the order to take the *Revenge* from Montauk Sound on the eastern tip of Long Island to Nantucket—a similar route to the final flight made by John F. Kennedy, Jr., two centuries later. In early December 1810, Perry met with Rodgers, who helped him secure a cushy mission to make an accurate survey of the coast between New London, Connecticut; Newport, Rhode Island; and Gardiner's Island, New York.

It was on this assignment that Perry proved about as trustworthy with command of a vehicle as I am. Rough winter weather had delayed Perry's progress in completing the assignment, and he decided to return to New London to meet with Rodgers and ask for an extension in January 1811. Three months earlier, Perry had hired a local pilot named Peter Daggett. Daggett had assured Perry that despite thick fog and winter weather, the *Revenge* would be able to make it through the channel between Fisher's Island and Watch Hill, the neighborhood where Perry had grown up after his mom had taken him and his siblings to town from the country house where he was born. With this assurance from a trusted and knowledgeable local pilot, Perry and the *Revenge* weighed anchor at five o'clock in the afternoon on January 8, 1811, bound for the meeting with Rodgers in New London.

Shortly after midnight the schooner was under way on what would prove to be its final journey. Perry had assumed when he went to bed that the *Revenge* was more than five miles from the coast near Watch Hill, yet in a thick fog and with a driving wind kicking up, the ship struck the reef near his old neighborhood, yards from the beach where he had played as a child. Echoing his demeanor during the *Diana* affair, Perry stayed calm and made several attempts to free the damaged *Revenge* from the reef to no avail.

Gale-force winds started to blow, and after fifteen hours of trying, he finally gave the order for his crew to abandon the *Revenge* as it was badly beaten across rocks. But he didn't give up there. As his crew gathered up the supplies from the ship that had washed up on shore, Perry joined the effort to free the ship now under way from other ships that had stopped to assist. All efforts were useless. The *Revenge* was lost, and Perry's first command came to an abbreviated and inglorious halt.

A court of inquiry blamed Daggett, who, as a local and seasoned pilot, should have known better than to attempt the route in such conditions. But for his part, Perry refused to blame anyone but himself, despite evidence to the contrary. Popular opinion among naval officials was that Perry had acted in the sinking of the *Revenge* with the same level-headed calm and honor as he had in wrestling the *Diana* from British control. The only criticisms ladled on him were that he had a tendency to be too lenient when it came to the mistakes of his subordinates, and too hard on himself.

☙·❧

I was thinking about Perry and the *Revenge* in between intermittent swipes of my wiper blades and clicks of my emergency flashers. I spotted the Home Depot about two blocks up and was hoping I would not find myself in a similar predicament—vehicle totaled and stranded on a reef awaiting public scorn and ridicule. I could have cried. Here I was finally chasing down my dream, and nearly from the start I was being thwarted. If I hadn't cried, I certainly could have screamed, and while my mind has worked to suppress some of those memories now, I believe I did just that. So much for my Perry-like calm in the face of adversity.

As I coasted through the semicrowded parking lot with my clutch engaged and gear set for reverse just in case a small child ran out in my way, I thought about giving the whole thing up. What, after all, would I tell my wife? But then the strangest feeling came over me, one I'm sure Perry himself must have felt from time to time—especially when staring down the *Goree.*

"Fuck it," I said to myself and then repeated the phrase I heard my grandmother mutter under her breath in Swedish—I won't even try to type it here, but it translates roughly to "Damn it all to hell." And then, the only Latin my dad remembers from high school: *illegitimi non carborundum*—"Don't let the bastards get you down"— which isn't even Latin at all, but it is strange how we remember things, isn't it?

I would soon learn that the situation would require a great deal more than cathartic swearing, foreign-tongue platitudes, and a determined attitude. I might just end up stranded on a reef after all.

≈11≈

The Unlucky Traveler: Concluded

A member of the hotel's maintenance crew had assured me that the water would be turned on by the time I returned from Home Depot, so I was a little self-conscious when I went inside. My face was covered in grime, my clothes too. I felt that a stranger—and everyone in the store was a stranger—might assume that I had gotten into some sort of altercation, perhaps with an oil rig. Not wanting to talk to anyone because I was filthy and my mood was even more soiled, I roamed the store in search of a restroom.

I am still amazed that this is what commerce in the United States has come to—stores larger than military forts in Perry's time. Arenas of retail, coliseums of spending, stadiums of debt. There's no such thing as a mom-and-pop shop anymore, unless of course you are Mom and Pop Walmart. The funny thing is, the big-box revolution never bothered me until that moment. I was an early adopter of Target and—cover your eyes, my indie book shop–loving readers—when a Borders opened near our house when I was in high school, I thought I had reached Nirvana. My wife and I make semiweekly trips to Costco to pick up the essentials—a crate and a half of toothpaste, a fifty-five-gallon drum of olive oil, you know, the basics—and I like the warranty service at places like Best Buy. But right here and now, in this moment of frustration, humiliation, and desperation, I absolutely fucking hated retail on a large scale.

After fumbling through lighting and appliances, a solid hectare of lumber, and nineteen linear miles of screws, nails, and other bits of binding, I finally found the restroom and managed, with great effort, to remove at least the outermost layer of grime from my tortured epidermis. I waved my hand for perhaps the seventy-fourth time in front of the motion-activated paper towel dispenser for the postage stamp–sized ration of drying power it dispensed, and steeled my nerve for my true mission to this godforsaken neon-lit hell. I needed a C-clamp in order to finish the repair of my brakes, and I remembered seeing one somewhere in one of the aisles.

I cursed myself for not having grabbed it when I had the chance, and, like a half-witted desert explorer passing on the chance for fresh water, I embarked back into the gloom, hoping the oversize signs demarcating the aisles would be useful in helping me find my way. But combined with my ignorance when it comes to do-it-yourself projects, the purposely vague signs were too much for my addled mind to bear. Was a C-clamp hardware? Or was it woodworking? Could it be with the power tools? One has to assume that it would come in handy should someone want to drill a hole through multiple pieces of lumber, but in time I knew I was grasping at straws and finally abandoned the search in favor of a new one—for an orange-vested member of the Home Depot team.

"Excuse me," I said, having found a member of that team after perhaps twenty minutes more of searching. "Can you help me find something, please?"

"I'll certainly try," said the man, who was approaching seventy and had the striking white hair and mustache to prove it.

"I'm looking for a C-clamp," I told him, "a rather large one."

He looked at me as if he were trying to comprehend why on God's green one someone would come to a hardware store looking for such a thing.

"What are you using it for?" he asked.

"I'm in the middle of changing my brake pads, and I need the clamp to push the caliper plunger thingy back in place."

"We don't have an automotive department," he said.

"Yes, I know," I said. I could feel tension rising from the pit of my stomach and was doing all I could to suppress the violent outburst I could feel coming on. "But I have done this before, and I know what I need and it is a plain old C-clamp."

"How'd you do it before without the C-clamp?" he asked. "And come to think of it, how did you get here if you're in the middle of changing your brakes?"

That's it, you doddering old fool, I felt like saying, I have decided that someone in this impossible sty of a town needs to die, and I have elected that you, as the dumbest, least helpful person here, are that person. Instead, I politely swallowed and paused before explaining the situation to the man, starting with the sound I heard and working to the present.

"Well, that wasn't smart," he said. "Driving with no rear brakes is dangerous as hell. Someone ought to report you to the cops."

And someone ought to send you to the home, I considered replying, but instead I mustered all the charm I had left in me to thank him for his help, which had been completely absent in the course of our interaction, and told him I would try myself to find the part I needed.

It took some doing, but I eventually did find what I needed and opted to use the automated self-checkout—ordinarily one of my biggest pet peeves since it removes the last shred of human dignity from the buying process—in order to avoid any potentially explosive interaction with another idiot working the night shift.

Back out in the parking lot, I remounted the jack and removed the tire yet again. I had left the brake caliper hanging on the ride over since it wasn't going to do me any good anyway and because I was in quite the snit to boot. The rain had stopped, which was a blessing, but the air was thick with humidity, and I was soon in a rather egregious state of sweat. I paused to remove the C-clamp from the white plastic bag, and to settle myself. I was nearly done, I promised myself, and when it was over and I was back in my hotel room I would celebrate with a hot shower—because in my mind Billy Bob or Jethro or whatever the maintenance guy's name was would be finished fixing the water by the time of my return—then a trip to a trendy restaurant in Ann Arbor for a nice, healthy meal followed by a good night's sleep. I'd probably burn my clothes, but that could be cathartic too.

Maneuvering the C-clamp over the top of the caliper plunger thingy in such a way that I would be able to tighten the clamp and push it back in, I should have known my luck would not, could not, possibly hold up. As I screwed the clamp down and its head touched the end of the caliper ever so slightly, I was anticipating five minutes of effort and then cleaning up, replacing the tire, and going about my business. Perhaps, if I could manage to keep it clean, I would return the C-clamp in the morning before visiting the Clements Library, the University of Michigan's historical collection and the largest archive of Perry papers in the world, in order to recoup some of the unbudgeted costs the afternoon had foisted upon me. But when the head made contact with the caliper, the plunger thingy fell to the ground with a clang, like the head of a statue assaulted by Odd Job's hat, and a Vesuvius of brake fluid tidal-waved from deep within the bowels of my vehicle onto my hands, my pants, my arms, feet, and chin. While reality would dictate it could not have been more than a few ounces, I was coated in the semigelatinous fluid like Bill Murray after his run-in with Slimer in the hotel hall in the first *Ghostbusters* movie. I screamed, a caveman scream, and though I could not feel them through the goo that had taken up residence on my face, I'm pretty sure hot tears began to fall from my bleary eyes.

And then panic set in.

I tried in vain to screw the plunger thingy back into place but eventually realized it was time to call 'no joy,' and a tow truck. The C-clamp was covered in brake fluid, having failed without use. I was covered in brake fluid. My life was, in that moment, covered in brake fluid. So I stepped soggily, keeping my legs akimbo in order that I not start some sort of friction chemical fire as I trekked back into the store and found my way, once again to the restroom. Fifteen minutes and nine hundred swipes from the paper towel machine later, I emerged still sodden and damp but clean enough to operate my cell phone. It had been seven hours since I first heard the crunch coming from the rear of my car, but already it felt like a lifetime. I walked back to the front of the store, passed the retiree who had been so unhelpful. He tried to say something, but I didn't slow, just whispered "fuck you" under my breath and stepped back into the putrid Michigan air to call for a tow.

As I was waiting for the tow truck to arrive, I surveyed the parking lot, only to notice that not two hundred yards from where my disabled vehicle now sat useless was a four-bay garage called Belle Tire that advertised brake service on its marquee. I looked at my watch and saw that it read 8:56. Belle Tire was closing in four minutes, so I sprinted across the parking-lot sea to catch them before the lights went dim. The last bay door was pounding shut when I made it to the shop. I knocked on the glass front door, but no one answered. Great, I thought, really freaking great. Just my stupid fucking luck, I thought. You know what? Fuck driving. Fuck Michigan. Fuck my car. Fuck my luck and fuck a duck. Fuck Oliver Fucking Hazard Perry and his little fucking ships. I quit. I'm done. Fuck this whole fucking thing.

After I had turned and walked away, I heard a voice calling from the direction of the front door. The Belle Tire manager apologized that there was nothing he could do that night but showed me where to leave my keys and instructions regarding what, exactly, was wrong with my car.

"It won't be too hard to tell," I assured him and gave him my phone number to call in the morning after he took a look.

I replaced the tire and, with no small amount of frustration, threw the tools I had purchased into the trunk. Fifteen minutes later, the tow truck arrived, and a nice man named Jim got my poor car rigged up.

"Where are we taking it?" asked Jim, a veteran of nine years in the towing game who had already towed three cars that evening.

I meekly pointed to the Belle Tire two football fields away with a sort of 'sorry, I'm an idiot' shrug.

"It's a shame," he said. "You could have just about pushed it there and now you have to pay for a tow."

"*What?*" I said aghast. "I thought my insurance would cover this! I can't afford all this. It's only my first day on this road trip . . . ." Just as I was losing it completely but before I began begging for my mommy, Jim interrupted to say he was only joking and that the insurance would cover up to seven miles.

"Lighten up, man," he said. "You get this upset about some bad brakes and who knows what will happen if something really bad happens."

Between Jim and the Belle Tire manager, Jeff, the previous half hour had been the highlight of my day. They were both friendly, empathetic. I sort of hope they read this, because I'm not sure I thanked them enough when I had the chance.

Now stranded and at least a mile from my hotel, I did what I tend to do in situations when there are limited but varied options and only a single acceptable outcome: the hardest thing possible. Both Jim and Jeff had offered me a ride to where I was going, but I felt the overwhelming need to walk. I thought it might clear my head after the afternoon's odyssey. And, at first, it did. I walked across the strip mall parking lot and purchased a Diet Coke from a gas station on the corner, drank it, and then crossed an intersection in the direction of my hotel.

I would love to say that I had found solace and perspective by contemplating the hardships Perry and men of his time faced when traveling by horse through harsh and infinitely big country, but I didn't. Mostly I thought about my pants and how squishy they were thanks to the oil, grime, and brake fluid that had accumulated on them. I wondered if I should burn them or if setting them ablaze might create the kind of fire that swallows the Iraqi desert in thick black smoke. I must have drifted off into my own little world for a moment, because when I looked up I realized there was no light on the sidewalk running along the four-lane road to my right and the neighborhood—which I had not noticed when driving past with no brakes an hour and a half before—was a bit, um, dodgy.

Carrying all my traveling money in cash in my backpack, which was now slung over both shoulders, I suddenly got the feeling I was being watched. So powerful were my delusions that I actually conjured up Michael Jackson "Beat It"-style gangs approaching from all sides. I felt threatened and hastened my pace toward the relative safety of my cheap, waterless hotel.

"That's just what I need," I thought. "End this day with a good mugging. That would be perfect."

I called my wife and related the whole story to her—the crunch, the repair gone bad, money wasted, and a car bill to come; right down to the walk back to the hotel, which was cleaner than I had remembered and now, thankfully, featured water.

"Is there a mirror in your room?" she asked.

"Yes."

"I want you to look in it. Do you see yourself? You're a six-foot-four-inch guy with broad shoulders and you probably look deranged. I'm pretty sure no one would even think of mugging you."

She was right, of course. The next day I would walk back the same way to check on the progress of the vehicle repair and see that the neighborhood was not that bad, even sort of homey. But in the moment, on that sweat-soaked and mentally broken night, I had myself convinced I was about to become an extra on *CSI*.

Having no way to reach Ann Arbor—I was not willing to spend money on a taxi ride—I settled for a hot shower and an entire pizza, washed down with a liter and a half of Diet Coke, and settled onto my bed to watch bad television. I had taken everything from my car—baggage, laptop, even camping equipment—and stuffed it in every square inch of floor space. Among my things and safely locked inside, I fell asleep with the lights on and Anderson Cooper on TV.

In the morning, I woke to several missed calls on my cell phone from a number I didn't recognize but assumed was that of Belle Tire. I knew the repair was out of my budget but vowed to myself over a cup of coffee from the machine in the lobby that I would not let it ruin my day. Today was going to be a good day—a little gassy from the garlic-crusted pizza of the previous night, but other than that a much better day than the day before.

"I've been trying to reach you," said Jeff. "I'm afraid I've got some bad news." He then went into a long speech detailing exactly everything that was wrong with my vehicle—at one point, I think he said that there was a problem with the compressor in the second quadrant of the ninth axle that needed to be removed with a flux capacitor—and I pretended to know what he was saying. In truth, I didn't recognize anything until he said, "It's gonna cost you about nine hundred and seventy bucks."

I should explain that just the week before, the axle on my wife's minivan had snapped for no apparent reason, a repair that ate up all of our discretionary spending for the month. I didn't have a thousand dollars. No way. I nearly wept telling Jeff the whole story again.

"Man," he said. "That sucks. And all this is for a book?"

"Ye-ye-yes."

"I'll tell you what," he offered. "I can get you out the door for six-thirty-five, but I'd probably cancel your trip and just get your ass back to Cincinnati right away."

"De-de-deal," I whimpered.

I had three hours to kill while Jeff and his able-bodied crew performed battlefield surgery on my car, so I arranged for a late checkout and grabbed my running shoes and swimming suit to check out the fitness center and pool I had seen on the hotel map. I wandered the halls, following signs like trail blazes, and, passing a room with a door open, smelled the awful scent of Ben-Gay and dust. I peered inside and saw an old man of about eighty or so with oxygen tubes connecting his nose and a tank on the floor. He was obviously upset and had been there a while. His room was piled floor to ceiling with the detritus of a life spent collecting. Clothes bulged and spewed from a closet built for no more than three hangers. Boxes were piled in the corner and the old man was on the phone.

"I'm a goddamn senior citizen!" he bellowed. "You can't fucking do this to a senior citizen! If I had my way, I'd come down there and kick you in the goddamn mouth, you sumbitch!"

I gathered that he wasn't talking to his grandchildren but was taken aback when he turned to me. "What the fuck are you looking at?" he yelled in my direction, and I was suddenly aware that I was staring at him and his junk from the doorway. "Get the fuck out of my face!"

It turned out that the fitness center and pool did not belong to my hotel but to the nicer one next door. A brasslike sign pointed from the hallway I had been roaming through a disused room, out the sliding door, and across an uneven concrete sidewalk to an outside door of the other hotel. I used my room key to get access and made it onto the treadmill, where I ran and watched an old episode of JAG before jumping in the pool for a few laps and quiet contemplation. I have always loved to swim. It helps me think. And on this particular day, the only things I kept thinking were, What the hell is this place, and how soon can I get the hell out of here?

≈ 12 ≈

The Perry Papers

I paid Jeff and retrieved my car. He had been compelled enough by my story to throw in an oil change but took the opportunity to tell me face-to-face how important it was that I scrap my plans and just go home. I assured him that I would do so, knowing fully that there was no chance I was going to come all this way and just abandon my trip.

It was almost two when I left my shitty hotel and its strange clientele and maintenance practices behind me and pointed my newly repaired vehicle in the direction of the William Clements Library. As an almost Ohio native, I have been bred to hate all things Michigan, particularly the University of Michigan. There's a subtle indoctrination process that starts just before puberty. First you're lured in by hot dogs at a neighborhood party on a Saturday afternoon in the fall. The hot dogs are especially good when Ohio State is playing the Wolverines. Maybe there are some peanut butter cups, maybe your neighbor lets you have an extra cup of grape Kool-Aid—whatever it may be, you are gently nudged to be a Buckeye fan. Then there are the Ohio-history classes that drive the point home over and over again that you live in the Buckeye State, the insinuation being that since you are a resident, you should therefore be a fan. All is positive until a kid like Billy Williams shows up to school in a U of M T-shirt and is so derided, so belittled, that he wets his pants and has to spend the afternoon in the nurse's office until his mom can come and get him. Billy is not the most popular kid to begin with—he tells weird jokes and, as the reliable sources in the rumor mill have confirmed, was once seen picking his nose and eating it—but this brazen sartorial slipup will forever make him an outcast. Years later, in high school, Billy Williams will be the only senior without a date to the prom. That's okay, he swears, his girlfriend is in college and can't be bothered with such trifling things as a prom, but everyone knows that no girl will talk to him because of that T-shirt he wore back in seventh grade.

You don't want to be like Billy. As an adult you might congratulate him on his individuality, but in the turbid years of adolescence, Billy might well have put on a Nazi armband, an Al-Qaeda beard, and relieved himself on the American flag. So you go along with it. You believe the hype—that the University of Michigan produced more communist agents during the Cold War than Moscow; that Michigan graduates are illiterate and have a fondness for pedophilia, necrophilia, and all the other -philias that shock your brain. You go along with the programming, you root for a school whose mascot is a nut named for the man who killed Julius Caesar, ignoring the manipulation and backstabbing. You drink the punch because you fear the reprisal of the angry mob. And then, before you know it, you are an adult hosting your own block parties. You spend hours tending the hot dog fire as "Hang on Sloopy" plays on a loop over the whole-house speakers you installed for just that purpose, until the unsuspecting youth arrive hungry and primed to learn, to be sponges for your own cruel mind control.

In other words, there is nothing more treacherous for an Ohioan like me to admit than this: I really liked the University of Michigan. It's beautiful, old, scholarly, just as an august institution of higher learning should be. I admitted this fact out loud as I drove around looking for a parking space amid the throng of students recently returned from summer break. My alma mater, Miami University, is beautiful, but in an incredibly designed way. The buildings, even the new ice arena, are built with the appearance of age in a uniform redbrick-and-cream pattern that exemplifies early-American architecture. The buildings on the University of Michigan campus exude age through their diversity. There's the old fieldstone halls and the modern performance centers, the Georgian-style brick buildings and the steel-and-glass edifices imbued with a certain contemporary chic that I found, in their side-by-side placement, wonderfully endearing.

I had called from the hotel to ask for directions to the William Clements library and was told to look for the building with the white pillars. The student aide who offered this advice neglected to tell me that there would be more than one, so parking my car in a place I judged to be central, I approached a young man waiting for a bus to ask for directions.

"I'm not really sure," he said. "What kind of classes are held there?"

"I don't know," I said. "I don't suppose many. The Clements Library is home to the university's special historical collection."

"I'm an engineering major," he said, by way of excuse. "But if I had to guess . . . "

He pointed vaguely in the wrong direction and twenty or so minutes later and having had three more similar conversations—it seems there are a lot of engineering majors at the U of M—I eventually found my way to the facility, small in comparison to surrounding buildings and bearing the aforementioned white pillars.

I had been directed to the Clements Library by Gerard Altoff, who confirmed my Googling by saying it was the largest repository of Perry's papers in the world. Upon entering, I was greeted by a middle-aged man seated at an ornately carved desk in a room of such splendor and fineness it nearly took my breath away. The library's reading

The Clements Library on the campus of the University of Michigan, a place so resplendent with academia I could hardly stand it. Damn you, David McCollough.

room is home to volumes dating back to the mid–sixteenth century, held on open shelves that display the works chronologically.

"Our collection starts over there," he said with obvious pride. "It spans five centuries of the printed word."

Without asking my name or purpose, he gave me a brief history of the room and the collection and then, like someone claiming pseudo-fame because their cousin once got drunk at a party and made out with a regular extra from *Melrose Place*, he asked me if I had ever heard of the book *1776*. Of course I had; David McCollough's history of Revolutionary America had been a mainstay on the nonfiction bestseller list.

"This is where McCollough did his research," the docent said. "He was here for months, in this very room." Beat that. It was as if he could smell the Ohio on me and just wanted to put me in my place. Feeling amazingly overmatched, I told him that I had come to see the Perry papers, and he directed me through a doorway and down a flight of stairs to a room in the basement reserved for research. The woman at the desk, an affable and smiley lady of about fifty, asked my purpose and told me to take a seat, someone would be along shortly to explain the rules and walk me through the paperwork. Having just spent food and gas money for the next month on car repairs, I was a bit distracted when a gentleman named David approached me with a clipboard to ask a bit more about my intentions.

"I see here you want to review the Perry papers," he said, referring to a form the receptionist had me fill out. "What is your intention in doing so?"

He was eloquent and bore the tendencies of not only a librarian but a librarian good enough at his job to be entrusted with such a valuable collection. David was like a wizened Major League veteran feeling out a rookie. While my minor in college had been American history, I had never set foot in a special-collections library in my life. I barely knew where the library was on campus, let alone the finer points of etiquette in such a place. He asked for two forms of picture ID, so I handed him my driver's license and passport. He then searched my bag and told me all electronic devices and ink pens needed to stay in a mahogany locker with a brass plate indicating its number. I told him I was just here to see some of the papers, that I was researching a book, and he immediately asked to know my publisher's name and address. He kept asking about my book, and I wondered if getting access to the Perry papers would require some sort of blood or urine sample.

"And how long do you plan on staying with us?" he asked in a semiannoyed, almost condescending tone.

"An hour or two?" I said sheepishly.

"I'm not sure how much research you'll be able to get done in such a short amount of time," he said. "Most authors spend weeks here if they are working on a book project. Did you know that David McCullough was here for months whilst researching *1776*?"

"Someone told me upstairs," I said. "That's really interesting." "Our collection is prized," he said.

"That's why I'm here," I told him. Gerard Altoff had told me that everything I could possibly want to see from the Clements collection had been photocopied and was in storage at Perry's Victory and International Peace Memorial. "There's no need to go to Ann Arbor to see the stuff," he had told me, and I was beginning to understand that his suggestion involved more than just helping me out; it was a means of saving me from hearing about David McCullough and the long list of house rules. But I needed to see the papers themselves. True enough, I could get all the facts from photocopies, but I couldn't touch the same paper Perry had touched. I wanted the visceral connection. You can't touch the Declaration of Independence—without being shot—and you can't touch George Washington's wooden teeth. But I had the opportunity to touch Perry's letters, and for reasons I still haven't quite figured out, touching them was important to me—important enough that I was willing, no, *called*, to make this drive despite an overwhelming desire to follow the path of prudence home. I appreciated Altoff's advice, but I couldn't follow it. I had come too far, and the opportunity was too rare to pass up.

Finally satisfied, David the librarian assigned me a seat in the middle of a room crowded with tables and card catalogs. He explained that I needed to find the documents I was looking for in the catalog and then fill out a research request form so that an aide could retrieve them for me. Dismayed by the prospect of yet another form, I was somewhat heartened to find several cards related to Perry's papers, just between those once belonging to Thomas Paine and those having to do with the founding of the U.S. Presbyterian Church. This was quite the collection indeed. I asked the research assistant seated above me at an elevated desk to retrieve Perry's documents from 1811 to 1814, then asked how big the collection was in its entirety.

"It's not that big," she said. "Only about four linear feet of shelf space, twelve boxes in all." It made me wonder how many linear feet it had taken McCullough to write *1776*. "I can bring it all down on a cart if you like."

I thanked her and told her that I was really just interested in 1812 and 1813. She jotted down a couple of notes and told me to have a seat. Feeling fully vetted, I was surprised when Barbara DeWolfe took a seat next to me. DeWolfe is the curator of the university's collection, which pretty much makes her the guardian of a priceless and irreplaceable assortment of one-of-a-kind objects. She was dressed in a red suit. With salt-and-wheat hair, she looked more like curio-shop keeper than a librarian. Meeting her, I gathered, was a rite of passage for all would-be researchers at the Clements Library, like meeting the royalty and offering one's self up for inspection. DeWolfe told me a bit about the collection itself. Much had come from estates while other pieces had been donated by benefactors. Perry, whose role in securing the Old Northwest for America in 1813 had just as much impact on Michigan as Ohio, was prized among the collection if not for outright fame then for sentimental reasons.

After instructing me in some basic practices for handling historical documents—always leave them flat on the table or flat against one of the foam reading stands the library made available, don't move too quickly for fear of tearing—Barbara asked me about the nature of my book.

"It's really more of a travelogue of curiosity," I said, hoping to convey that I was not, in the strictest sense, a historian but just a guy with some time on his hands.

"I see," she said. "How long do you plan on staying with us?"

"What time is it?" I said.

She looked confused. "Ten minutes to three," she said.

"About an hour, give or take. I'm hoping to spend the night in Canada tonight." She seemed a bit taken aback. It would take the better part of a week to wade through the collection properly.

She shot a doubtful look at me, and in my mind I cursed McCullough and the exhaustive hours he spent hunched over these very tables.

"I'm not really doing serious research," I said. "See, the idea of the book is that history lives all around us and that access to it does not require exhaustive research or degrees or published papers on currency rates of nineteenth-century India. It just takes a little effort."

I braced for Barbara, whose obvious pride in her work I feared I had just offended, to have me forcibly removed from her sacred stacks by armed guards, but instead she smiled. "I think that's great," she said. "Not enough people make the effort. They're satisfied to watch The History Channel or not care altogether." She then said something about the nature of the university's collection and how it was not meant to collect dust in a back-room storehouse. "So what are you hoping to accomplish in such a short time?"

"More than anything, I wanted to see his handwriting," I said. "And there may be a letter that I'd like to see." Just then the nice young woman from the front counter returned with two boxes slightly larger than a big family photo album and set them on the desk in front of me.

"I'll leave you to it then," Barbara said. "I hope you find what you're looking for." And with that, she was gone, but I felt satisfied to have made my case effectively enough to impress someone like Barbara DeWolfe, even if I only earned her version of a pat on the head.

My hands trembled when I opened the first box of documents. I felt caught up in something and, honestly, a bit overcome. Oliver Hazard Perry has been a curiosity of mine for years but not a full-blown obsession, so I hadn't expected this visceral response. Perhaps it was nerves—handling two-hundred-year-old, irreplaceable documents might have that effect on a layman—or maybe it was anticipation. I can't be sure. All I know is that I was switchgrass trembling when I opened the box.

The first thing you notice when you look at documents like these, letters mostly, is the fineness of the writing. Not the penmanship per se, but the actual fineness of the strokes. I'm fond of fountain pens. I use them all the time. Something about the feeling of the nib skating over the surface of the paper, the weight of the pen, is sublime to me. And yet people in Perry's era didn't have heavy lacquer pens; they had feathers, quills, and pencils. In the first letter I looked at, a letter written by Christopher Raymond Perry, I noticed the fine lines made by the nib of his pen, the geometric swirl of his calligraphic cursive, and I admired it. I may be the only person in the world who can read my handwriting, and even that is pretty sketchy. So to see letters written on heavy paper in a fine hand sparked esteem in my heart. It was obvious that care was taken in writing letters back then, and I admire that, particularly in an age when POMS LOL banged out on a cell phone keypad counts as interpersonal communication.

I read several more letters as well as communications from navy and other government officials, and it felt, for some reason, like I was trespassing. I wondered if a couple hundred years from now some overzealous person would go traipsing through my things. Never was the sense that I was invading Oliver Hazard Perry's life stronger than when I came across a letter Perry had written to his mother from Hampton Roads, Virginia, on June 14, 1804. He was a young naval officer, a nineteen-year-old lieutenant home from the Barbary Coast and on leave. As with any other man in his situation—having been on board a ship with a couple hundred other men for several months and, like I said, nineteen years old—the subject on Perry's mind was women. When we think of shore leave today, we think of sailors in white uniforms hitting up the strip clubs and country bars on the prowl for something. An evening? An hour? A lifetime?

Endless possibilities in terms of the duration and quality of relationships sought with the fairer sex.

But Perry lived in a different time, almost on a different planet. This was pre-Victorian Earth. The sexual revolution would not happen for another hundred and sixty years. In many ways it was a repressed time, a time when decorum would lead men to do all sorts of dumb stuff. Think of powdered wigs, for God's sakes. The appearance of propriety, however, was more important than actual propriety. Men and women of the time were certainly not asexual. Ben Franklin, the venerable old man with the key in the storm and the vision of a bicameral government, was by many accounts a horny old dog who probably had the clap. People did it back then, but they didn't talk about it. Men of actual propriety—and I have no reason to believe Perry was not among them—held down their sexual vigor like bullies in the schoolyard. Instead they fought wars and sought honor and, in this case, wrote egomaniacal and oddly beautiful letters to their mothers.

"I know I have a chance," Perry wrote, "but I consider myself to [sic] young as yet, the last gentlemen is immensely rich—he has a daughter who has taken a liking to the cut of my face. I have been obliged to promise to return to this place when I come back from the Mediterranean. You will consider it vanity, when I tell you that I am in great demand with the young ladies."

> Dear Mom,
>   I am the man. This rich dude has a daughter who thinks I'm hot. He made me promise to come back when I wrap up this war with the pirates. Don't mean to sound arrogant or anything, but I am a pimp. Tell Dad I said hi.
>   Later,
>   O

This was Perry's world. He makes no mention of the woman herself, only that her dad has money. And aren't you proud that older rich men find me attractive enough to whore their daughters out to me?

I'm getting cynical. Maybe it's the romantic in me, but there seems something so calculating about those times, something so irretrievably businesslike that I am glad I come from the modern middle class where love can last a night or a lifetime and is largely in control of the people doing the loving. And yet, for as retentive as Perry's world was and for all the calculus of marriage as partnership that went on back then, I can't help but marvel over the beauty of a sentence like "You will consider it vanity when I tell you I am in great demand with the young ladies." I listen to eighties hair-metal and even some rap, and I promise you there is not a Bret Michaels or Jay-Z out there today who could load so much ego into a single sentence, and Perry wasn't even a writer.

I have never been the alpha-male type. Never the high school jock or the barroom Casanova. I married a girl I met when I was seventeen. And as for glory? I have a hard enough time putting my name on the cover of this book. I grew up an upper-Midwestern Lutheran. Glory was for God. The only way to win among the congregation was to demand the least attention. While glory and fame were capital in Perry's world, they were nothing in mine, not when compared with a hard day's work and some good tuna hot dish. Then again, it would probably be more pious of me to not write a book at all. If it were simply about the adventure, I could have had it and not written word one. If it were about the story, I could have closed my eyes and told it to myself. And yet here I am writing, hoping that someone will read it, that many someones will, in fact. So perhaps there is a bit of me, a bit of everyone, that seeks glory—even the person in the front pew.

I do hope for a small bit. It would be disingenuous for me to state otherwise. I hope for enough glory (read: Book Sales) that my publisher asks me to write another book, then another, and a whole library shelf more. Does that make me like Perry? In a way. We both seek a bit of glory to live lives according to our own dictates. I want to provide for my family and be able to do so doing something that I love. Perry probably wanted something very similar. In a way, don't we all? But there's something about the way glory is described in the early nineteenth century that seems so distant, so alien. It is as if glory is some sort of currency, as if the measure of the man is taken by the number of statues erected in his image. I've never wanted a statue of me. I don't even like to have my picture taken. But I get a sense that somewhere, deep inside, Perry did want to have statues built in his honor. He did want to be known through the ages. And I wondered then, as I do now, if that was because he wanted to feel important in his father's eyes.

His dad was a war hero and a hothead. He was alpha male, and that disregard for authority got him kicked out of the navy. Maybe Perry wanted to show his dad he could succeed in an organization in which his father failed. Oliver Hazard Perry worked the system from the inside while his dad was unwilling to give deference to those above him. And the younger man eventually proved more successful. It's like that with me but probably opposite. My dad is an engineer who has been practical and has made smart decisions his entire life. He doubted that I could make it when I told him I had changed my major from marketing to journalism. And for more than ten years I have tried to prove him wrong. I have tried to show him that I could be successful as a journalist and writer, even though he never demanded such proof. It's Freudian as hell, but maybe the reason I wanted to write this book is the same reason Oliver Perry burned with such a desire to attain glory in a navy uniform. Maybe, at the end of the day, we were both just trying to make our dads proud.

But reading Perry's letters, I realize that I am very different from him. He seemed like more of a gamer, more like someone who would do whatever he could for advancement. Me, I don't want advancement, I just want to be left alone to do my thing and raise my family. And yet I find myself drawn to him. I can't help but like Oliver Hazard Perry. For all his self-promotion and striving, for his bombast and stubbornness, for writing letters like the one to his mom, I still want to meet him. I know it's not possible—not without a time machine or, as Matt Damon says in *Good Will Hunting*, "some serious smelling salts and a heater"—but reading his letters gives me a glimpse into who this guy was, and I try to imagine who he would have been today. Would he have been in the military? Probably not. I'm guessing Wall Street. Goldman Sachs or Lehman Brothers. He'd be making a bunch of money and spending it on the kind of suits you see in *Esquire* and GQ. He'd be marble. Smooth and cold. He'd be the guy who takes it upon himself to find the loophole in the tax law. He'd be the guy you want to go to a football game with because he could get you into the locker room. He'd be, he'd be like one of those go-getter contestants on *The Apprentice*.

In the Perry collection the letters and documents followed a general time line. A letter from William Jones dated 6 March 1813—just about the time Perry was building the Lake Erie fleet in Pennsylvania—told him that he had been commissioned as a captain in the navy:

> Dear Sir,
> The Senate having confirmed your nomination as a Master Commandant in the Navy of the United States, I have the pleasure to hand you herewith your confirmation as a Master Commandant in the Navy dated 9th Sept. 1812.
> I am respectfully Yours,
> Wm. Jones

Just like that—and, again, the language. The letter basically says, "You've been promoted and we're giving you back pay for seven months," but that sense of formality of the times influenced the way people communicated, and I liked it, even if it bored the hell out of me in high-school and college literature classes.

There were several letters from William Henry Harrison, and it felt strange to idly finger notes originated by a future president of the United States. Some letters were naked; others had been covered in a sort of Glad wrap, which I assumed was for protection and to prevent decay. The ones that weren't covered felt like vellum, résumé paper that had gotten wet and then left next to a space heater to dry. You could feel the quality, but they were sort of stiff. I imagined that if I had crumpled one up, it might have broken into a thousand little pieces. The ones that were covered felt slightly more plasticine, grainy, like duct tape. I tried to be very careful touching them because I didn't want to be the guy who destroyed an irreplaceable piece of history. Every time I shifted in the only-sometimes-comfortable wooden chair, I worried about knocking the boxes of documents to the floor and having to explain to Barbara DeWolfe why I had been so careless. But I didn't fixate much on what could go wrong, nor about the time.

And after a half hour I found myself transfixed. Who doesn't like to snoop? And to think that all of this was free, just sitting in the basement of a special library at a public university, it made me start to hate the Internet. I probably could have found all of this stuff on the Web, but would it have been nearly as gratifying as holding the actual documents? I think not. The Internet, I realized, gives people the illusion of being satisfied without ever actually topping them off, like a diet pill to make you feel full when you really wanted a meatball sub. The tangibility of holding these things made me feel like I had access to the world of their authors. But like the music writer Chuck Klosterman once said in an interview, giving a kid in Fargo the ability to look at the pictures from a Hollywood party may give him more of an idea of what it looked like, but it didn't give him more access to the room. He's still sitting in Fargo. And as my time waned in the basement of the Clements Library, I realized that the accessibility of the documents was illusory in terms of understanding the lives of those who wrote, read, and handled them. Simply reading Perry's papers would not allow me to get to know him any better than I already did—nor would it make me any more like him or make me like him any more—but I was glad that I had come just the same. Particularly when I read some of the correspondence he received directly following the Battle of Lake Erie.

There were letters of congratulations from a wide range of people following the battle. The first came from officers of the *Niagara*, followed over the course of months by the New York Common Council, the New York Society of the Cincinnati, and the Savannah Common Council. In a war that had few reasons for celebrations up until September 10, 1813, it seemed like Americans grabbed the opportunity to celebrate.

I kept reading, skimming most things and flipping back to the letters that were dated earlier. I was looking for a particular letter I had hoped to find among the pile—Perry's missive to Harrison following the battle, the one containing the famous words "We have met the enemy and they are ours." But it wasn't there. I asked a library aide if there were more papers from this time, perhaps some kept in a special collection somewhere. But she said no. Everything they had was in the boxes. There were two more boxes in the back room that she offered to retrieve, but they were from later years and more than likely did not contain anything from the time of the battle. I thanked her and returned to my seat.

I read for another twenty or thirty minutes and then, without much fanfare, packed up my things and headed out. There had been five or six other researchers in the library when I had arrived, and as I left I could not be sure that any of them had moved. I understood how historical works could suck you in, but there was, for me, something claustrophobic about the research room. Something about being in an enclosed space below ground level with all that old stuff, I don't know, it just felt like death. I thanked the staff members whom I recognized and retrieved the things I had stowed in the locker outside the reading room. I couldn't wait to get out of there and out of Ann Arbor. I was itchy, ready to move on, and as I climbed up the stairs through the grand lobby and library room, I paused for a moment and doffed my imaginary cap to David McCullough. I had lasted about an hour; he had lasted months. I took one last look around the room, with its rich old wood and ornate carpets, with the substantial tables and green-glass reading lamps. It was the kind of room a bad mystery writer might come up with if describing a death in a library, almost a cartoon version of the things people love or hate about academia. I loved it. The main room of the Clements Library was a room as self-important and over-the-top as the people who make history. And that's the sense I got being there, as if it were the final resting place of historic books. I had never seen a place quite like it—beautiful and grand and ornate and sophisticated. It wasn't the kind of place where a guy like me, with my love of dogs and kids, could ever really reside, but it was an experience to visit. I was half-tempted to sit down on one of the overstuffed sofas and read, maybe even take a nap. But I had better things on my horizon, better places. Ann Arbor and this library had been a mere pit stop.

I was Canada bound.

∼ 13 ∼

Crossing Over

I love Canada. I always have. There's just something about a country so massive yet so sparsely populated and so near to where I had
grown up. It's wild and strangely beautiful, and you need a passport
to get there now, so it's also kind of exotic. Plus, people are nice
in Canada, and I like nice people. I come from a long line of nice
people, and it feels good to know that there is an entire nation that
(with the possible exception of French-influenced Quebec) values
niceness.

I know it's cliché to call Canadians nice. It's like saying the
Brits are uptight and the Irish are drunks and the Brazilians like
to dance. But here's the thing—they *are* nice. I have visited Canada
more times than I have visited Pennsylvania. When I was a young
lad the legend of my grandfather, father, and uncles packing up
a couple trucks and a trailer with fishing equipment and heading
straight north from Mason City, Iowa, through Minnesota and into
western Ontario for manly undertakings loomed large. When, at
the tender age of ten or so, I was invited to attend one of these
annual pilgrimages, it felt like an initiation. Land a northern pike,
sleep in a tent, shit in the woods, and you will be one of us, boy,
a Heimbuch through and through. And I did all those things. I

fished in tiny boats on small lakes so far removed from the world I had known as to seem alien. I had stared breath-struck at a black bear that had come into our camp and found amusement with the firecrackers my grandpa was lighting and throwing at its paws. (The desired effect would have been for the bear to hightail and run away, but we were the visitors on his property, and he seemed to want to make us feel welcome.) I shat in the woods.

Those early impressions of Canada were of a land unfinished by modern hands, of a world left to its own devices where the nearest town was forty-five miles and more than three hours away and where bald eagles soared among the treetops, hunting the same northern pike and walleye I was. I loved this Canada for its solitude and stoic grace, for being the setting of the first real book I ever read, Gary Paulsen's *Hatchet*. And for a boy naïve to the real dangers that spring up when solitude and seemingly endless wilderness collide, it was a fantasyland. This part of Canada felt somehow like it belonged to me, to my dad and his brothers, to my grandfather, who had discovered the lakes in the region by filling up every gas can he owned and driving north from his Iowa farm until they were halfway empty. I had no right to invade, to eat the blueberries that would help the black bears recover from a long winter's sleep, or to plod along the former logging roads that had become little more than bare traces in the decades since they had last been used. I had no right to feel pride in myself for enduring, especially since I really hadn't endured anything. Still, I felt pride just the same, in my land, my wild corner of Ontario north and west of Thunder Bay, and when I tried to describe it to my friends, they would stare at me with a certain dumbfounded I-just-crapped-my-pants-thinking-about-the-bear face. They couldn't understand the vastness of it all.

But the wilderness of my Canada was only one aspect of this brilliant country. I first visited Toronto when I was in junior high. Every year, our eighth-grade class took a trip, and each year the destination alternated between Toronto and Washington, D.C. Nothing against our nation's capital—I would live and work there later, and it would become second only to Chicago on my list of favorite U.S. cities—but I am sure the Toronto trip was in God's plan for my adolescent development. Unlike the supposed melting pot of the United States, where immigrants shed the shackles of their national heritage in order to build a more perfect union, Toronto represents a different way for people of the world to coexist. Canadians seem to view their culture not as some strange type of homogametic fondue but as a national salsa, where everyone brings the ingredients of their past to the collective, and in that mixture—where individual flavors can be identified—something new and better is created. There was nothing more interesting to me as an early teen than to see the plucked geese hanging in the windows of Chinatown shops and to hear the tones of a Pakistani man speaking English with a French accent. Perhaps it was an indication of my future world curiosity or perhaps it was just my inner polyglot, but my first experience of Toronto and its rich tapestry of people was a refreshing eye-opener, like a first cup of coffee in the morning.

Twice more I visited Toronto in high school. Both times were for band trips in which the mighty Marching Shoremen of Avon Lake High School performed our halftime show on the field of the SkyDome before meager crowds of Toronto Argonauts fans. Once, after our performance was finished and we were loading the vans with our uniforms and instruments in the bowels of the enormous stadium, two of the team's owners came down to visit us. Meeting John Candy and Wayne Gretzky was like an audience with the Queen, the Pope, and the Dalai Lama all at once. But because the men were Canadian and because we were just high school kids, the experience was probably a lot friendlier and a lot more fun. I played "Hail to the Chief" for the elder President Bush with that marching band during one of his visits to Cleveland in the run-up to the 1992 election, and while that experience had magnitude and weight I have yet to equal in my life, it paled in comparison to the sense of awe and wonder I felt shaking the sausagelike hand of the star of *Planes, Trains and Automobiles* and the decidedly more delicate mitt of The Great One.

Later on that same trip, I would finally get together with the girl who had beguiled my fancy for more than two years. It was in a maze just outside the Ripley's Believe It or Not on the Canadian side of Niagara Falls. We were coming from opposite directions, unaware of each other's presence, and then I rounded a corner just as she did and she kissed me. It was an early addition to the list of the best moments in my life. And it was in Canada. God bless Canada.

Those early experiences stirred something in me, a sense of being nearly Canadian. Born in north-central Wisconsin and raised for the most part on the shores of Lake Erie, I've always felt the near-presence of the Great White North in my life. It was always there, just across the water, and I felt a certain kinship with Canadians through their pop culture. *You Can't Do That on Television, Degrassi Junior High, The Kids in the Hall* were the television shows I looked forward to watching in my youth, the ones I channel-surfed for when I was home sick on the couch. And later, in high school, it was music by the angry (if misinformed about the definition of the word *ironic*) Alanis Morissette and the quirky but talented Barenaked Ladies that provided the soundtrack to my nearly drama-free life. While many of my friends and classmates were growing out their hair and forgoing showers to be a part of the jaded, self-aggrandizing movement spawned by my generation, the aptly, if stupidly named grunge of the Pacific Northwest, I was into something a little more wholesome and clean-cut. While they mourned the suicide of Kurt Cobain, I was singing BNL lyrics like "If I had a million dollars / I'd buy you a monkey / Haven't you always wanted a monkey?" in my car.

Nearly all of us have people or places we identify with and idealize. My dad has Iowa, my friend Rob has the U.K. I have Canada. Once while playing a board game with my wife and her cousins, I drew a bad card and muttered "fucking Canadians." It was something my wife understood but her cousin seemed perplexed by.

"What's your problem with Canadians?" she asked, but before I could answer, my wife jumped in and said, "He doesn't have one. He loves Canada and Canadians."

"I don't get it," said her cousin.

"He's just pissed that he can't be one."

That pretty much sums up my attitude about our neighbors to the north and may help explain my excited state as I eased my newly repaired Jetta away from the curb in Ann Arbor and pointed it east. The trip had been pretty heartbreaking so far. Car problems, a strange hotel, and the only real letter I had been looking for among the Perry papers—the envelope on which he wrote his famous words to William Harrison following the Battle of Lake Erie—was nowhere to be found. So far, things had been a bust. I was already homesick, missing my wife and kids, and the excitement of the road trip had drained like my brake fluid, but my spirits brightened when I realized that in an hour or so, I would be crossing the Detroit River via the Friendship Bridge and touching down in Windsor.

Border crossings have always been a little scary for me. I've read too many John le Carré novels, seen too many spy movies, and I think maybe the idea of passing from one country to another makes me want to believe that I am somehow a fugitive. Did I pay that electric bill from five years ago? Oh shit, I don't think I did. They'll probably haul me off to some windowless prison in New Mexico to keep me from fleeing. But as crossings go, my experience with the tollbooth-style border at Windsor has always been pleasant and easy. It's usually some nice-looking guy in a crisp uniform with his cap tilted slightly back on his head and his Canadian Customs and Immigration badge glinting in the sun. He usually takes my license and smiles and asks, "Aboot how long are you planning on staying?"

And I tell him I'll just be there for the night to celebrate my friend's bachelor party or my fraternity's semiformal dance. He waves me through and I won't think another thing about it an hour later.

But if you really want to know the effects of the Bush II administration on international goodwill, try crossing that border today. For one thing, Doug (and for some reason I always think of the old border guard as being named Doug, though it is just as likely his name was Steve) is gone and he has been replaced by an angry red-haired pixie in full body armor, packing a nine-millimeter in a serious-looking holster and eyes so piercing they seem to examine your soul. She spoke with long pauses in between her sentences, like a poker player sizing up her competition. And within two seconds of her taking my passport, I was awash in that feeling of paranoia. For one thing, I wasn't washed—I had skipped out on the shower after swimming in the hotel pool that morning. I was already a bit frazzled from the previous two days' activities and felt a bit like a nuclear-fallout survivor after navigating through Detroit's postapocalyptic, the–Big Three–are–not-invincible warren of burned-out buildings and abandoned streets. But there was something in the way she looked at me, something accusatory, something skeptical, something I had never before seen on the face of a Canadian—something American.

After the usual questions about whether or not I was carrying any fruit (I had remembered to get rid of the bananas I had brought from home) and how long I planned on staying, she waited for a moment and then set into a line of questioning that was strange and uncomfortable. As it so happens, I had turned on my tape recorder, hoping to capture Doug's voice. I left it running after pulling up to the guard shack, and the following is an actual transcription of the scene.

"What's your purpose in visiting Canada?"

"I plan on visiting Fort Malden and then driving all the way around the lake to Buffalo."

"For what purpose?"

"I'm researching a book on the Battle of Lake Erie."

"A real book? You have a publisher?"

"Yes."

"When is it due out?"

"Next May."

"Are you planning on meeting anyone in Canada?"

"No one in particular. Maybe a park ranger at Fort Malden, I'm not sure."

"Do you know anyone who lives or has lived in Canada?"

"Um, no, not really."

"Do you plan on meeting anyone here?"

"No," I said, but I was thinking, Didn't I just tell you that?

"Do you have anything to deliver to someone living in Canada?" And it was right here that my paranoia seemed a little less crazy and a little more perceptive. I couldn't tell if she thought I was a drug mule or a terrorist. I'm six-four and so white I'm nearly see-through. But I'm also clean-cut. And besides, who would use researching a book relating to the War of 1812 as an excuse for ferrying illegal substances across international borders?

"No," I told her. "I have nothing to deliver in Canada."

"So, something to pick up then?"

"Excuse me?"

"Are you picking something up here in Canada to bring back to the States?" Like what? Strong beer? A hockey puck? By this point, I had been talking out the window to the guard for more than ten minutes. The three cars previous to mine had taken less time collectively to get through, and two of them had American plates. Maybe I was being too obscure. Maybe I should have just lied and told her I was going to Windsor to visit the Caesars Palace casino and the all-nude titty bars jokingly referred to as the "Windsor Ballet." But it was too late to change my story now. Besides, I had nothing to hide. I literally could not have possibly done anything wrong, and yet I felt like I was being persecuted. This was such a strange type of profiling that I wondered what profile I fit. Too Nordic-looking to fill the stereotype of the Mafia, too fat to be the military or the CIA. Too old to be a college kid looking to score some weed, too poor to be a kingpin, and, forgive me for this one, too everything non-terrorist to be considered a terrorist.

"No, I don't plan on picking anything up."

"I see. Where will you be staying?"

I held back the urge to sigh for fear of pissing this woman off and told her that my plan was to find a campground near Fort Malden and sleep in the tent I had in my trunk.

"Did you bring other camping gear? A knife perhaps?"

Huh? This lady was just looking for a reason to bust me. "I have a Swiss Army knife."

"May I see it?" I took the knife from the pocket on my vest and handed it to her. She looked at it as if it may have contained a small nuclear device or kilo of cocaine. As she studied it, she said not a word. As a nervous talker, I wanted to say something, anything, to break what felt like whole weeks of silence. I was just about to say something about my camping plans when she thrust the knife at me and waved me through the gate without looking in my direction.

"Thank you," I said. "Have a nice day."

"Be careful with that knife," she said from the corner of her mouth with a strange sort of "I'll be watching you" sneer. And just like that, I was through. But the experience, which I had built up in my mind for the preceding few hours, felt sullied, dirty. I had just met the only unfriendly person in Canada, and it made me sad that she might be some kid's introduction to the country I had grown to love. She was doing her job, or so I thought, so I couldn't really blame her. But things had changed the mood along the border. It was as if high alert was the order of every day, like Canada was becoming Americanized in the post-9/11 world, and, rounding the turnabout and steering in the direction of downtown Windsor, I immediately began missing Doug.

⁓ 14 ⁓

The Great Campout That Never Was

A little shaken and in desperate need of a pee, I delayed my journey's next leg and stopped in Windsor at the Caesars Palace extension, which was new since my last visit. There had always been a casino there, or always as far as I was concerned, but it used to be called Casino Windsor. I had visited the city on at least two other occasions; there may have been a third, but alcohol was usually a key ingredient of my Windsor dalliances. The first—or the first I could remember—was for a fraternity semiformal my sophomore year in college. It involved massive amounts of powerful Canadian beer, a casual stroll to the casino from the hotel without actually going inside, and an early night for yours truly.

The next trip was for my friend Rob's bachelor party. By this time we were out of college, and I was working as a city-government beat reporter in southwest Ohio. The plan was for two nights of drinking and gaming and general tomfoolery, but I got a phone call from an editor on the second morning telling me that the mayor of the city I covered was planning to resign later that day and I needed to be there to cover it because I had been the one covering the scandal leading to the resignation. I stayed just long enough to wipe away the previous night's cobwebs with a hearty breakfast with the guys. We had checked in late the previous afternoon and had hit the hotel bar immediately, so I had little recollection of the city itself, and yet, walking to my car and driving through the morning streets, I noticed something different about Windsor. It's a bit like a low-rent version of Reno built on top of an aged city. For all the check-cashing establishments and litter-strewn minimart parking lots, there are small moments of great European charm. Cafés with giant windows that open like French doors set in ancient-looking stone walls. The menus were displayed *en français* with English subtitles, and for some reason that seemed very Continental and cool. I remember making my way back to the Friendship Bridge and thinking how graceful the city was, to have so much French influence in a town so obviously named for and by the English. It made me want to be European, or more accurately, it reinforced my love of all things Canadian.

But none of this was on my mind as I drove along the banks of the Detroit River—that lifeblood link between Lake Huron and Lake Erie that played such an important role in the campaign of 1813. Instead, I was thinking about the pressure that had been building in my bladder since Ann Arbor and how the distinctly easygoing attitude of Canadians should not be applicable to their driving. Still, I stole a glance or two across the water toward Detroit, and from this vantage point—a mile or so away and on foreign soil—the hellhole nestled just above the plumber's crack of the Rust Belt looked almost inviting.

I found a space on an elevated floor of the parking lot and did a full-tinkle sprint across the connecting breezeway that led to the casino at Caesars. The two security guards must have sensed my urgency because they waved me through without checking my ID and after finding the men's room—located conveniently on the other side of the gambling floor—I decided to have a look around. It was late in the afternoon by this point, and I knew I had to get moving if I was going to find my campsite before dark, but I just couldn't bring myself to rush. I've never been much of a gambler, though had I chosen a more lucrative career path, I suppose that I might have been. Journalists, you see, are the only working professionals who marry schoolteachers for the money, so I've grown accustomed to a certain frugality that in many ways contradicts my nature. But how can you go to a casino without playing at least one hand, right?

Earlier that year, my parents had gone on an Alaskan cruise with my sister's in-laws—friends of theirs. Somewhere along the coast of the Canadian Yukon, my sister's father-in-law, a man on whom luck seems always to be shining, had won more than twenty thousand dollars playing video poker. This was in the back of my head as I scanned the blackjack tables looking for one with a cheap minimum bet. Blackjack is a simple game. Even I, the English major, can count to twenty-one, but the wallet sting of my car repair still lingered, and I found myself unwilling to pony up five bucks for a single hand. So I found the video poker machines and sat down at one with a one-dollar minimum bet. All I had was a twenty, so I put it in—the machine gladly accepted my American currency—and lost five dollars in under a minute. That was enough for me, so I cashed out and took my receipt to the teller window to retrieve actual cash.

The man behind the counter—who it turned out was named Doug (what is it with Canadians and Doug?)—handed me the Technicolor currency of the Great White North. He was friendly, the first Canadian I had spoken to since the bridge, and a quick glance at my watch sent a sudden panic through me. I had to haul ass.

"How far is it to Amherstburg?" I asked.

"Less than an hour," Doug said. "Are you heading down to the wine festival?"

This was news to me, though if I had listened to the radio for more than five seconds while I was driving I would have heard about the Shores of Erie International Wine Festival, which was scheduled to start the next day. "No," I said. "Just going to see the fort."

"You're a man after my own heart," said Doug, who continued for about five minutes telling me about the trips he had taken to Fort Malden with his young son and how much he enjoyed sharing that sort of history with his boy. It made me think of my dad and the trip to the Perry monument that would serve as the genesis—two decades later—for this book. Doug was warm and friendly and seemed genuinely pleased to speak with me, traits I have yet to find in any person working the cages at an American casino. In some ways, Doug reassured my faith in Canadians as a loving people. I thanked him for his time and the directions he had scratched out for me on casino stationery and set off across the breezeway, this time at more of a trot than a full-on sprint.

⁂

The drive to Amherstburg, the city that surrounds Fort Malden, was relatively easy, though I had to keep checking my speedometer because I had forgotten the signs would be in kilometers-per-hour, not miles. Immediately south of Windsor is the kind of industrial wasteland you find just about everywhere in and around Detroit, but soon enough the road levels out and you pass cottages and small commercial centers reminiscent of northern Minnesota. Even here, in close proximity to the major industrial and commercial centers of Detroit and Toledo, the population disparity between the U.S. and Canada is evident. I once read that more than 80 percent of Canadians live within a hundred miles of the U.S. border, and driving through this southern corner of Ontario, I imagined that the people were spread out on a long, thin line stretching from Newfoundland to Vancouver, interrupted only by the occasional city like Toronto, Ottawa, or others where NHL teams play their home games. It was quiet, almost tranquil, and I soon felt my blood pressure—which had been elevated because I was worried about finding my campsite—ease a bit.

True to Doug's word, Amherstburg was slightly less than an hour south of Windsor, and the evening sun cast long west-to-east shadows across the main drag. I saw a sign advertising directions to Fort Malden and followed it through a sleepy residential section of town that was eerily similar to the streets of Vermilion. With cottages lined up in neat but not overly planned rows and more-stately manors tucked among well-groomed shrubs and wrought-iron fences, this place reminded me of a pensioner's dreams. And amid the charming homes along the river stretched a stone-and-iron fence with a historic marker mounted on it announcing, in French and in English, the presence of Fort Malden.

The gates were closed because the fort had shut down for the evening, but I could see, standing back among old maple and oak trees, the main buildings, and they looked like they had been plucked from the English countryside and dropped gently along the Detroit River, half a world away. Unlike the Spartan log camps at Fort Meigs, Fort Malden, or what I could see of it, appeared to have been built with a sense of permanence and grace missing from the American counterpart less than a hundred miles away. Fort Meigs was thrown up in haste as a defensive shelter for William Henry Harrison's starving and ravaged men. The buildings at Fort Malden looked like they had been built by a foxhunting party riding up after a long day to sit by the fire and sip brandy. It was dignified, proper in a way that underscores the idea that even back then Americans could be viewed as boorish compared with the English. If Fort Malden was Savile Row, Fort Meigs was the discount rack at Tom's Big and Tall.

I spent only a few minutes reading the signs outside the fort's walls, testing my rusty and dusty high-school and college French but inevitably turning toward the English versions. All federal signs in Canada are bilingual, further evidence that it is a country that embraces its roots rather than excavates them. But with the sun setting fast, I knew I needed to find my home for the night before it got too dark.

In my rush to get the hell out of Ann Arbor, I had left behind my planning notebook. I had spent weeks laying out this trip and kept all my notes, numbers, and maps in a notebook, figuring that keeping everything together would make it less likely for me to lose something. That is, of course, unless I lost the whole thing. I tried to flash back to where I had seen it last. Did I have it in the library? No, I didn't think so. I probably left it in the hotel, and an icy chill washed over me as I began praying that it would not be found by the crazy old war vet, who would follow my itinerary to track me down and kill me in the night. (It is amazing how paranoid I get when I'm tired.) Most of the stuff in the notebook I could remember, but the name of the campground I had selected, its location and telephone number, escaped me. I stopped at a gas station—even this was made of stone and exuded a sense of age and gravity that shocked my American minimart sensibilities—to ask for directions. The kid working the pumps—he could not have been more than twenty—told me that he had just moved to Amherstburg from Quebec and he didn't know where I could go, but he called a friend at a pizza place across the street who delivered pies to campers all the time, and they pieced together a map for me to follow.

The campsite was in a national park, a bird sanctuary, and was located about eight or nine miles outside of town, two miles off the main road. I was glad the gas station boy and pizza delivery guy were there to help me, because I would not have found this place on my own. But the directions were immediately moot when I pulled in the park entrance to find the ranger station dark and a sign that told me the campground was closed that night thanks to the shift to winter hours. I had purposely scheduled my trip for after Labor Day because I didn't want to deal with tourists anywhere I went, but I had neglected to check if that meant anything in Canada. There was no gate at the park, so I probably could have just driven right in and snuck into the campground, but the sign expressly warned that trespassing visitors would be prosecuted to the extent of Canadian and provincial laws. I didn't expect to end up at the Canadian version of Gitmo for sneaking a night in a provincial park, but my trip had been fraught with piss-poor luck to this point, and pushing it any further, I decided, would be something less than idiotic.

Luckily, the pizza guy had given me directions to a second camp-ground, a Jellystone-themed place with signs depicting Droopy Dog and Ubu on the frontage to the road. I found the place with some difficulty as the terrain and roads on the outskirts of Amherstburg are decidedly rural, and anyone who has ever taken a drive through Iowa can tell you that you'd better know where you're going because you can get lost pretty easily once you step off the beaten path. Through a combination of double-backs and blind luck, I found the Jelly-stone Campground, and though I had been warned that it was a lit-tle seedy and more expensive than the provincial park, I decided it would do just fine. I just wanted to set up my tent, eat a granola bar, and go to sleep after a long, kind of shitty day. Of course, this plan, too, was eliminated as an option since the park offices had closed at 5 and the clock in my car read 6:45. Fuck, I thought, watching smoke rise from the cooking fires outside two or three dozen camp-ers, what the hell was I going to do now?

≈15≈

The Worst Hotel in All of Canada

I remembered seeing a sign for a historic hotel on the road leading into Amherstburg, the Royal Arms Inn, or something like that. It sounded expensive, but I reasoned that if there was one hotel in town, surely there had to be more. I aimed my car toward the remnants of the setting sun and headed back west in the direction of town—or the Detroit River, I didn't really care which one I reached first, so long as there was a place to lay my head and maybe something to eat. I had not eaten anything all day and was ready for the meal I had promised myself in Ann Arbor but never enjoyed thanks to my broken brakes. A lucky stab at road selection led me back into town, across the street from the gas station I had visited more than an hour before, and closer to a temporary home. I turned right and cruised the main drag looking for a place to stay but quickly found myself outside of town. I turned around in the parking lot of the Amherstburg visitors center—closed for the season—and headed back south until I saw a shabby-looking sign that read HOTEL, BEST FISH AND CHIPS IN TOWN.

Perfect, I thought. This place had to be cheap. It looked cheap, a one-story L jutting back from a kind of fisherman's bar with almost no windows to view the junk lot abutting it to the rear. I could probably even save money over camping. I parked and followed the backlit yellow sign pointing toward the "office" only to find that the check-in desk was also the main serving area of the aforementioned bar. It was a big room with two pool tables, some shoddy lounge furniture, and ancient stand-up video games scattered throughout. The bar itself was stocked with less-than-well-standard bottles. One, a plastic bottle about a gallon large, had a white label with *vodka* handwritten in black. Judging by the two patrons—a man who looked like he had fallen off a motorcycle at considerable speed and a woman who might have been in the sidecar—this was not the kind of place I wanted to be hanging out in. I pictured bar fights and meth deals happening over booze-soaked games of pool, not to mention low-grade pornographic sex in the bathrooms. I thought about fleeing, sucking it up and finding the Royal Arms regardless of the price or maybe just sleeping in my car, but the owner-manager bird-dogged me from behind the bar on the other side of the room.

"Yes sir," he said in a Pakistani accent that sounded like he had learned English from a Frenchman. "What can I do to help you?"

"Um, well, I um," I stammered. "I'm, uh, looking for a room. Any vacancies?" Please say no, please say no, please say no so I can justify getting the hell out of here.

"Plenty of rooms," he said. He pulled a dog-eared and tattered notebook from under the bar. It was his guest registry. He asked for my name and address, which he scribbled in, well, not English, before I had a chance to protest or even ask the rates.

"Ah," he said after taking down my address. "You are American, sir."

"Yes, that's right." I nervously giggled as I could now feel the eyes of the beaten couple turn on me. "But I love Canada." I hoped this would somehow subdue any kind of anti-American sentiment that might linger in the hearts of the two toughs at the end of the bar. "So do my kids," I added just for good measure. Maybe they wouldn't rob and kill a father who loves their homeland?

"Very good sir, so do I."

"How much is it?" I asked. "Just for one night."

"Sixty-five, sir."

At this moment two things came over me. Number one, was this guy serious? Sixty-five dollars a night to stay in this place? He should pay *me*, I thought. And second was a reinforcing terror. I had thirty-one dollars in my pocket, more cash in my wallet. If I took out my wallet and exposed the other bills I had, would that make me more of a target for the people I was now convinced were homicidal maniacs sitting at the far end of the bar?

"What if I pay in American?" I hoped the exchange rate had plummeted since cashing out at the casino, where it was $1.10 Canadian for every American buck.

"American cash, sir, why don't you give me fifty and we'll call it even?"

I did my best to hide my wallet as I took out another twenty and combined it with the bills from my pocket. I slipped the cash to the owner-manager, and he stuffed it in his shirt pocket, replaced his notebook ledger, and pulled a key from a hook hanging amid the cheap bottles on the bar.

"Number twenty-three, sir, like Michael Jordan," he said. "Please, follow me, sir."

We walked down a narrow, dark hallway to an even narrower and darker one, and he showed me to the room at the end of it. The cheap, hollow door and linoleum tile matched the stench—like old cigarettes, booze, and sadness. The room was tidy but not necessarily clean. The beds were ancient, like those at your grandparents' place, and covered in mismatched spreads and pillows thrown askew. I got the feeling the owner was also the housekeeper and maintenance man. He turned on the only lamp in the room, which burned a single forty-watt bulb, and gave a quick tutorial on the television remote and operations of the primeval full-size refrigerator at the end of the dresser. The man, who said his name was Jim (probably short for Hajim), told me he would be in the bar all night if there was anything I needed, then left with a courteous bow. I looked around and tried not to touch anything. Someone had been murdered in this room, maybe more than one person, I thought. I turned on the television and the bathroom light and headed outside to get my bags. When I got to the parking lot, Jim and the woman from the bar were looking at my car with a certain fascination that worried me to no end. Steal the car, I thought, take what you want, just please don't let me be the next victim in Room Twenty-three.

"I have never seen these plates before," said Jim. "Where is Ohio?" There was something sweet in the way he asked. Sweet in the innocence behind his question and sweet in the image it conjured in my mind. Shortly after the attacks of September 11, 2001, I had seen an AP news photo taken in Vancouver. It was of Canadian students rallying on campus. One student held a sign that read, NOW MAYBE AMERICANS WILL LEARN GEOGRAPHY. I remember being offended, not only because I am an American who loves geography, and not only because the sign was an obvious jab at perceived American jingoism, but because it was coming from a Canadian. It left a bad taste in my mouth, but standing in this dark and ominous parking lot and hearing Jim ask the whereabouts of a state just twenty or thirty miles as the crow flies from our present location somehow redeemed that image from years before. I explained Ohio's location gently to Jim, who thought Toledo was a state, then watched as he and the woman went back inside.

Nervous as hell and wondering if the sweetness of Jim's question was just a bad cover-up for him and the lady patron casing my car and the possessions it held, I carried everything I had with me—including my tent, CDs, and road maps—into the room in one agonizing trip. Once inside, I barricaded the door with my bags and settled in for one of the longest, most sleepless nights of my life.

I started off pacing the floor with my shoes and coat on, waiting. What for? I don't know. But I listened for any sound, any clue that I was about to be accosted by Canadian bikers, maybe a sleeper cell of some kind. After an hour, I sat on one of the chairs that looked like it had been sold by the sheriff's office after a building had burned to the ground. It smelled about the same way. Eventually, I could feel myself getting tired. There were two queen-size beds in the room, and I played eeny-meeny to decide which one had the lesser infestation of bedbugs beneath the sheets. I had been in the car a lot in the previous two days and had been sitting in an upright position for too long not to lie down. I thought about the floor but then wondered what residual evil might still be on it. No, I reasoned, the bed would be better. Surely the police would have taken blood-soaked sheets as evidence, right? I put on another layer of clothes and removed my camera bag from the barricade at the door, using it as a pillow. Still, I couldn't settle down. My mind was racing, and I hesitated to toss and turn on the mattress—which was stiff and floated on the box springs like a can of tuna on Jell-O—for fear of making skin-to-sheet contact. So I lay perfectly still and watched television. President Obama was presenting his health-care priorities to a joint session of Congress, and I heard Joe Wilson call him a liar before deciding to switch to something a little more mindless. I ended up watching French-language television from Quebec, doing my best to translate with a sleep-addled mind. I must have nodded off at some point, but I know that it wasn't before four in the morning because I remember looking at my watch and wondering what time the sun would come up so that I could safely take my things back to my car and run. When I did wake up, the sun was bright, shining through the moth or ash holes in the curtain I had drawn the night before to keep unknown persons from watching me sleep.

With the sun shining through the curtains of the half-windows at the rear of the room, I got a good look at the place and wondered if I should wait until I got back home to have a hepatitis test. Everything in the room seemed timeworn—or at least vintage in the way that vintage can be when it is not cool. The faux-gilding on the mirror, the leaky and rusty bathroom sink. The chair and table from the burned-out building. I turned on the shower hesitatingly and only because I knew I had a long day ahead of me, and the water leaked out onto the floor. I used one of the towels, which felt overlaundered and yet oddly unclean, to sop up some of the mess, and kept my sandals on when I got inside. The small bar of soap was sticky when I peeled away the paper, as if it had been used and rewrapped in a cost-saving measure only an immigrant could dream up. The wallpaper was stained and peeling. The number on the door, which I had not noticed in the gloom of the previous night, was handwritten and had been scratched out several times. At any minute, I fully expected a cockroach to squirm out of my ear where it had nested the previous night. And for the second day in a row, I dressed in a hotel counting the seconds until my departure.

⁙

Once again, I had to get the hell out of there before something really bad happened. It occurred to me that I had been feeling that way quite a bit since leaving my parents' house—the need to flee. Oliver Hazard Perry sailed full-speed toward danger and the unknown, yet almost everywhere I had gone I wanted to run at the slightest hint of either discomfort or uneasiness. He probably would have loved that hotel. He would have gone down to the bar and challenged Jim to a fistfight just for shits and giggles. I walled myself in the room and counted the minutes until I could go safely out.

When he was a young man, my dad took a co-op job with a company in Wisconsin. Away from home and making an intern's salary, he stayed at a YMCA and wrote glowingly about the accommodations to his parents. Toweling off and cramming my things back into my bags, I wondered where some of that spirit was. I loved the idea of adventure, on paper anyway, but the actual doing of it was nerve-wracking to me. Could I really be such a soft suburban snob? I hoped not. I wrestled with myself while packing up my things, with my guilt, with the feeling that I had been somehow discriminatory toward Jim and his hotel. The chances were very good that he was doing the best that he could, that he was working hard and building a life. No one died in Room Twenty-three, and he had no intention of selling my kidneys on the black market. I was being paranoid. Then, just as I was about to laugh at my small-mindedness, my scaredy-cat paranoia and the way I had judged the poor proprietor of this hotel with the best fish and chips in town, I heard someone shout out in the hallway. Shriek, really. And I decided that I would never again second-guess my instincts and never again forget to see if the campground was open during the week.

≈16≈

Fort Malden

After a quick breakfast at a Tim Hortons—these places are as common in Canada as, say, trees—adjacent to the motel's parking lot, I made my way back through town and found a parking spot near the public parks that line Amherstburg's shore along the Detroit River. I walked along the beautifully manicured waterfront, taking in the gardens and the historic markers relating to British military history in the city, and trying to let a gentle early-fall breeze wash the previous night's filth off me. Strolling along the narrow, straight residential street that connects the fort with the central business district—a street that once served as the rope walk for the shipbuilding efforts that took place here—I noticed a small sign outside a white cottage called the Park House and decided to stick my nose in.

Ordinarily a place like this would be a walk-by for me. Military history is one thing—major places are fine—but I tend to shy away from historic kitsch. Early in my journalistic career, I lived and worked in Winchester, Virginia, a small town at the northwestern-most tip of the Commonwealth. Everywhere you went, a historic marker announced something supposedly significant but usually nothing more than simply old. You couldn't throw a rock without hitting a battlefield or a house that was once used as a hospital or an inn where one of George Washington's cousins spent the night. At first, I tried to take it in. I felt it was my duty as an outsider to accept what was being offered to me by the locals. But eventually it got boring. You can only look at so many quilts and step on so many creaky floorboards before you decide enough is enough. In general, I am interested, sometimes even enthralled, by history, but history is like tequila—you have to know when you've had enough before it really starts to bite you in the ass.

I would love to say that I was drawn into the Park House by its majesty or by innate curiosity, but the fact of the matter is that it doesn't look like much. It doesn't even look that different from the houses up and down the main street. But here's the thing—I was antsy. It was only a little past ten when I strolled by the sign, and the main buildings at Fort Malden were not set to open for another couple of hours. Maybe I was bored, maybe I was restless, maybe I was a little pissed-off that up to that point my trip had been a relatively colossal failure, but however you slice it I think I was looking for a little redemption, a little compensation for the previous night, when I stepped inside. What I found was a slight, redheaded woman in her late sixties named Valerie who spoke with the same Glasgow lilt as that teacher in the Harry Potter movies. And it was better than redemption, it was connection.

Valerie had lived in Amherstburg for a little more than two decades and had gotten involved with the Park House as a way of volunteering in the community. Apparently civic pride is pretty big in Amherstburg, which once boasted a fairly robust manufacturing base, but all the industry and its ugly remnants had cleared out of town, leaving behind what was, for all intents and purposes, a retirement community. Pensioning Canadians seeking a little rest and some time-tested charm headed to Amherstburg to enjoy the tranquility and its location at the intersection of the Detroit River and Lake Erie.

I followed Valerie as she guided a middle-aged couple from the Toronto area around the house. She showed off the furniture and the handicrafts—tinsmithing was still done at the Park House, and the work of local tinsmiths dotted the décor and was available

The Park House, in Amherstburg, Ontario, was built near Detroit and dismantled piece-by-piece when hostilities broke out. It was rebuilt on this site and served as a general store and residence for more than a century.

for sale in the foyer-turned-shop where I had come in. The couple bragged to Valerie about how they spent every free moment traveling around the Canadian Midwest to see historic sights like this one, and the wife—who had a talent for talking if not listening—bragged about her work in her local writers' guild. Apparently she had already finished three novels set in thirteenth-century Scotland and was fairly excited to be talking to the real honest-to-God thing. Valerie seemed engaged in the conversation, and I wondered if I would ever get a chance to ask a question. The man and I perused the postcards and knickknacks while the woman bragged about having a better grasp of Scottish history than most Scots. Shrugging off what could be an insult, Valerie—who was, after all, Scottish and spent a good deal of time working with history—smiled and nodded and smiled and nodded as the verbose visitor regaled her with the intricate wonderfulness of her written works.

Valerie must have noticed me loitering, because she excused herself from the conversation, saying, "If you don't mind, dear, I believe I owe this young man a tour." As we walked away, Valerie didn't speak ill of the annoying previous customer, but I did catch a prolonged sigh that could be mistaken for relief as we walked through the living room and into what appeared to be a den.

"What brings you to the Park House today?" she asked, and I almost immediately fell in love with her accent and the grandmotherly way she looked at me, as if I might be lost and in need of a cookie. I told her about my little adventure and my hope to discover the remnants of the Battle of Lake Erie by driving around it. "That's very nice, dear," she said. "I presume you've come to Amherstburg to see the fort, then?"

Valerie then launched into a history of Fort Malden—how it had been built as a trading outpost and used as an Indian-affairs office by the Brits; how it had been the place where the great Shawnee leader Tecumseh had plotted with British ground forces to devise a way to counteract the buildup of American strength under Harrison at Fort Meigs; and how it had been something of the British-Canadian version of the Alamo, where the poor, tired, and starving British forces had hunkered down after having supplies cut off from Forts Erie and Niagara on the other end of the lake by an American raiding party that included Perry. It was the clearest ten-minute history lecture I had ever heard, and hearing it in that sweet, melodic accent made it all the better.

"Wasn't this where HMS *Lady Prevost* was built?" I asked. The HMS *Lady Prevost* had been built as the British equivalent of the American ships built to fight the Battle of Lake Erie. The other big British vessel out of Malden, the *Detroit*, had been taken from the Americans at Detroit. Together the *Lady Prevost* and the *Detroit* were the mirror of the American brigs *Lawrence* and *Niagara*. Early in his station at Presque Isle (Erie, Pennsylvania), Perry had volunteered to help lead a raid against Forts Erie and Niagara from Black Rock, near Buffalo. The raid was designed to cut off supplies from reaching Fort Malden and was a huge success. From midsummer through the battle at Put-in-Bay, Malden was essentially left on its own, though Commander Robert Barclay—the big cheese in the British Lake Erie fleet—had been able to patrol the lake, stalk it really, since the American fleet was still largely under construction.

It had been something of a race against time to see who could get the big gunships ready in time to fight. Barclay was cut off from weapons and food on the other end of the lake, but he didn't consider Perry much of a threat. Not only were the *Niagara* and *Lawrence* being built in a rush, they were being built on the wrong side of a large sandbar that he believed would prevent the Americans from launching them into the lake proper. Barclay, who had lost an arm at Trafalgar, prowled like a cat outside a birdcage as Perry and his crew of shipbuilders worked feverishly—literally—to finish the big ships before the Americans lost any chance of taking Lake Erie. But he never attacked the shipbuilding efforts. He knew they were there, he knew what they were doing, but Presque Isle, an arm that wraps around the bay leading into the lake, proved daunting. The Americans didn't have much to defend themselves with, but Barclay didn't want to risk his ships before they could be joined by the *Lady Prevost* for a full-on battle. He also knew about that sandbar, and he didn't think Perry would be able to get the heavy ships over them.

Perry's luck—the same luck that had seen him change ships midbattle at least twice during the attack on Forts Erie and Niagara and guided him through the hectic bloody firefights that ensued—came through in a big way. A fog rolled in, and Barclay had turned his back like a parent to a precocious child for just long enough for the brigs to be helped over the bar by brilliant engineering and lightened loads. Perry launched before Barclay could do anything about it. The British commander hightailed it back to Fort Malden and hid there, waiting for the right moment to attack, while Perry and his men cooled their heels at Put-in-Bay and met with Harrison in Sandusky to plan an attack.

Though the wind across Lake Erie is unpredictable, it generally moves from west to east with a slight north-to-south influence. That's why the winters in Cleveland are so bad. Cold Canadian air picks up steam and a whole lot of moisture whipping across the lake, then dumps a temperamental load of snow on Cleveland and its east side when it makes landfall again. Perry was sitting essentially downwind of Barclay, making a full-frontal attack difficult at best. So the Englishman had the wind advantage—an important one in the Age of Fighting Sail—but some difficult realities to face.

Valerie told me that while Barclay had big ships, he couldn't get enough guns to arm both them and the fort. "And there had been a terrible drought that year," she said. As mentioned earlier, the farmland surrounding Amherstburg had not produced nearly enough food to provision more than two thousand men, so Barclay and Major General Isaac Brock—commander of the land forces at Malden and the captor of Detroit—relied on resupply from the east to keep their stores stocked. When that resupply line was severed, the English were on their own.

To this point in my research, the perspective I had found on the War of 1812 and the Battle of Lake Erie had been largely American and more than a little defensive. Americans wanted to believe in the heroism of guys like Perry and Harrison and Winchester, who had stood up against the evil British Empire and the hordes of savage warriors they had fueled with alcohol and empty promises like a sleazebag cruising for chicks in a bar. We want to believe that the war, when we think of it at all, was a struggle, a second struggle, for the independence of our young nation. It's part of what we do. We root for the guys in the white hats because the guys in the black hats have to be bad. And that may have been the prevailing feeling in the East, but on the far western front, Valerie claims the sentiment was different.

"Look, this house had once stood in Detroit. It's made from wood that only comes from a certain section of land along a certain section of river on the other side," she said. She showed me an area under the stairs where the wall paneling was removed to expose the beams underneath. I was shocked to see that in the wood, at the joints, were carved Roman numerals. Apparently the Park House had been a precursor to prefab houses of today. To simplify building and, later, dismantling, each board had been marked individually. When war broke out, the house was transported across the river and rebuilt on the Canadian side, where it had been ever since. "Barclay and Perry and Brock and Harrison were all warriors, and people died, to be sure. But they were under orders from Washington and London. They were fighting here because some men with a map decided this place was important.

"But the people from around here, the Americans and the Canadians that actually lived here had no problem with each other. There was a lot of intermarrying across the river. The war was really more of a skirmish," she said, "like a fight between two brothers. Nobody really wanted to kill anybody."

She illustrated her point by telling me that after the Battle of Lake Erie, when Brock had fled with Tecumseh and his warriors and Harrison had pursued, a contingent of British soldiers were left behind to burn Fort Malden to the ground so that it didn't fall into American hands. Most of the burning party escaped, but a few were captured and taken back to the recently liberated Fort Detroit as prisoners of war. "And do you know what happened?" she asked.

I didn't know, but wanted to. "They were let go with a wink." She winked at me and walked me to the door, where she wished me luck with my book and asked me to send a copy when I finished it. I promised I would, and just as I was leaving, she told me to remember not to be too gullible when it came to believing the war stories. After all, what separated us then was nothing more than what separates the U.S. and Canada today, and we needed to remember the spirit of brotherhood that set the British firestarters free. Otherwise, we're doomed to repeat our past.

"Don't forget to visit the American fort on your way out of town," she said from the doorway. "It's just south of here, across from a Tim Hortons and a scruffy-looking motel."

Back into the morning sunshine, I made my way up the old ropewalk street toward the fort and was almost pleased to find it abuzz with activity. Tents were being erected, speakers were being set up, and wine was being brought in by the vanload. Apparently when Parks Canada holds a Fort Malden wine-and-arts festival, they don't use the green space along the river but the actual grounds of the fort. I approached and, as I did, walked past a tour bus, the kind where groupies submit to the carnal longings of rock stars on queen beds bolted atop the diesel tanks. I assumed it housed the evening's entertainment. Everywhere I looked, hundreds of volunteers and booth workers were setting up for the festivities, which were set to kick off later that day, long after I had planned to be gone. They were too busy to notice a solitary traveler strolling through the open gates and onto the fort grounds without any identification, and once I was in I kept to the periphery, trying not to be noticed.

The original fort was burned to the ground by the retreating British in September 1813. What remains today was rebuilt in 1838 and used as staging area for the 34th Regiment of Foot, of which I know nothing though I really enjoy the name. It remained a military outpost until 1851, when it was demilitarized. Eight years later, it was turned into a lunatic asylum and served in that capacity until 1870. Many of the large trees that dot the site, so says Wikipedia, were planted during the asylum years to provide shade. It was acquired by the Canadian government in 1937 and has been a historic park since.

I was sort of glad I didn't know about the lunatic-asylum bit when I was walking the grounds—that stuff gives me the willies—but I certainly enjoyed the shade. Many buildings still stand from the

If you look past the tents and volunteers setting up for the Fort Malden wine festival, you can just make out the earthworks built to deter invading armies.

1838 rebuild, but perhaps the most striking features of Fort Malden are the earthen bulwarks that were dug to discourage land attack. Precise hills meet at arrowhead points in a geometry designed to maximize field of fire on an enemy attacking from below. It's not enough that these hills are six or seven feet higher than level ground. No, that wouldn't be hard to surmount at all on an eighty-five-degree angle under the watchful eye of cannon stationed at crossfire positions all around. No, not hard enough at all. The heights of these mounds were emphasized and extended by moats that added seven or eight feet to the already imposing climbing. I looked down from one of the cannon positions and thought to myself that it didn't look that bad. Might be a bitch to mow the lush green grass growing down the trough, but not too bad at all. Then I climbed down to the bottom of the moat and looked up.

Imagine standing at the base of a wall that is almost but not quite perpendicular to the ground. It's slick with dew and mud and the blood of those guys who stood there before you and who thought, "If I can just get a hand hold, I can probably get up there." And you have the same thoughts, only you don't get past "I can probably" because in your moment's hesitation some limey on top has put eight pounds of hot lead right through you.

Military technology has come extraordinarily far in the two hundred years since the War of 1812, but I realized as I huffed and puffed up the embankment that even though they didn't have stealth fighters and nuclear bombs, military planners back then knew how to ruin their enemy's day.

I spent another forty-five minutes or so meandering the grounds and reading the handy bilingual signs, waiting for the fort buildings to open up or for someone to kick me out for not having an exhibitor's pass to the wine festival. Then I realized that the fort was closed for the weekend. Under any other circumstances I might have been pissed that I had wasted a half day without getting to where I needed to be, but for some reason, I wasn't. Maybe it was the beautiful weather, maybe it was that the time I had spent walking was peaceful, but more than likely it had been talking to Valerie that made me realize half the fun of this trip was just seeing where things were going to take me. I had spent months planning and dreaming and making lists, and in the blink of an eye those lists were gone. Once I got over my need to feel rushed, hurried, behind schedule, I would probably have a lot more fun and experience something a lot better. Valerie was right, and the shit-ass hotel had proven the point. I had been clenched then, rushed, and look where it had landed me.

I decided to take it easy from this point on. I knew that in my book I had scheduled a day of driving—all the way around the Canadian side of Lake Erie, then crossing back into the states at Buffalo and arriving in Erie in time to eat dinner. But I wondered to myself, why bother? Why worry so much about getting to Erie when I had a whole lot of ground to cover? Why rush? Why not enjoy it a little bit?

I threw a quarter into the Detroit River and snapped a few pictures of birds and boats passing by on the emerald green water. Then I took a couple of deep breaths and got back in my car and on the road.

I didn't go more than a couple miles before I stopped at the American "fort" Valerie had told me about, and damn if it wasn't right across the street from my shit hotel. I had walked right past it on my way to Tim Hortons, too consumed by blind fury and haste to have noticed it even a couple hours before. I put *fort* in quotes because there really wasn't one. After experiencing the pristine preservation and maintenance of Fort Malden by Parks Canada, I sort of expected every historic sight to be held in such sacred esteem. This one apparently didn't qualify.

A vacant lot big enough for a couple doublewides, the area once home to Fort Covington is situated between what appeared to be a senior citizens' home and a building belonging to the Amherstburg Public Works Department. All that remains of this fort, which served briefly as a staging area for American troops under Harrison's command and in pursuit of Brock, is a concrete slab no bigger than a hopscotch board, with two miniature cannon and a small plaque donated in 1996 by the Amherstburg Bicentennial Committee. Unlike the cannon along the river and in Fort Malden, which were period-authentic, these two minis were stamped with the insignia of the Ford Motor Company. One had fallen off its rotted wood base; the other was nearly alive with a swarm of bees. It didn't take a detective to figure out the American presence here was something no one wanted to remember. The plaque differed from those at Fort Malden not only in size and overall quality but in the fact that it was only in English. It seemed our Canadian brethren were tossing a bone to the occasional American willing to brave a crossing from the Tim Hortons parking lot to check out Fort Covington and not wanting to have to deal with Francophile Quebeçois who might question why on earth any public money should be spent to honor an American invasion.

I tried to be offended, tried to feel besmirched, but then I remembered all the sites I had seen in America related to other occupiers of our great land. They were few, far between, and often not nearly as dignified as the plaque erected by the Bicentennial Committee. I snapped a couple photos and headed back to my car, glad that Valerie had told me about this place. Even if it was an afterthought, it was a nice gesture for an obviously frustrated traveler.

⁓17⁓

The Long Way Around

When I still lived with my parents, I made a point of going weekly to the park near the mayor's office, the one on top of a cliff overlooking the water, to visit the lake. Lake Erie. My lake, my ocean, the refuge of my dreams. Some days, I would sit for five minutes—usually when it was blisteringly cold—and others I would while away an hour or two, reading, collecting driftwood from the meager patch of sand and stone at the bottom of the concrete stairs that led directly down the cliff, or writing terrible, juvenile poetry in black-and-white Mead notebooks that I would fold in half and carry in my back pocket. It was ritual, like visiting a bedridden grandparent in the nursing home. Not an obligation, exactly, but something I was compelled to do.

Lake Erie has played a prominent role in my life. On our first date, my wife and I got sandwiches from my favorite deli on Cleveland's West Side (may you rest in peace, dear Max's) and went down to the lake to eat and flirt and have the awkward conversation friends have when they decide to make their relationship romantic. When I was young and hypodermic needles were washing up on the shore, I swam and body-boarded and punched waves at the only beach I have ever really known—Huntington Beach. I was undaunted by the medical waste and the threat of AIDS or severe infection from punctured skin being filled with dirty lake water, too young to do anything other than blithely go about being young. I celebrated birthdays and graduation on the shore and spent hundreds of summer and early-fall hours bobbing up and down on the waves in my dad's boat, waiting for a fish to take my line and the nausea to subside.

The lake was a friend of mine, and I don't know too many people from my hometown who felt the same way. For me it was romantic and endless, like a private ocean devoid of dreaded sharks and other wee beasties that have always terrified me when not on my plate. I have been away from Cleveland for more than a decade now, thanks to college and jobs and family, but I visit my parents and siblings and in-laws often and always make special time to visit those waters that call to me from my dreams.

I had a lot of fun on and in the water of Lake Erie growing up, but it was during those weekly visits—sometimes on a Sunday morning, other times on Fridays after school—that I did my best thinking. It was on the bench overlooking the water that I learned about growing up, where I pondered my life, my future, and the nature of love. It was in one of those quiet moments alone when I decided which college to attend and, on a visit home from my first real job in Virginia, that I knew it was time to propose. To me, true peace happens when I'm bundled in a sweater and parka with the persistent but un-angry wind blowing off the water onto my face. This trance is only deepened by the maroon-and-gold sunsets to the left and invading purple sky coming in from the right.

I did my best thinking there and still probably do, but often my mind was clearest in its most empty moments, when I would just sit and stare and wonder, rather romantically, if there was another searching soul on the other side staring back. It was something I had wondered about for years, like wanting to know what the inside of a Rubik's Cube looks like. The only way to find out was to take it apart, and the only way I could ever know what was on the other side of the lake would be to go there. But it was more than curiosity that brought me there, more than simple wondering. I had to know. I had to see it, to look back from another person's vantage point. It was innate. It was woven into my fiber. I was driven to drive. Surely there was someone else over there, right? A person who wondered the same thing?

It turns out, there was.

Almost two hours and a couple of wrong turns after leaving Amherstburg, I had been following the lakeshore, traveling at odd speeds for an American driver (who knew that sixty-five kilometers per hour is something like forty-two miles per hour?) and zoning out at the sheer emptiness of the north side of the lake. Part of me had always held a fantastical idea that the Canadian side of Lake Erie would somehow resemble Marseille or Nice or even Quebec, that it would be somehow more Continental and refined than the American side. In part, this fantasy has to do with my lifelong obsession with Canada and, well, no that's pretty much all it has to do with.

I had inflated expectations—let's not forget about the museum in Vermilion here—of a meandering lakeside drive through pretty country dotted by charming towns built around central squares and three-hundred-year-old cathedrals. I imagined a drive on the other side of the lake like being on a drive through Bordeaux and had built it up a great deal in my mind for a long time, because I have wanted to drive around Lake Erie since I was old enough to drive. This was a dream come true for me. And I had intended on living that dream to the fullest.

Amherstburg had been a nice start since it largely met my expectations of a quaint town where the people were friendly and patient with my money-counting and ten-years-rusty French. So, leaving town, I expected more of the same for the rest of the day and into the evening. Google Maps estimated my trip around would take something like eight hours, and I was ready, particularly after the misfortune in Michigan and the long nights in two bad hotels. But as I put Amherstburg in my rearview, I was surprised to find a landscape that was both shockingly flat and remarkably empty.

Hoping for something half as pastoral and quaint as the Côte d'Azur, what I got what something as thoroughly empty as Nebraska. Endless stretches of open land edge either side of the road. Corn, tobacco, the occasional fruit stand, or clumps of trees dot the vast expanses. It is bucolic and flat, like the surface of still water, but broken in places as the road bends and winds. Every so often—an intersection, with the other road stretching farther in the distance in another direction. Time seemed to slow, and not just the seconds ticking by on my watch, but time as in era. I wouldn't say that this part of Ontario is stuck a generation back. It's not. But the bustle of urban life is built on a framework that is fragile, an infrastructure prone to decay. Out here, things seemed to last. I had expected France and gotten the heartland, but I wasn't disappointed. Not really. True, I got frustrated when I considered the landscape's monotony, but more often than not it was a steady pulse of beauty. Calm and serene and a little lonely, but the kind of lonely you come to appreciate. I had wished I could be with my kids and my wife when I had woken up that morning. At home, making coffee and breakfast for the family. But when I got out of the towns and as far as I could from the cities—it was hard to believe Detroit was so close, let alone on the same planet—I appreciated the stillness.

I stayed as close to the lake as I could, doing my best to follow the maps in my Walmart atlas that was accurate in the States but surprisingly unreliable north of the border. I spent miles looking for a turn that should have been right in front of me, and whole hours seemed to pass before I saw a sign indicating which road I was actually on. But as flat and empty as this part of Ontario was, I found myself pretty jazzed to be there. Like a boy with his dog skipping stones along a bubbling creek, it was romantic, avoiding the expressways, taking a route that would force me to take my time, awed by the immensity of the world and my miniature proportion to it.

I had done some math. Toledo is at the western tip of the lake and roughly an hour and a half—ninetyish miles—from my parents' house. Amherstburg is slightly east of Toledo, and the two shores in the western basin are relatively parallel. Taking my best guess to compensate for the speed differences from km/hr to mph, I figured two hours east of Amherstburg, I should be pretty close to directly across from Avon Lake. A mathematician or an engineer might use better logic, but I was blessed with an English major's brain, so it was the best I could do.

I looked for places to stop—public beaches, a park, an abandoned lot, anything—and checked off the small towns listed on my map as I saw signs for them. Signs were about all I saw for most of them, as the definition of town in this part of Ontario is slightly different from my own. In my mind a town requires some sort of central business district, a fire department, a police station, and maybe a place to get some gas. In Canada, I gathered, the definition was a bit more biblical: wherever two or more are gathered, we shall call it a town. And the droning monotony of occasional houses and vast open expanses, coupled with an often impeded view of the lake to my right, began to test my resolve. That is, until I saw something off in the distance. It was tall and white and appeared to be spinning. I watched for more than ten miles as the windmills grew larger until I was eventually among them. There were more than fifty, all of them at least two hundred feet tall with huge propellers spinning silently, gracefully, yet almost violently in the breeze, generating power to fuel, what? I had to assume the electricity eventually made its way to Toronto or Windsor, because there wasn't much need for it in the vast emptiness of this part of Ontario.

Suddenly snapped back from the dreamlike trance of the giant windmills, I checked my odometer—which I had mentally marked with my calculations of where the lakeshore opposite my hometown might be—fearing I had overshot my goal. It felt like hours ago that I had approached that wind farm, hours more that I was engulfed in its immensity. Turns out it had only been a few minutes. Time marches slower in this pastoral land. I had yet to pass my goal but decided to stop anyway, just to double-check. The first place where I could pull over was at a crossroads, a collection of three prefab houses tucked behind an empty two-story structure with a road-side sign announcing the best lunch buffet of homemade cooking in Canada, or something like that. I pulled in, led as much by my desire to eat as by my curiosity. Visions of meat loaf and macaroni and cheese with ketchup set my mouth adrool and must have been sufficiently distracting for me not to realize that there were no other cars in the lot, no lights on inside, no sign of life anywhere. I stepped out of the car and onto the homey wraparound porch only to be greeted with a handwritten sign announcing that the lunch spot was COMING SOON. The paper it was written on was yellow and looked brittle; the tape holding it to the glass door was cloudy and cracked. Canadians must use a different dictionary than I do, because not only were their towns severely lacking in townliness, but *soon* must mean before the next ice age rather than in the next couple weeks.

Discouraged by the lack of lunch and afraid to push through the doublewides blocking access to the shore, I reassessed my map and decided that my Lake Erie doppelganger, the person looking back at me during my weekly visits, must live somewhere near a placed marked "Deaftown" on my map. Strange name, I thought, but perhaps it had once been home to an institution serving the needs of the hearing-impaired. Anyway, it didn't look far from where I estimated myself to be, so I hopped back in the car and returned to the road. Within five minutes, I saw signs for "Dealtown"—and why does this typographical error not surprise me?—as well as a couple for a winery that seemed like a promising spot to look for access to the water and a reverse-angle view from my beloved perch.

Mary-Jane Smith was standing on the ramp leading from the gravel parking lot to the tasting room at the Smith & Wilson Winery, talking to two customers when I pulled off the paved road and laid my car under a tree near the center of the lot-turnaround. I got out and thought I would just have a quick look around, maybe walk through the tasting room and then get back on my way. For some reason, I was suddenly interested in my schedule again. I wanted to make it all the way around the lake and back to Erie, Pennsylvania, by that evening in order to camp and then visit the *Niagara*, which had been sunk in early 1814 but raised in 1913 by the state and turned into a working, floating museum of the battle. I didn't have time to waste at a winery. I had a commodore to chase and a book to write.

I tried to slip by unnoticed, but the parking lot held only two other cars and one of them belonged to Mary-Jane. And I have never been very good at being unnoticed. I wasn't three steps from my car when she called across the lot to me.

"Hello there!" she said, her voice the bubbly and friendly kind you hear at church picnics. "Welcome to Smith & Wilson, come on inside."

The Smith and Wilson Winery near Dealtown, Ontario, my refuge on the lonely road around Lake Erie. In the distance is the lake. I strolled this road with a glass of white wine, enjoying an Under the Tuscan Sun *moment.*

Mary-Jane was slightly earthy in her fleece vest and blue jeans.
I guessed she was in her early forties, but it was hard to tell because
of her youthful smile. She reminded me of the kind of woman who
had Golden Retrievers as pets. Not one, probably two. Relaxed,
casual, warm. She was exactly what you might think of when you
imagine a winery owner in south-central Ontario. I followed her
into the tasting room, which was warm and quaint and had picturesque views from a huge plate-glass window overlooking the vineyard that lay between it and the lake beyond. I was happy to see the
water, if for no other reason than it confirmed I was still heading in
the right direction.

"What brings you in today? Would you like to try some of our
wine?"

"Um," I said, "I'm not sure that I should. I have kind of a long
drive."

"Where you heading?"

"Home, back toward home."

"An American, huh?" she said, though I wasn't sure what gave
me away. It was probably my guarded posture, a giveaway in this
friendly part of the world. "You're the second American car that's
pulled in today. There was a couple from Milwaukee in about an
hour ago that said they were stopping by on their way home from
Chicago."

"Huh?" I said. "But this place is nowhere near being on the way
between Chicago and Milwaukee."

"So you know where Milwaukee is?"

"It's about two hours north of Chicago, which is every bit of
seven hours west of here."

"I see," said Mary-Jane with the kind of chuckle that says,
"What a strange world we live in." Not content, or perhaps unable
to simply let me browse and be on my way, Mary-Jane began asking about what brought me to her neck of the woods, and when
I told her about Oliver Hazard Perry and the Battle of Lake Erie

and the book, she seemed genuinely interested. She asked me questions and told me stories about her experiences living along the lake before asking why, specifically, I had chosen to stop at her establishment.

"Well, it's really sort of starry-eyed and romantic, but I grew up in a town that I think is directly opposite of you, on the other side, and I've always wondered what was over here."

"No way!" she said, as if I had just given her the Christmas present she always wanted. "My husband and I like to sit on our porch and look across the water. We've always wondered what was on the other side too!"

Mary-Jane pulled a map from below the counter, and I showed her that, sure enough, we were shore twins. We figured we had probably been looking at each other for years without knowing it. Suddenly I didn't care about my schedule, about Erie, about the *Niagara.* This, I thought, was what I wanted to do for most of my life, to see the other side and confirm my suspicion that there was indeed a doppelganger over here, a romantic enthralled by the lure of the lake, who whiled away hours dreaming as I had.

True, she wasn't quite what I had expected, but then what about this trip had turned out that way? For some reason I had imagined a lumberjack or a teenager like me when staring across the lake. But having met Mary-Jane, I was pleasantly surprised. There was something comforting about her, like she was the kind of person who really believed everything would, eventually, be okay. And I suppose that I am too, so maybe it's fitting that we've been making eyes across the lake for such a long time. Still, I held out a little hope that her husband at least moonlighted chopping down trees.

"This may seem a bit forward," I said. "But would you mind if I walked down to the water and had a look?"

"It's almost a mile," she said in a way I thought was meant to discourage my meandering. "You should probably take a glass of wine with you. Red or white?"

She poured me a glass of white, and I set off down the dirt tractor-tire ruts leading south toward the shore, sipping and taking in the late-afternoon sun. I was alone on that dirt track, a few acres of corn to my left, a few acres of grapes to my right, and it felt like one of those *Under the Tuscan Sun* moments—romantic and improbable, a brief respite from the world. Every few yards I stopped and took a small, savoring sip of the sweet white wine, readjusted my camera strap on my shoulder, and had a look around. The house-turned–tasting room was above me on the gently sloping road, and I tried to see if Mary-Jane was watching me, but it seemed that she was not. When I was certain no one was looking, I pulled a couple grapes off the vine and popped them into my mouth without regard to pesticide or agro-chemical poisoning. They were almost inedible, and I thought, not for the first time, who came up with the idea of crushing mass quantities of these funny-looking berries, squeezing out the juice, and letting it sit in a wooden barrel for a while before drinking it? I often find myself asking these kinds of "how the hell did we figure this out?" questions when I'm alone and relaxed. Like crabs—who the hell thought the ugliest beast in the sea would be a delicacy? Now before you fire off some letter with the right and proper answer, I'll tell you that I don't really care. Not about the crabs and not about the origin of wine. What I did care about was the feeling that, for the first time on my little escapade, I was relaxed. No stress about ghosts or broken cars or border guards, just that peaceful feeling you usually see only in magazines and catalogs.

I took my time walking the rest of the way down to the lake, cutting across a row of corn and walking along a tree line until I found a path going toward the shore. Mary-Jane had warned me that there was no beach, so I was prepared mentally when I reached the edge of a cliff twenty-five feet or so above the water. No Wile E. Coyote moment here. The wine had kicked in, and I felt a slight buzz forming in the middle of my brain. Mary-Jane had cooked up some high-test stuff, and a couple more glasses might have put me out for

Somewhere across the water and through the smog is my hometown, Avon Lake. Mary-Jane Smith, my dreamy-eyed Canadian doppelganger, was nice enough to let me walk her property.

the night. Instead, the first just had me looking for a proper tree to piss on and, once it was found and soaked, I scrambled through the trees a couple more yards until I found a place to sit down.

The view from Mary-Jane's shore should have been a mirror image of the one from my little park bench at the mayor's office, but it wasn't. The lake seemed somehow different from the other side. Gentler, maybe, more mysterious. And the horizon, too, was different. Looking toward Canada on a cloudy day is like looking at hypermodern art, just two slightly varied tones of gray separated by a thin dark line of horizon. But from here, with clouds over the lake—if none were above me at the winery—the image was tweaked. The line between water and sky was more defined. The water—green beneath me—was the same gunmetal shade I had looked at for most of my years, but the sky was different. Dusky, brownish, like a sandstorm was blowing somewhere out over the water. And then it hit me: pollution. The Ohio side of the lake was populated, developed. Except for a few breaks of open space, the shore is lined with villages and towns, suburbs and cities. Power plants, cars, houses, and other pollution factories sully the air, and from where I sat it looked like it should have been unbreathable. For all those years I spent staring across the water, I had no idea I was looking at relatively pure air. But Mary-Jane, in her wistful gazing, was staring at Al Gore's worst nightmare. It was creepy, like realizing that the life you live is nothing more than a peep show for some Kurt Vonnegut aliens. Only the peep show didn't include boobs, but slow death. I wondered if I could ever feel the same way about Lake Erie's recovery, seeing in full view just how directly its destruction was caused by us.

My thoughts were getting heavy; thinking about environmental destruction was killing my baby buzz. So was the tree I was sitting on, which seemed to want to check my prostate, so I snapped a few pictures to show Mom back home and stepped out from the trees back toward Mary-Jane and the tasting room. I was thanking her for being gracious and allowing me to play out my whim when she introduced me to a couple of other people from the winery. They all apparently shared our mutual fascination with life on the other side. And one told me that at night, when the humidity is low and the air is crisp, she can see stoplights changing across the lake. I didn't have the heart to tell her that such a sight was impossible, given the curvature of the earth. And I didn't have the heart at the time to admit to myself that what she had probably seen was the aircraft warning lights on top of the smokestacks at the coal-fired power plant blinking on and off, just below the source of the haze that had recently broken my heart. Instead, I played dumb and feigned amazement, returned my empty glass, and exchanged business cards before heading out on the road.

After my experience at Mary-Jane's place, I felt like I should be just about finished driving, but as the kilometers wore on and the scenery stretched for miles ahead—that bucolic emptiness of farmland inter-rupted only by clusters of houses and the occasional town—I began to get a sense of just how big Lake Erie is. Hours rolled by, and the sun continued in its lazy arc toward the horizon. I paused every once in a while to check my progress only to think, "Jesus, and this is the *small* lake?" The Great Lakes hold something like 20 percent of the world's fresh water. That includes the Amazon, the Nile, the Mis-sissippi, and all ten thousand of Minnesota's lakes. That includes the glaciers of Alaska and the streams of Africa. Only the polar ice caps represent a larger concentration of fresh water, and you can't begin to understand the scale of it until you try to drive around one of the lakes in a day. These lakes are huge. They are inland seas that have provided recreation and drinking water, transportation, and, in the case of Oliver Hazard Perry, strategic advantage for hundreds of years. It's amazing to me that with the power the Great Lakes repre-sent—controlling these waters could be one hell of a power trip—they have been fought over only briefly. For most of the two and a quar-ter centuries of the United States' existence, they have been peaceful havens, diplomatic victories.

The border between the United States and Canada is more than four thousand miles long—not including Alaska, which takes the length past 5,500 miles—and it is not militarized. There's no con-flict, no fighting. Apart from the occasional crossing with an over-zealous customs guard, it is wide open. The U.S. border with Mexico is less than half the length—under two thousand miles—and there are people who want to build a wall the entire length of it. There are assault rifle-toting yahoos who spend nights in their pickups with night-vision scopes claiming to be patriotic defenders. The contrast is striking. The U.S. is capable of peaceful relations with our neigh-bors to the north, but a sense of hostility is rampant among some at the mere mention of those to the south. This doesn't have much to do with Perry, or even where I found myself cruising at awkward speeds across the Canadian heartland, but the contrast between the attitudes regarding our borders made me think about what it meant to be an American then and now.

Perry's America was a nation divided. In the post-Revolutionary years, Americans were united by little more than the common hangover following the throwing-off of imperial bonds. New Englanders wanted to trade with the world. Southerners wanted to be left alone to raise their crops and own their slaves. Federalists wanted to elect a king to serve for life, and Democrat-Republicans wanted every decision to be left to the will of the people. But Perry's America was powerful, too—if not in the size of its military, then in its potential for resources and trade, and the potential to repeat its recent history. Perry's America had the potential to be great and was taking steps toward greatness and might.

My America seems like a place that hasn't learned a lot of lessons. We are still a nation divided between conservatives and liberals, between war hawks and peaceniks, between right and left. We are united under a common flag but are torn asunder by extremists on either side of the aisle whose purpose in life seems to be to prove the other side wrong and thus be more right. And after the attacks of September 11, 2001, we are a paranoid nation. We're scared of our own shadow and apt to place stock in silly things like a color-coded threat index. But unlike America two hundred years ago, our might is felt around the world. Our military might is unsurpassed, but our economic might is even greater.

−.−

I stopped twice more before reaching the eastern terminus of my trip. My first stop was along the side of the road as the sun beat out its final rays of the day before leaving the skies to become dark and immense. I decided I had overestimated my ability to circumnavigate the lake in a day and overplanned my schedule to camp at Erie. I would have to make it to Pennsylvania another day to visit Perry's second flagship, the *Niagara*. And after a couple bad nights and three long days, during which my mood shifted from the thrill of travel to missing home with the frequency of a traffic light, I can't say I minded the thought of spending the night in my parents' guest bedroom and eating breakfast with my kids.

The second stop was in the town of Fort Erie, where Perry had helped overtake British forces in the spring of 1813. Everywhere I looked, I saw familiar names like Walmart and Wendy's, soldiers in America's economic army. It seemed that the potential of America had spilled across the unprotected border with Canada and across every other border in the world too. In a way it was comfortable to be surrounded by the familiar, but I also felt a shock of return to the neon glare of modern life. I had only been in Canada for two days, and already I could feel my pace slowing a bit. Confronting that glare of economic globalization was akin to realizing you are related to a serial killer, even if he is an uncle you have never met. I wanted to go home, but I didn't want to go back.

The border crossing at Buffalo was like a scene from a bad movie. Hellish floodlights cracked cool evening air, and commando guards armed to the teeth with Homeland Security weapons patrolled the crossing. I pulled up to wait my turn at the booth and looked out my window to see four cameras staring at me like inquisitors in Torquemada's private dungeon. I tried to imagine what was happening on the other end of those feeds. Were customs cops taking retinal scans and digging through my personal history? I hoped they overlooked my unpaid parking ticket and noticed that I had been giving religiously in the offering plate.

The guard on the Canadian side, the one who had given me the stink-eye when I told her I was writing a book, seemed like an elementary school lunch lady compared with the American man who took my passport. He questioned me about why I had gone to Canada and what I was carrying. He warned me to stay in the car when he said he wanted to search my trunk, and he shined his flashlight so directly and brightly in my face when he was done that I thought he was trying to look into my soul. But eventually, he waved me through and back onto the fast-moving and properly speed-limited American highway system. Seventy miles an hour felt like warp speed compared with my amble through Canada, and for three hours I drove silently across New York, Pennsylvania, and Ohio under a dark sky devoid of stars.

I was tired when I got home. Tired from driving, tired from having so much time to myself to think, tired from being away, and only mildly disappointed that I had missed such an important stop on my trip. I kissed Dylan on the head and snuck into bed with my eldest son, Jack. I knew there was time. I would make it back to visit Perry's ship. It was history, after all, and it wasn't going anywhere. But after running from ghosts and fixing my car, surviving two interrogations at the border, and a night in a crime scene, I was ready to rest if only for a night. When I put my arms around Jack and pulled him closer, it felt like I hadn't been gone for more than a couple of hours. That was the amazing transformation I discovered when he was born: fatherhood is portable. True, there are things you miss about your home—your favorite chair, your well-organized pantry— but when you are a parent, home is and always will be wherever your children are. I can't remember a time when my dad came home from a business trip and climbed into bed with me, but I remember him always coming in and tousling my hair the next morning, like he wasn't really home until he saw me. I used to think it was annoying, particularly because he is such an early riser and I preferred to sleep late, but now that I am a father, I understand.

There's so much I understand now that I have kids, so much about my dad that I could never have understood otherwise. I understand his impulse to share with me, even if he was born without the emotional mechanics of what I consider intimacy. His waking me up the morning after a business trip or dragging me to see places like the Perry monument was his way of telling me he loves me. And I know for a fact that he never got even that much from his dad. Fatherhood has changed a lot in two generations, or at least the expression of it has. My dad has four kids and eight grandkids and has never once changed a diaper; I have changed hundreds in five years of paternity. But that doesn't make me a better father. It doesn't make him a worse one. Because what makes a father is the feeling you can't describe, the one that I felt when I got into bed with Jack that night. What makes a father is the feeling like you want to protect something with your own life, that you want to teach them everything you know how to express, that you feel somehow safer being around them. I love being a father, and I loved the way I felt when my head hit the pillow that night. It was as if something inside me, slightly askew, had been set right. And for the first time in three days, I didn't have to want to fall asleep. I just did.

≈18≈

Drinking with an Englishman

I woke up the next morning feeling refreshed and spent the morning with my kids. Mom wanted to hear the details of my trip. Dad had left a note saying he would see me when he got home. Because I was scheduled to spend the night in Erie and the morning visiting the *Niagara*, I had only one stop planned for that day in Cleveland, but it was the one I had been looking forward to the most for more than a year.

When I was first contemplating doing a book about Oliver Hazard Perry and Lake Erie, I knew there was one thing I wanted to include in my research—beer. One beer in particular, the Great Lakes Brewing Company's Commodore Perry India Pale Ale. Because I'm not a historian and because this book has as much to do with my relationship with Lake Erie as it does with the battle for it, and because I really like beer, I had made a point in the planning stages to put Great Lakes Brewing's headquarters on my list of destinations. Located near the historic—and by *historic* I mean old and in a bad part of town—West Side Market, Great Lakes Brewing's offices, brewery, and pub-restaurant are key to the burgeoning gentrification of Ohio City, a neighborhood on the Near West Side around West Twenty-fifth street. This is a part of Cleveland that, ten years ago, not many suburbanites would have visited. And only slightly more do today, but it's definitely a neighborhood in transition. Restaurants and bars cater to the lunchtime business crowd and weekend market-goers and also to the young and daring at night, and at the heart of it all is Great Lakes Brewing.

During the 1990s, when the microbrew craze was sweeping the nation and everyone with some yeast and hops and some time on their hands seemed to be getting into the act, the owners of Great Lakes Brewing decided to become Cleveland's brewery. They made and continue to make hearty, heavy beers that stand in sharp contrast to the watered-down offerings from Big Beer in St. Louis and Milwaukee. Great Lakes beers are like Clevelanders—they are a little harsh and can be hard to swallow if you're new in town, but once you've survived a blisteringly cold winter along the lakeshore, you find yourself craving them because you understand them more, you become a part of them, one of them. As if flipping the bird to Budweiser and Miller and anyone who dared ferment ingredients outside of town, Great Lakes also took on a marketing strategy designed to appeal almost solely to Clevelanders by drawing upon local history in the naming and labeling of their beers. The Burning River Pale Ale pays homage to the most notorious of Cleveland's myriad environmental disasters and is labeled with a photo of the skyline at night that appears to be burning from below. The Eliot Ness Amber Lager evokes the famous lawman who, after nailing Al Capone on tax evasion, became Cleveland's public-safety director and retired in shame when he couldn't solve a mass-murder case known as the Torso Murders. The Edmund Fitzgerald Porter dares to imagine what might have happened had the ship made it to Cleveland—its destination—had it not sunk and made Gordon Lightfoot famous. The label for Conway's Irish Ale features a photo of an early-twentieth-century Cleveland beat cop who happens to be the great-grandfather of the Brewing Company's owners, Patrick and Daniel Conway.

The beers and the labels are distinctive and personal to anyone who has called Cleveland home. And one summer, when visiting my in-laws, I made a run to the grocery store and noticed a new offering from the brothers Conway—the Commodore Perry India Pale Ale. India pale ales were so named because they were made in England with extra hops to help them survive the long passage from, say, London, to the empire's claims in India. They were sailors' beers, hearty and highly alcoholic. The label on the IPA features a painting of Perry in mid-transfer from the *Lawrence* to the *Niagara* during the Battle of Lake Erie, easily his most famous moment. I bought a six-pack and drank it during a family get-together before passing out from the heft and high alcohol content on a backyard lounge chair—easily my most notorious moment with the in-laws. And when the time came to do this book, I decided that I needed to know where the painting came from and why, with all of Cleveland's maritime history, Great Lakes Brewing Company decided to name their sailor's beer after Perry.

Entrusting the kids to my mom's able care, I left around lunchtime for the twenty-minute drive to the Near West Side. The car felt different than it had for the previous few days, more like a mode of transportation than a gateway to adventure, but I didn't mind. I had some drinking to do.

I hadn't made an appointment with a media relations person, so when I arrived at the front door of Great Lakes Brewing Company I decided to use the only reporter's trick I ever really mastered—playing dumb. The company's offices are a warren of cubicles and desks on the first floor of a building that was once probably pretty grand, but in the last century has gotten a bit down in the mouth—the sort of postindustrial, postwar structure that one day, when gentrification sets in, will fetch a huge sum in rent for studio apartments and lofts. Seated behind a glass partition, like the ones in inner-city gas stations, was a middle-aged woman who seemed ready to eat her lunch. I stood at the window and smiled, but she ignored me (God, I love

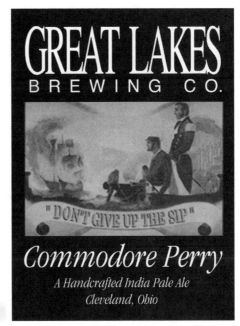

The Great Lakes Brewing Company's Commodore Perry India Pale Ale. Note the homage to Lawrence's famous words: "Don't give up the sip."

Cleveland). She took notice when I knocked, and she made a half-hearted attempt at feigning interest in what I was after.

"I was hoping to speak with someone in media relations about your Oliver Hazard Perry beer," I said. "But I'm afraid I don't have an appointment."

Stupefied look and obvious expression of longing for the fast food sitting on her desk.

"I'm an author," I said, "and I'm only in town for the day. Do you think you could point me in the right direction?"

"Um-hum," she said and turned to a colleague sitting out of view amid the cubicles. She said something about me being a writer and needing to talk to someone about one of the beers. At this, her coworker popped her head around a corner with a "what are you talking about?" look. When the second woman came to the window, I made my case again and politely asked—though I'm not sure it would have mattered had I demanded—to speak to someone in marketing or media relations.

"They're all in a meeting over in the pub," she said. "Probably be busy all day. You should call first next time."

"Do you have a phone number where I might reach someone?" I asked. "Or a name?"

"You should be able to find that on the Web site," she said. "I don't know who you need to talk to."

At this point a couple of thoughts crossed my mind. First, how big of a company could a regional brewery be that they don't know each other? And second, why is it that everybody gets nervy when you say you're a writer? I've come across this phenomenon time and again as a reporter and magazine editor. I could be working on a story about puppy dogs and rainbows, and the minute I tell someone I'm a writer they get all clammy. Do they assume I'm there to do an exposé on them? Some people might think press-shy people are just that, shy, but maybe we all tend to believe we have something to hide or that we're important enough that journalists are trying to seduce their way into our deepest thoughts. Let's face it—most of us aren't all that interesting, and our secrets aren't going to shock the world.

With a curt nod in place of a good-bye—the standard Cleveland get-the-hell-out-of-here-so-I-can-scarf-my-McDouble-in-peace gesture—she sent me on my way. I left the main offices and crossed the employee parking lot and loading docks to another, more gentrified building housing the Great Lakes Brewing Company pub, restaurant, and gift shop. If the offices and warehouse are vestiges of a once-proud past, then the pub is the public face of a currently proud future for Great Lakes. It's a cool building, all old brick and narrow passageways. The bathrooms are in the basement, which has old pictures on the wall, private dining rooms, and low ceilings, the kind of place you might expect to see on a ghost-hunter's show, but cleaned up a bit to make it charming. The bar is old and dark, the tables line the windows facing the street, and an outdoor patio makes the perfect place to blow a two-hour work lunch with burgers and an illicit beer.

I loved it instantly. Even the gift shop, which is chockablock full of enlarged and framed beer labels, posters, glassware, and restaurant swag is great, divided down the middle by a staircase under which the cash register sits. I asked the woman working behind the register if it would be all right if I had a look around, and in my meandering casually brought up my intentions for coming here.

"I was hoping someone might be able to tell me more about the Perry beer," I said.

"What would you like to know?" she said in that charming way only people who work in hospitality can muster.

"First, the label," I said, pointing to an enlargement hanging on the wall. "Where did the artwork come from?"

She told me that it was a painting that was hanging in an upstairs dining room, that it had been hanging up there for years, and when I asked if I could see it, she said the Rockefeller Room—how awesome is that?—was in use for a managers' meeting, which is where my press contact was at present.

"Any idea why they chose Perry?"

"I'm afraid I can't help you there, but you might want to ask the hostess if she can get the person you need out of the meeting. They can probably tell you."

This was more like it. Service, not paranoia.

For the third time in ten minutes I told my story, this time to the hostess who asked me to have a seat, maybe some lunch, and said she would see what she could do. Right then I panicked a little because I only had six bucks in my wallet. Gas, tolls, car repairs, and fast food had drained my funds in Canada. The last time I had filled up—somewhere in New York—I had worried I wouldn't have enough money to get home. I don't carry a credit card—been burned there, but that's another book and another temptation—so I worried that I would have to take a table during a busy lunch rush only to drink water and leave my remaining money as a tip to a pissed-off server. Instead, I took a seat on a bench inside the front door and waited for the hostess to return from upstairs with the verdict.

Ten minutes later, she came back and told me that I probably wouldn't be able to meet the media relations person because she had a meeting after the one that was going on, but I was welcome to stay and wait for the Rockefeller Room to clear so I could see the painting myself.

"We'd be more than happy to get you a Commodore Perry India Pale Ale," she said. "It's on the house." I swear to God she winked at me, and I was almost smitten. I sidled up to the bar, taking a seat at the elbow. The hostess went to the other end and let the bartender know what was happening and patted me on the shoulder when she returned. "You're all set," she said and went back to her station before I had a chance to thank her.

The bartender said his name was Tony (not really, but I have to protect his identity a little here). He spoke with that perfect northern-England accent—thicker than the one in the south—that makes words somewhat indiscernible, with a tight-lipped mumbling action that completely belied his obvious Americanized posture. He poured me a pint of the IPA and leaned against the bar top like Sam Malone on *Cheers*.

"They tell me you're interested in Oliver Perry," he said. God, I wished I could talk like that, all casual and intrigued. "Why's that, then?"

I told him I was a writer working on a book about the Battle of Lake Erie and the lake itself, and then an uneasiness came over me. I felt that talking to an Englishman about the War of 1812 would be like talking to an African American about the Emancipation Proclamation or a Jewish person about the Holocaust—as if I were unqualified to discuss such things as a white American male of German and Swedish extraction. But Tony had been behind the bar at Great Lakes for more than two decades. He knew how to handle my obvious sheepishness.

"War of 1812, that's an interesting topic right there," he said. "Do you know much about it?"

"Can't say I know too much," he said. "You see, the English have fought a lot of wars and some are more memorable than others, but it was a hell of a thing that Perry did that day." A helpful gift-shop clerk, a charming and equally helpful hostess, and a gracious barman willing to talk about old wars with a complete stranger? This was what I had imagined my trip was going to be like. After the first beer went down like water and the second was starting to hit me like a ton of bricks, I decided that I didn't want to leave that barstool, possibly ever.

Tony and I talked for more than an hour, the conversation continuing after each time he left to help another customer—a paying customer at that. We talked about the battle, about England, about Cleveland and how it had become a real home for him. We talked about the legacy of war and how perceptions of it can be so different from either side. For him, the entire War of 1812 was a skirmish on the heels of the great Napoleonic conflicts. For me, it was a seminal and overlooked piece of American history. When the hostess finally returned to tell me I could go upstairs to see the painting that became the label, I felt obligated to Tony not only for the beer but for the conversation. I took out my last six dollars and slapped it down as a tip. It wasn't enough to get me through my next three days of traveling anyway, and it certainly wouldn't get me and my sons back home to Cincinnati, but it felt like a gesture of gratitude I could not afford to not make, although I'm certain to him it carried as much weight as the little skirmish carried in his home country's long and storied history.

Up in the Rockefeller Room, sitting at a long table amid papers and a laptop and his iPhone, was a man with his back to the window, the sunlight obscuring his face like some Hollywood Mafia don. He barely looked up when I came in but asked if I was the one who wanted to see the painting. He introduced himself as Dan Conway, who with his brother Patrick had founded Great Lakes Brewing Company in 1988, though he didn't look old enough to have been in any business for more than twenty years except maybe as a paper boy. I gave him my story, and he pointed to the other side of the room where, hanging on the wall, was the massive painting from which the Perry beer label had been taken. But unlike the label, which bore the image of Perry in his rowboat, the painting itself yielded a near-panorama of the battle. It had to have been four or five feet tall and at least seven or eight wide, oil on canvas and oddly familiar. Perry was in the bottom-right corner, the battered *Lawrence* torn to pieces in the background and other ships charging with guns blazing. I'm no artist—I can't paint my way out of a bathroom—but it seemed strange that the painting was done in yellow and brown hues. I looked at it for a couple minutes, took some pictures, and felt strangely satisfied at having accomplished my goal of finding the actual piece that had inspired the label. Then I turned to Dan and interrupted his careful study of a spreadsheet that held either sales figures or employee schedules.

"Excuse me," I said. "But do you mind if I ask why you chose Perry?"

Dan explained that at Great Lakes, the beer comes first. When they wanted to do an Irish-style beer, they came up with the recipe before deciding to name it after their grandfather, an Irish beat cop from early in the twentieth century. For the Perry beer, they wanted to do an India pale ale and came up with the recipe before working on the title.

"It wasn't all that hard to pick Perry," Dan said. "IPAs were sailors' beers that were around during the time he was. It made sense to use Perry since he's so closely associated with Lake Erie and the North Coast and at about the right time."

Funny, I had hoped for a slightly nuanced answer. A childhood obsession like mine, a fondness for the Age of Fighting Sail, something, but Dan is like so many Midwesterners—practical to the core. They had a beer based on those consumed by sailors around the turn of the nineteenth century, and they had a naval hero who gained fame on the waters a few dozen miles away. Simple math.

The painting was a little more intriguing. I asked him where it had come from, since it didn't seem like they were committed enough to the Perry legacy to have something commissioned solely for a beer label. He explained that the painting had once hung in McGarvey's, a restaurant on the bank of the Vermilion River in Vermilion. I remembered the place from trips with my dad, whom you'll recall docks his boat just up river from there, and we had stopped a few times for burgers after fishing. It was the kind of place you could park your boat dockside and go in for beers before heading out or home.

"The owners really helped us get up and running here, and when they went out of business, we got the painting from them," he said. And once again I was fascinated, no completely taken in by the Great Lakes Brewing Company's spirit of local connection, personal touches, and practicality. We chatted for a few more minutes before I felt like I was intruding on his work and then bid farewells and luck. I was half-tempted to push it a bit further and try to nab another free beer from Tony at the bar but worried that the freebies only lasted as long as I waited, and if I ordered another I wouldn't be able to pay. So I made my way back to the car and back to my parents' house to spend the evening with my kids and my mom and dad before continuing my adventure the next morning at the penultimate destination on my list—Put-in-Bay and the annual celebration of Perry's victory over the British in the waters near there. Still, I was a bit sad to say good-bye to Great Lakes Brewing Company. It had been my most successful visit of the trip to that point and had quickly become one of my favorite places in my favorite town.

~19~

Ferries, Flags, and One-club Golfers

The ferry dock was empty when I arrived in Sandusky the following morning, except for a couple crew members and a teenager working the ticket booth. Excited and perhaps a bit zealous to take in everything I could in a single day on Put-in-Bay, I had gotten up before dawn and driven in the cool early darkness the forty miles from my parents' house in Avon Lake, along the lakeshore on the same route I had taken earlier in the week. But it seemed different now. When I set out four days earlier for my big circumnavigation, I had felt like I was on an adventure, a Kerouackian meandering through time and space. I was so fixated on unearthing the shards of Perry's legacy that lay buried along the lakeshore that I had sort of forgotten to enjoy a nice drive on a pretty road. That attitude had changed for me in Canada, and on this second trip along Route 6 I felt a little more at peace. It might have been that I had finally relaxed, it might have been that everything that had gone wrong I had survived, so maybe I was willing to go a little more gently with the flow. I can't be sure, but what I can be sure of was that I enjoyed myself a hell of a lot more the second time around.

There was only one little problem. I was broke. The car repair and the tools, the gas, the extra night in a hotel room had all sapped my financial reserves. I was stuck with two choices: go home or borrow some money from my dad. The first seemed like a defeat and the second was painful for me to do. Dad has always been supportive. He has never said no when I or Rebecca and I have needed help. But it was hard to ask him for it. It was hard to face him and admit that I needed something because I wanted so badly to be my own man. I knew that he had gotten no help from his parents—not that they wouldn't, but they had nine children on a farm-implement salesman's salary—and my dad had put himself through school and bought his first house and cars and developed his nest egg all on his own. I wanted to be like him. I still do, so badly in fact that admitting I need help is like admitting to myself that I can't be like him. But I wasn't going to give up.

The night before, standing in the driveway where I greeted him as he arrived home from work and telling him about my trip, I had told him I needed to ask him something. I shifted awkwardly, not making certain eye contact, uncomfortable in my own skin. But Dad has a constancy about him that I have always admired. He never seems upset, never changes his facial expression unless it is to smile or laugh—usually when he's talking to his grandkids, especially when they say something adult, something beyond their young years.

"Dad, I was wondering if maybe," I said. "I mean, I need to buy a ticket for the ferry and, uh . . . "

"Don't worry about it, we've got you covered," he said, not letting me face my own humiliation. "You've had a rough week."

"It's just that I don't want to ask, but I . . ." I paused and shifted my weight back and forth. I'm as big as Dad, maybe an inch or two taller, but in that moment, I felt like a little boy. "I can pay you back as soon as I get—"

"No, it's no problem," he said, again not wanting me to grovel. He was smiling, that narrow toothy grin he shares with his siblings, the same one I see in the mirror, the same one I see on my sons' faces. To him, my request was small. Still, I think he understood the gravity of my asking. He knew how hard it was for me. "I've got you covered."

"I haven't been wasteful," I said. I always feel the need to justify with dad, to try to explain that I was doing my best to be like him, when I'm not certain that is something he has ever wanted or expected of me.

"I know," he said holding the grin. "Shit happens and it's happened to you this week."

Shit happens? His response was so matter-of-fact, so easy. I don't know why, but I had expected a lecture, perhaps an implicit request for a pro forma detailing my spending and the logic behind my budgeting. I'm always like that with him. And my sisters seem to be too. We want so bad for him to be proud of us that we sometimes overlook the fact that he already is. I must have looked pretty defeated and I felt that way, that combined emotion of gratefulness and shame. I looked away. "Look," he said. "You'd give it to Jack, right?" Of course I would. Absolutely, I thought, but surely he couldn't think of me the same way I think of my son, could he? I have never given my dad enough credit for being a dad. He's an engineer, an army guy and a successful senior executive at a company he helped build nearly from the ground up. I look at his credentials and take them to be the measure of him as a man. I never seem to give him enough credit—none of us does, except maybe my mom. Yes, I would absolutely give my sons the money if they asked. I wouldn't think twice. And maybe, just maybe, this little exchange helped me understand how my dad looks at me, through the same paternal lenses I view my own children through. I never understood that before. I extended my hand, which, while larger than his I'm sure, still feels small when he shakes it. He pulled me in for an Iowa hug, the kind you get from relatives who grew up without parental affection. It's tough, firm, accompanied by a slap on the back and lasting no more than a second, maybe two if it's a holiday or a funeral. "Don't worry about it," he repeated. "I think

it's cool what you're doing. Now, let's go inside. Mom's got dinner waiting."

Having borrowed some money from my dad, which I promised to
repay with book proceeds (thank you for doing your part to help
pay back that hundred bucks), I decided to take the Jet Express over
to the islands. It was a bit pricier than the ferry that had taken me,
my wife and kids, mom, dad, brother, aunt, uncle, and cousins over
the first time, but at least it landed right in the middle of the island,
near town and the Perry Memorial, and I wouldn't have to walk a
couple miles along the side of the road before I could even start for
the day. Plus, it was a little longer trip from Sandusky, which would
give me a bit more time out on the lake. I bought a ticket for the first
ferry out and the return on the last ferry of the day, which would
give me about sixteen hours to tour the island and do the research
I wanted to do out there.

"Do you expect it to be busy?" I asked the teenager behind the
ticket window. She had a look that was both perky and glazed over,
like she'd had a long night with friends the night before.

"Yeah, probably. They've got that Perry weekend going on, plus
Ohio State is playing USC tonight, so there'll be a lot of people who
head over to Put-in-Bay to watch that." Great, just what I needed,
a town full of drunks. But it would probably be fun, barring the
possibility of being knocked overboard by a Buckeye fan who had
drunk his breakfast.

Leaving Sandusky, the Jet Express, which clips along at a speed
sufficient to drown out all noise but the monotonous thrum of huge
twin engines and wind when you sit on the top deck, rounded Cedar
Point ("America's Roller Coast") and left Sandusky Bay en route to
Kelleys Island to pick up more passengers before pushing across to
Put-in-Bay. On the trip over to Kelleys, the boat had been nearly
empty, just me, an older couple, and a few guys who looked like they

were college students getting off campus for the day or picking up a few final shifts at their summer jobs. So I pretty much had the top deck to myself. I love that feeling of being buffeted by the wind and humidity out over the water. It was relatively cool, and I had a jacket on, the fabric snapping in a popcorn burst of quickly moving air. I surveyed the water, looked to the west toward Johnson's Island—a notorious Civil War prison for captured enemies—and to the east where open water rolled out in a seemingly endless carpet of carbon blue. I smiled to myself with the knowledge that I had been to the other side of the horizon and seen what was there. This was now, officially in my mind, my lake.

We landed at Kelleys and took on forty or so passengers. Some were obvious tourists who had probably spent the night in one of that quaint island's bed-and-breakfasts; others were clad in Ohio State's scarlet and gray, and among them there were obviously some early-morning revelers who had tied one on with their breakfast. These guys should be interesting, I thought, hoping none of them would puke on me before we made it to Put-in-Bay. The group that stood out consisted of maybe ten or twelve middle-aged men and women. They were dressed as if on their way to a country club, and each carried a single, lonely golf club. I watched them for a while and tried to figure out, as they took seats on the benches in front of and next to me, what they were up to. Each of them had a different club. Some of the men had drivers and some of the women had wedges. It was almost as if they had split a single set of clubs for the day to break up the caddying duty like so many Sherpas on the climb up K2.

After ten minutes of watching, I had to know. I approached one of the men, a barrel-chested icebox of a man in black Nike golf shoes, tan shorts, a black Nike wind shirt, and a black Nike golf cap. He was leaning against the rail opposite me along the stern of the ferry and listening to his buddies talk about something evidently hilarious that had happened the night before.

"Can I ask you something?" I said. He turned his eyes toward me, and his broad face and walrus mustache made him seem probably ten years older than he actually was. "What's the deal with the golf clubs? Why only one?"

"It's the annual one-club tournament on the course over at Put-in-Bay," he said. "We've been doing it for ten years."

"I can't imagine that the scores are all that good," I said, realizing only afterward that my comment came across as crass and a bit snide.

"Neither are the players, or the course for that matter," he said. "Besides, it's just an excuse to swing a club, drink beer, and not have to carry all that much. It's our salute to Commodore Perry."

The last part surely was a joke, but it reinforced the ambience of the Lake Erie islands. Catawba, Middle Bass, and a couple other smaller islands are where people live. Kelleys is where you go to visit a winery or camp or spend the day strolling around the outskirts of the island. Put-in-Bay is the adult playground. Home to both the longest bar in the world and the only round bar-barn I have ever seen in my life, it's the kind of place where middle-aged former hell-raisers go to spend the money they didn't have in the seventies doing the things they loved to do back then. There's no casino or anything, no strip clubs that I know of. Hell, there's a school there for the island children who live there year-round, and the central business district isn't much more than a block long and a block wide, but there is always beer. Lots of beer and lots of food and lots of boats carrying people looking for beer and food. This is where the parents go when the kids are away at camp.

The trip from Kelleys to Put-in-Bay was filled with shouted chatter and a whole lot more people. It was one thing to stand at the rail when the top deck was empty; it made me feel like Leo DiCaprio in *Titanic*, but having to stand at the rail because there was no place to sit down sort of sucked. Still, I managed—I'm tough like that—and kept my eye on the Perry Memorial jutting from the narrow part of the island, watching it grow larger as we got closer. For some reason it seemed bigger from the water. Three hundred feet is a long way up, especially when the nearest tall object is a tree one-fifth the size. We rounded the eastern point of the island to make our approach to the dock in the shallow bay downtown. This was the same bay where Perry "put in" (hence the name, not that the beer-chundering masses much care), but nearly two hundred years later it is almost unrecognizable. Hundreds of white specks—the fiberglass hulls of fishing boats and pleasure boats—dot the shallow waters leading to a town that is one part Martha's Vineyard and two parts old-timey circus. As we drew nearer, I watched for the clearing at the base of the monument to come into view and when it did, it looked like REI and L.L.Bean had had a kid, and that kid had thrown up all over the ten acres of green grass. Tents were pitched every-where—tents in colors ranging from military khaki to purple to early-1990s teal, stacked like sardines in a cramped tin box. Surely there couldn't be that many partygoers willing to bivouac to catch a pre-game buzz, right?

Right.

In addition to being an annual golf outing for either the plea-sure seekers or lazy drunks I met on the boat, and a weekend dedi-cated to the memory of Oliver Hazard Perry's victory in the waters seven miles northwest of the shore, the second weekend in Septem-ber is also an annual Boy Scout Jamboree on Put-in-Bay. A better writer might be able to describe my sick excitement as I imagined War of 1812 reenactors, Boy Scouts with pocketknives and know-how, and drunken Buckeye fans prowling the streets in search of gaining territory, but suffice it to say, I pictured a train wreck in the making.

I was hungry, but one of the ferry's crew had casually men-tioned that this was the last weekend the observation deck atop the Perry Memorial would be open, so I decided to head there before the other ferries started arriving with people who might want to kill some time before the big game, or before joining in on "Kumbaya" around one of the Boy Scout camp fires. To get to the top, you go into the base of the structure—which I will never be able to think of again without thinking of my aunt's dish-soap-bottle comparison—and step around the marked graves of six soldiers and sailors (three American, three British) killed during the battle to a narrow staircase that follows the inside circumference of the giant column. Up these stairs there is a room, a dark room lit by ominous orange lights, with an ancient-looking elevator—the kind that has been around for a hundred years and its age is obvious. Give the park ranger at the desk three dollars, and you get a paper ticket to ride to the top. Sounds simple, only I hate elevators and, worse, I really hate old elevators. It's not that I'm claustrophobic or even necessarily afraid of heights (though they aren't my favorite things); it's just that I have known too many engineers and architects to ever be able to trust a building this tall. Two of my best friends are architects, which might sound cool, but I knew them as undergraduate frat boys who were just as likely to throw up on themselves as put on matching socks. No offense to Dave and Adam, but I don't think I'll be in line to climb their first skyscraper. No, no thank you.

But at least my guys have computers to keep them in check. When the Perry monument was built in 1913, they were probably using slide rules—and (I might be mistaken on this one) weren't heroin and marijuana still legal back then? I tried to clear my mind. Just an elevator ride, nothing more, and I had just about convinced myself that everything was going to be all right until some mouth-breathing knuckle dragger in line ahead of me asked the ranger why the monument was closing for three years.

"We're going to be making repairs to some structural damage," said the volunteer ranger, a retirement-aged, no-nonsense guy in a green trucker cap and matching "Ranger" windbreaker. "When the monument was built, it was designed to drain rainwater and snowmelt off the side, but some time back in the seventies, they decided

Perry's Victory and International Peace Memorial. The three flags represent the U.S., Canada, and Great Britain. The water to the left is the shallow harbor where Perry waited for Barclay to come out and fight.

they couldn't have water pouring over the edge from three hundred and seventeen feet up. So they installed an internal drainage system, but the engineers weren't too smart about it and forgot to heat the pipes. So thirty or forty winters of water thawing and freezing has done some damage."

Done some damage? This was a giant concrete column. Ever seen a driveway that's been cracked by ice? Now, wrap that driveway into a gigantic paper towel tube and put it in the middle of a lake known for the severity of its winter storms, add an ill-designed drainage system and an apple crate of an elevator, and it becomes a death trap. I wanted to bolt, just say "screw it, I don't need to revisit the site of a childhood expedition that ultimately was the inspiration for this book" and run the hell away. But I had already paid my three dollars, and that represented a certain sacrifice to me at this point. That three bucks was a cup of coffee, and I love coffee. I had to try and get my money's worth, even if it meant dying a horrific death.

The ride up was cramped and scary. I shared the elevator, which was sort of elegant in a grandmotherly way, with two other riders and the volunteer—Dave or Skip or Filbert something like that. He prattled on about the history of the monument and gave us a brief overview of the battle, but for what seemed like incomprehensibly long stretches he didn't say anything. It was almost as if our presence was somehow bothering him. As we reached the top, he warned us that it would be considerably cooler—I think those were the words he had used—at the top than it had been at ground level. Then he held out his arm as an invitation to get off his rig. I stepped out of the cabin and up into the frigid early-fall wind that whipped and tore at me like some kind of demon. *Considerably cooler?* That was an understatement, but the sun was out, and the sky was that cerulean blue you really only get in the fall when the haze of summer has burned off and cooled and the winter clouds are still forming somewhere over the Yukon. It was nice. And crowded.

Because of the shape and the height, it's sort of hard to see how crowded the top is from the ground. I had assumed it wouldn't be crowded, but I apparently made an ass out of you and me. The observation deck was lousy with Boy Scouts and scoutmasters, all clad in khaki and green, their kerchiefs flapping in the arctic wind. But, true to the myth, they were all courteous, and I began wondering what they put in the water to make a bunch of adolescent boys behave so well? Was this Jamboree really just a time for them all to put on matching sweat suits and Nikes and wait for the mother ship to arrive? Kidding aside, when I wanted to read a sign or cling close to the building for fear of falling through the badly deteriorated concrete—which bore no visible signs of deterioration, but I knew they were there—the boys moved politely to the side and managed to stay on their best behavior.

The view from the top of the Perry Memorial is, at the risk of sounding like Rick Steves, breathtaking. It is a panorama unlike any a skyscraper in Cleveland or Detroit or Buffalo could possibly match. I could see thirty miles into the clear distance, over the string of islands both American and Canadian, past Point Pelee to the mouth of the Detroit River, where the British had launched their desperate attack that made Perry famous. I could see the timeless beauty of water and rock and trees and the decidedly modern visage of our lust for all things electric in the form of two nuclear power plants—one in Ohio and one in Michigan. Standing at the northwest corner of the observation deck, looking past Gibraltar Island and Rattlesnake Island and another ten or so open miles of water, I could see the actual battle site. I had intended on visiting this noble patch of water, but time and life and job and family and all the commitments that make being an amateur travel writer nearly impossible got in the way, so I had to settle for reading the sign that diagrammed the battle and making do with imagination.

And here's the funny thing. For all my trying, all the stops along the side of the road and gazing off into the horizon, for all the times I tried to imagine the battle, this was the first place where I could just see it. I could see Perry and his squadron tacking against light winds, trying to gain position against the British, who were bearing down with long guns and cutting the American ships to ribbons. I could feel the violence of the echoing guns. I could see, in a way that no painting or diagram or heroic poem could ever describe, the violence and desperation of the moment. For a long time I stood there watching, as if through a personal portal to the past as Perry charged and looked back over his shoulder wondering where Jesse Elliot was with the brig *Niagara*. I could sense the depravity of the scene as more than 80 percent of his crew lay dead or injured and he was forced, ironically, to strike his colors—the deep-navy-blue flag with the slogan "Don't Give Up the Ship" emblazoned on it, and carry it with him. I could feel the madness of the moment as he set off in a rowboat across a half mile of open water, through the shots of cannon and musket to take command of the *Niagara*, the wind, and ultimately the battle. And I could hear the echoes of the American carronades, the short, powerful ship-killing guns that boomed so loudly there were reports they could be heard in Cleveland—fifty miles away. Then I could sense the grief-stricken, panic-addled peace that came when the final shot was fired and victory was declared.

I had spent more than a year reading everything I could get my hands on about this battle and a lifetime trying to make sense of why it meant something to me, and it was only here, standing atop the monument in the gusting wind, that it actually made sense. I'm not a scholar or even a person with a strong inclination toward the past. I'm not a military guy who studies tactics and strategies. I'm just a guy who grew up in Cleveland, a guy who had a romance with a place that no one else thought was important. When you live in New York, you think the world revolves around you. When you live in L.A., you're convinced of it. But what are you if you're from Cleveland? Or Ohio for that matter? More than likely the butt of a joke. The burning river. The forever-losing Browns. The Rust Belt, the boring old heartland—at best a backdrop for a Michael Moore documentary or the setting for a sitcom in which nothing much happens.

The Battle of Lake Erie and Oliver Hazard Perry mean something to me because they are ours. This is *our* thing. This monument was a place where my dad took me; this history it was devoted to could only have happened here. And I guess for most of my life I had been proud of it without knowing it. Proud that my dad was the kind of guy who thought it was important to do this kind of stuff with me; proud that such an amazing story happened right here; proud that Lake Erie is a place that I can and will always call home— and there is nothing more important that trying to understand the place you come from. Even if you are a transplant, even if you are from somewhere else, home is the place where you find yourself wanting to return. It's why I still go to the mayor's office and sit by the water when I'm visiting town, why I have a collection of beach rocks in a bag in my drawer. It's because I am as much a part of this place as it is a part of me.

You know, maybe Robin Williams had it right in *Dead Poets Society.* Maybe we all need to stand up on the desk and get a new perspective of our surroundings to really understand them. Only I needed a road trip and to stand on that observation deck, to look out at the water that had held my gaze for a long time and allow the image of Perry's victory to come to me, to really understand why it had been in the back of my head for all these years. I wished I could stand there again with my dad and talk about the battle and the water and the wind. I wished my sons could have been there with me, even if it meant nothing to them at the time. But I know it would not have been the same for them as it had been for me. Their lives will take them in different directions, call them to other places. I just hoped that it will be me who introduces them to that place someday and that later on they will silently thank me for it, the way I was thanking my dad at that moment.

⁓.⁓

My nostalgia and the flood of emotion washing over me were interrupted by two things. The first was a woman who couldn't read the sign I was standing in front of, and the second was the fact that I was freezing my ass off and wanted to get out of the wind. I walked around the rest of the observation deck, pausing at each corner before falling into line for the elevator behind what had to be the result of some cosmic experiment in niceness, the kind of thing that is so pure it is almost creepy—Canadian Boy Scouts. The elevator must have been running slow, because the line didn't seem to move at all as I was bombarded with friendliness. The scout leader told me about their drive from the Niagara region around the lake and the troops' trip across on the ferry. He told me that more than 1,500 scouts were encamped on the island and that this was a trip his boys looked forward to all year long.

"Is it something to do with the significance of the memorial?"
I asked the long-socked and gangly scoutmaster. He stared at me
blankly. "You know, this memorial was built to signify the lasting
and mutual peace between our two countries," I said. "Is that why
it's so important for your troop?"

More blank stare, then, "Really, I just think the boys like having
the chance to get away for a weekend before school starts back up,
ya know."

All right, maybe I was being a little cynical. Maybe I was tired
and had hoped the elevator would move faster. I didn't intend to be
snide, but it had been a long week, and despite my pillar-top revela-
tion about the Battle of Lake Erie, I was feeling cranky. An island
full of Boy Scouts and drunks, frankly, had my skin crawling a bit. I
backed off and made chitchat while we waited. The scoutmaster, I'll
call him Doug since that's my go-to Canadian male name, was a nice
enough guy. Judging by the Blackberry on his hip—which he bragged
about having service for even in the bowels of the Perry Memorial—I
guessed he was an engineer or in computers in some way.

After a slow descent we made it to the ground floor, and as we
parted ways—me toward town, Doug and the Boy Scouts toward the
warren of tents to the east—I heard him mention that it was time to
get ready for the big parade. Oh goody, there would be a parade. I
asked a park ranger for a timetable for the day's activities and noticed
that I had an hour and a half to kill before the parade and ceremony
honoring both the scouts and Perry's victory, so I decided to right a
wrong I had committed on my previous trip to the island.

I decided to rent a golf cart.

Downtown Put-in-Bay is a mishmash of T-shirt shops, bars, restaurants, and trinket stores spread over no more than ten or so
acres in the center of the island. Among these establishments are
rental centers that offer golf carts and bicycles and strange three-
wheeled cars that look like something left over from the filming of
Moonraker. And oddly enough, all these rental places, along with the

Dairy Queen and a couple knickknack stores, seemed to be staffed by Russian teenagers (or at least natives of former Soviet Bloc countries) who had very little grasp of the English language. So it was with a bit of confusion that I listened to the young man, Sergei (of course), detail the specifics of my rental agreement. What I did understand was that for less than twenty bucks (one-fifth the price they were asking at the ferry landing a year before), I could rent a golf cart for an hour. I handed him my license and signed a waiver of some sort and set off exploring the island, which had awakened and become densely crowded since my arrival thanks to the influx of ferry passengers and the cannon fire coming from the reenactors' camp at the base of the monument, which had to have been hell for the hung-over weekend party crowd.

I had been to Put-in-Bay a couple of times and, apart from the hike to and from the ferry on my previous visit, had never been outside of town, so I started toward the eastern end of the island first, figuring if I had time I would head back to the other end to see what was there. Along the main road stood great old cottages and farmhouses, each with porches occupied by revelers or multiple generations of families taking in a late-summer weekend retreat. It was nice, no, better than nice, it was lovely. Everything seemed peaceful on the island. The electric-powered traffic was slow and quiet, the breeze at ground level was refreshing. Maybe I had underestimated Put-in-Bay. Maybe it was more than just drunks and sailors and drunken sailors. Maybe this was the way life is supposed to be, provided you are wealthy enough to live this way. I stopped by a couple of houses that were for sale and read the flyers stuffed in Plexiglas boxes on the front of the signs. A three-bedroom, run-down shack could cost more than half a million dollars here. I tried to imagine how much some of the nicer homes cost. Clean island living is damn expensive, even without the golf-cart-rental fees.

It took maybe five minutes to reach the eastern terminus and turn around. There wasn't much to see, just a rocky promontory

My trusty steed, one of hundreds of golf carts that choke the roads of Put-in-Bay. Having learned my lesson the first time, I decided to atone for past mistakes the second time around.

and a sign noting the fact that, unless you have gills and flippers, you couldn't go any farther. So I turned around and headed back toward town, all the while taking in the unique—if rarefied by property prices—atmosphere of the island. I could see myself, bestselling author of travel books and historically themed thrillers, sitting on my front porch with a notebook on my lap, a fountain pen in one hand, and a tall glass of sun-brewed iced tea in the other. I'd spend three seasons in Vermilion and summers on the island. Maybe that was the kind of glory I would chase. Perry could have his presidential commendations or whatever. I wanted real estate along Easy Street. I made a mental note to buy a lottery ticket, just in case the bestselling-author thing didn't work out.

In town I experienced what must be one of the few problems with island life on the weekends—a traffic jam made up entirely of golf carts and those three-wheeled contraptions (which I vowed to rent next time I visited), complete with an island police officer in his sharp blue uniform directing with hand signals and a whistle on the corner. From there, a seven-minute drive led me to the western tip of the island, where a state park, golf course, cozy, futuristic-looking rental bungalows, and a beach were crowded with weekend partiers. I took a few minutes to find the one-club golfers on the course, but no dice. So I headed back the way I came—past Perry's Cave adventure wonderland, crawling with Boy Scouts in line to tour the cave the commodore had used as a source of mineral-filtered water during his stay on the island, and to sneak in a round of mini-golf before the big parade.

I hung a right near town and followed an access road that led me to the long, straight stretch we had walked fourteen months earlier from the other ferry landing to town. It felt sweet, jamming along the road—which was as close as the island had to a superhighway—at the just-faster-than-you-can-sprint clip of my trusty steed. I cruised past the airport and to the other ferry landing, then turned around, confident I had made up for my egregious oversight in not renting the cart on the first trip. But I also felt like I was wasting my day. I needed to be more productive. I needed to get back on the Perry track.

What I needed was a parade.

❧ 20 ☙

Marching On

I make no bones about it, no apologies or excuses. I'll shout it from the rooftops, I don't mind. When I was in high school, I was a band geek. That's right, marching band, concert band, symphonic band. I've done them all. Four years with letters, if you can believe it. So it's fair to say that I know a thing or two about parades. And this one, with fifteen hundred Boy Scouts and hundreds more high school kids toting their marching instruments, was pretty good. Very good, in fact, and my nostalgia for my long-gone youth nearly brought tears to my eyes.

Even as the drunks hooted and hollered and parents elbowed their way to the front row to get pictures of their kids as they passed, I couldn't help but smile. There must have been two thousand people crowding the narrow street through downtown Put-in-Bay. Many waved banners as their band or scouts passed. Hundreds of cameras and camcorders. It all made me look forward to the day when I can be one of those parents capturing such a moment for posterity, which I would drag out as part of a pre-wedding video presentation. (A Helpful Rule for New Parents: Collect Evidence.) Even the denizens of the tented booths set up on the central park, where they were selling paintings and craft work, took a break to witness that most hallowed of small-town Norman Rockwell American traditions. And it was just that, pure Americana. Boy Scouts and marching bands, dignitaries in classic cars being driven by their owners. Who can really complain about a marching band parade?

As I watched the parade march toward me through the center of town, I noticed a familiar face. Leading the line of scouts and bands and local dignitaries was a park ranger in green pants, a green sweater, and a Smokey Bear hat. He had a beard that hadn't been there before, but I was positive that it was the same ranger who'd given my dad, uncle, and me a history lesson the previous summer. He was the one who went to my college and was studying to be a teacher. What was his name? Matthew? Mitchell?

"Marcus," he said. I walked up to him after the parade led to the base of the monument, where a tent had been erected for a presentation honoring the anniversary of Perry's victory. He looked at me like a deer in headlights when I said, "You don't remember me, but I was here last summer with my dad and his brother." Of course he didn't remember me. Perry's Victory and International Peace Memorial gets more than a hundred thousand visitors a year. But seeing a familiar, albeit recently bearded face made me relax a little.

"So is this still a summer gig for you? Haven't you graduated?" I asked.

"I graduated, but I decided to put in another summer," he said.

"What are your plans?"

"Hopefully, I'll get a job here," he said. "This is what I want to do, but I won't know until the end of the season next month."

This lucky SOB. He'd figured out a way to live the good life, the Lake Erie island life, without writing a bestseller. I felt like I had a friend now, someone I could ask questions and who could help me if necessary. Marcus was friendly and professional, a real Dudley Do-Right, but also, I think, he recognized our loose collegiate bond. I wondered if he too was glad to be speaking to someone other than a Boy Scout or a drunk. He told me that I should take a seat in the tent before they were all gone and pointed me toward a teenage girl who was passing out flowers with little slips of paper attached. The flowers, red and white carnations, represented a soldier or sailor killed or wounded during the battle. Each slip of paper bore the name, status (killed or wounded), nationality, and ship of a casualty. She handed me a carnation, and I looked at the tag: a British marine killed aboard the *Queen Charlotte*. I don't know if it was the pure Americana of the marching bands and Boy Scouts or just the fact that I was fully immersed in Perry, but this didn't sit right with me.

"Excuse me," I said to the girl, who had moved on to someone else. "But would you mind if I got a different flower?" She looked at me puzzled. "I don't mean to sound rude or anything, but it's just that I would really prefer to have one off of Perry's flagship, the *Lawrence*."

Marcus let out a bemused chuckle. I had told him about the book and my reason for visiting. He gave me a look that said "man, that's cold," but he didn't stop me from exchanging my carnation. She shuffled through the slips of paper like a Vegas dealer and pulled out one that fit my request. "Thanks," I said, and I went under the tent to take a folding chair in the third row.

Seaman James W. Allen, U.S. brig *Lawrence*, Killed in Action. I made a note to look up Allen when I got back home and wondered if there was a coincidence that James Allen is my dad's name. Could have been blind luck, but I thought it was kismet and decided I was, after all I had been through, finally in the exact place I needed to be. (Incidentally, I couldn't find Allen's name in the honor rolls listed in either Gerard Altoff's or David Curtis Skaggs's books. I e-mailed Marcus, who told me that because Perry's fleet had been so hastily put together and relied on volunteers, the records were filled with holes. He also told me to trust him—James W. Allen was indeed aboard the *Lawrence* that day and was killed. Phew, that's better.)

The ceremony was, in some ways, a lot like any small-town ribbon cutting or groundbreaking, no different from hundreds I had attended over the years as a reporter. Dignitaries sat up front, and there was a master of ceremonies—in this case it was Perry Memorial Superintendent Blanca Alvarez Stransky, who was oddly striking and bore a resemblance to a tall Eva Longoria in her green uniform and Smokey Bear hat—and the presentation of the colors by crew members of the USS *Lake Erie*, a navy ship based in Pearl Harbor. A Boy Scout led the Pledge of Allegiance, and three of the marching bands from the parade combined to play the National Anthem, which was also (and separately) sung by Anne Parker, an octogenarian resident of Put-in-Bay. The National Park Service Reenactor Gun Crew—how would you like that on a business card?—gave a cannon salute, and then a middle-aged man dressed in early-nineteenth-century clothes stepped up to the podium to perform the "Ballad of Lake Erie," an epic poem–song written by someone named Phoebe Boorman.

Accompanied by his wife, Linda, on piano, Robert Bell launched into an atonal, a-rhythmic retelling of the battle in verse, complete with a refrain that including lyrics like "The ships sailed high, the ships sailed low . . . ." I wasn't trying to be a music snob, but I found myself wide-grinned halfway through the performance—which was part acting, part singing, and part surreal tomfoolery—wondering what exactly the hell I was listening to. It was like watching someone try karaoke on a song he'd never heard before. Don't get me wrong, I could tell that Robert and Linda had nailed what was written, but I had never heard anything like it. Someone later explained that the song was written in the style of the dirges of Perry's day, and I thought, "No wonder we lost Michigan. If that was how we sang to keep our spirits up, I'm amazed we won anything at all."

Superintendent Stransky thanked the Bells for their performance and then said, "They have to be going. They have another engagement on the mainland." Really, these guys were double-booked to do that?

The ceremony became more ceremonious when the Honorable George C. Smith of the U.S. District Court, Southern District of Ohio, took the microphone. Wheelchair-bound, Smith was an active board member of the Perry Group, a nonprofit organization that puts on events like the memorial weekend to raise money for the preservation and maintenance of Perry's Victory and International Peace Memorial. The way Marcus explained it to me, the Perry Group was a booster organization that provided funding for programming and other projects not covered by the shrinking federal budget for national parks. I was moved that such a group existed, and Smith's speech moved me further when he spoke about a friend and fellow Perry Group board member who had recently passed away: Rear Admiral Wayne E. Meyer.

Meyer had no connection to Lake Erie aside from the fact that he was once the captain of the USS *Lake Erie*. Meyer was a passionate man, according to Judge Smith, and a genius. A successful naval officer, he was a brilliant engineer who conceptualized, designed, and built the Aegis Missile Defense System. Aegis—the word is derived from Greek and describes a collar worn to protect soldiers from battle—is one of the most advanced weapons systems in the world, and it all started with Meyer, who had an idea for a computerized sea-to-air missile system that could shoot down intercontinental ballistic missiles. Mind you, he had this idea in the 1960s, when computers were as big as houses and as powerful as calculators. He spent a lifetime developing it and used his ship, the USS *Lake Erie*, as a launch pad for the system. The *Lake Erie* was the ship that fired the missile in 2008 that blew up a satellite before it could reenter the earth's atmosphere. It took some serious math to work out a system that complex, and Meyer was the guy who did the calculations.

But he was also a student of history. When he took command of the *Lake Erie*, Meyer apparently studied Perry to get a sense of the legacy of the ship. Perry's name had been lent to a class of ships by the navy, but the *Lake Erie* was the only one floating that celebrated the history of his achievement. Meyer flew Perry's flag, the blue banner with the words "Don't Give Up the Ship," and made a point of visiting the monument every year—provided he was not absolutely needed elsewhere—to honor the anniversary. So here was an important man with no connection to the North Coast or Put-in-Bay who recognized the importance of Perry's victory and went quite a long way out of his way to honor it.

Smith said that Meyer was a friend and an active member of the Perry Group. He died just weeks before the ceremony I was attending, but not before he could be the first man in U.S. naval history to have a ship commissioned and named after him while he was still alive. Yeah, I thought, that is impressive.

Meyer's belief in history and Perry's history in particular was so strong that he set a precedent after he hung up his sea legs for an office job as a rear admiral. All new captains of the USS *Lake Erie* reported to him before reporting to their new ship. During these meetings, he would tell the new captain of his old boat and of Perry's story and would order them to make every effort possible to be at Put-in-Bay on the second weekend of September to take part in the historical weekend at the monument.

After remarks from the director of the Put-in-Bay Chamber of Commerce, a fit man in crisp dress whites with a U.S. Naval Academy ring and a smile like Tom Cruise's stepped up to the podium. Captain Ronald A. Boxall was relatively new to the *Lake Erie* and had made a dire error by not calling Rear Admiral Meyer first thing after learning of his commission.

"I put it off," he said, "I forgot about it for a couple weeks. Big mistake. When I finally sat down for lunch with Admiral Meyer, he looked right through me and said, 'You're late.' And then he gave me the long version of the story."

Boxall is from upstate New York. He's a career navy guy, and he said it took him some time to understand why he needed to bring his master chief, color guard, and select officers and crew halfway around the world for a weekend like this. But, he said, after visiting for the first time and getting a sense of the place and the history, he understood.

"The Battle of Lake Erie should be among battles like Pearl Harbor, Gettysburg, and Lexington and Concord," he said. "But for some reason it is not. Commodore Perry's victory represents the first and only time in history an entire British squadron is captured completely. The greatest naval force the world had ever known, and the only time they suffered defeat like that was right here."

Boxall said he has a hard time imagining what it must have been like to fight that way, tall-masted ships facing each other at point-blank range, especially here. "You know," he said, "I've been sitting here an hour, and the wind has changed direction three times already. There's no place else that I have been to where sailing is like this." His admiration for Perry is obvious, but it is his admiration for Meyer that oozes from his words. Like Judge Smith and others, he speaks reverently, passionately, about Meyer, and I felt a little cheated to have missed out on the opportunity to meet the man. Later in his talk, Boxall said that he had embraced Perry's legacy as captain of the *Lake Erie*.

"Every time I sign off on the intercom, I tell the crew 'Don't Give Up the Ship,'" he said. "We fly the flag, and I am constantly drilling that into the back of the crew's heads. It's gotten so bad that I can't even get them to practice an abandon-ship drill anymore."

After the ceremony, I approached Boxall behind the front table.

"Excuse me, captain," I said, not introducing myself or putting my question into context. I had a couple of questions, ones that had nagged me for some time, and I had hoped he could answer. I asked him about Perry's legacy. Was he important within the navy? Was Perry a person they taught at the naval academy?

"Yes, absolutely," he said. "His battle flag hangs just inside the front doors."

"The real one?"

"Yes, in a glass case."

"So, I don't really know how to say this, but what do you study about him? His tactics? His strategy?"

Boxall smiled a toothy grin and then tried hard not to sound condescending when he said, "Naval warfare today isn't really all that much like it was then. The tactics don't translate, but we study Perry because he embodied so much of what the navy is about today. Courage and honor." His answer sounded a bit like a greeting card, but I could tell he was being sincere. Oliver Hazard Perry was gutsy and smart, and as a result he had pulled off the biggest upset in the history of naval warfare to that point. There was something so red, white, and blue about it, something so electric. I stepped out from under the tent and looked up at the tall monument and realized it wasn't tall enough. The height, which had tossed my stomach as a kid and sent tingles down my spine earlier that morning, wasn't high enough to do Perry justice.

My moment of reverie was interrupted, however, by the sound of gunfire coming from the west lawn of the monument and the chest-thumping boom of a cannon. Shit. Were we under attack? Then I remembered—reenactors.

~21~

Farb-tastic

They like to be called *living historians* or, for brevity, *interpreters* and my first experience with weekend historic warriors came when I lived in Virginia. It was big news when the production crew of the epic sequel to the movie *Gettysburg,* called *Gods and Generals,* was going to be filmed in town. So big, in fact, that my editor, Bob Wooten, assigned me to cover the story for an entire day. Rare were the days when I filed less than two or three stories for the *Northern Virginia Daily;* even rarer were the days when those stories would be half as interesting as spending a day on the set of a major Hollywood production. So I didn't mind when I was told that it would probably be just a lot of mingling with extras and working the crowd.

And was there ever a crowd. Hundreds of behind-the-scenes people—grips and best boys and craft-services people—mixed with several dozen living historians in full costume (lots of wool and leather and hobnails, despite almost oppressive heat). The scene they were filming was taking place in winter, and so sudsy soap was sprayed along the streets, which were covered in dirt for period effect. As I understood it, the scene was basically filler. Stephen Lang, who played General Thomas "Stonewall" Jackson, would be exiting a carriage, greeting his wife, and walking through a door.

Two days of setup, an entire day of waiting, all for about seven and a half seconds of Hollywood magic. The reenactors were basically street filler, something to make the movie seem more authentic, and after spending a day with these people, I came to understand just how much authenticity means to them.

If you've read *Confederates in the Attic*, Tony Horwitz's amazing account of traveling through the modern South in search of the Civil War's legacy, then you know reenactors are a breed apart. Among them you are either gung-ho or a wannabe, a *Farb*. Those who wish to avoid being Farbish spend every free moment and every bit of extra income on perfecting their uniform, finding period-accurate buttons and boot straps. They obsess over the past in order to preserve it, they say. And in a way, they are nostalgic for a long-ago time and place that they could not possibly understand. They seem to wish they had been born a hundred years earlier, to be their own great-great-grandfathers. And it always seemed a bit curious to me. I understand wishing for a simpler time, but not at the cost of antibiotics, lattes, and the Discovery Channel. It would seem my nostalgia has limits.

In the pantheon of living historians, those who spend their weekends reliving the Civil War era usually get top billing. People go to see the Confederates lose at Gettysburg, even if the "battle" is being "fought" in a public park in Illinois. I think this billing has to do with the importance placed on that war and the seemingly noble causes being fought for at its root. Slavery, in a sense, is a sexier historical topic to tackle than, say, tariffs. Flip on The History Channel on any given day and you are bound to see something about the Civil War, and it will inevitably involve a reenactment of some kind. Appearing in a documentary is, for many, a reenactor's dream come true. It gives the noble Yanks and cantankerous Johnny Rebs of the weekend warrior world a certain elevated position among the eras—Wild West, Revolutionary War, even those nuts in Alabama who play Vietnam on snake-infested tracts complete with Vietcong-esque tunnel networks.

Boys and their toys. ABOVE: A carronade, like the ones carried by Perry's ships, is fired, demonstrating its ship-killing reputation. BELOW: Reenactors and members of the park service's historic-weapons-demonstration teams show visitors the mechanics of war in 1812.

So it was with a particularly keen eye that I watched the interpreters who had set up camp on South Bass Island for the weekend. Shortly after the ceremony honoring Perry's victory and our long-standing peace with Canada, they resumed what they had been doing all day—firing weapons, performing drills, putting on a show. An area of the west lawn near the base of the giant monument had been cordoned off for use as a demonstration ground, and a team of five men loomed about a snub-nosed cannon pointed southward toward the main land. As they did, two men in period military dress roamed the broad rope line, showing off details of their costumes and early-nineteenth-century muskets. Around the perimeter, green-sweatered park rangers roamed, chatting on walkie-talkies and warning tourists not to get too close.

Even at a distance, I could see the obvious pride the men—and they were all men—took in the ritual of loading their big guns, and I imagined they devoted the same relish to dressing in the morning, mending their uniforms, and assuring just the right tilt of their hats. And what hats they were. The gun crew featured a mix of headwear, ranging from a straw stovepipe to a more traditional wide-brimmed straw hat. A couple of men even wore *Cat in the Hat* striped stocking caps with long tails that hung down over their shoulders, giving the impression that the men tinkering around with antique weapons of destruction were on holiday from banging out toys in Santa's workshop. With the white pants, the shirts billowy and slightly ornate in the same vein as a pirate's, the scene was reminiscent of a drunken office party in late October. I stood transfixed, even as the cannon erupted into a violent burst of smoke and light and the concussive boom quite literally changed the rhythm of my heart. I no longer wanted to talk to one of these men, but I had to talk to one. I had to know why: Why spend your free time doing this? Why choose a war that almost no one seems to care about? Why, dear God, all of it? I managed to get the attention of one of the men on the gun crew and called him over for a

chat. It took about fifteen seconds for me to ask the awkward question about the Civil War and why it seemed that war's living historians got so much attention.

"Civil War guys have it easy," said Dave. We were standing along
the roped-off presentation area where members of his carronade
crew had been demonstrating the short, heavy cannon's destructive
power. Dave, dressed in white pants and a gunner's red vest and a tall
straw hat, had been willing to talk to me. When I asked why he chose
to get involved with the War of 1812 instead of the more popular
Civil War, he said it was a matter of circumstance, but that didn't
prevent him from getting his digs in on the guys who "do" the War
between the States. "It's so much easier for them to find gear. By the
time the Civil War came around, things were being mass-produced
and steel had become more prevalent, so things didn't rust like iron
does. A guy who's into the War of 1812 knows he's going to have to
work harder to find authentic equipment."

So he was basically saying that any fool with a credit card could
do the Civil War, but the War of 1812? That took persistence and
study and careful scrutiny. I was beginning to detect a whiff of an
inferiority complex, like a high school tennis player feels with regard
to the star pitcher on the baseball team, but Dave laughed it off.
"It's all in good fun," he said.

"But how exactly did you get into doing this?" I asked. "What
prompted you to spend your weekends dressed in funny clothes and
firing blanks from big guns?"

Dave looked at me with a "well, duh" grin on his face. He looked
like a manufacturing engineer, the kind of guy who wears Dockers
and oxford shirts to work with steel-toed boots. Definitely educated
and certainly clean-cut. The only real clue that he was not actually
a gunner during the War of 1812 was his glasses—wire-rimmed and
relatively small, though not fashionable. More practical. Workaday
glasses. He was perhaps six feet tall and relatively fit, but his odd grin
in response to my question gave me the idea that being part of the

gun crew was a way for him to relive his youth. What boy wouldn't want to shoot cannons and play with gunpowder?

But the real story behind his involvement with reenactment was not unlike the stories of men who get involved with bowling leagues or the Masonic Lodge up the street. Dave and his family were new to town—near Columbus—and he was looking for a way to make friends. Someone at work mentioned that he was a living historian and invited Dave to "do Valley Forge." Like all beginners, he was Farb to the core, but someone instructed him to strip off his clothes and tie two itchy wool blankets around him—"We're supposed to be suffering through a brutal winter, after all"—and he was hooked.

"It turned out to be a great thing to do with the family," he said. "The wives got involved. They helped us with uniforms but also liked dressing up in period clothes themselves. At the time, we had young kids, and they got a kick out of spending the weekend at an encampment."

The Valley Forge weekend was his only encounter with the Revolution, but when Dave returned to Columbus, he quickly fell in with a local cannon crew—circa 1812—and had been playing his part and firing his big gun for slightly more than a decade. He and his family would pack up their gear and head to places like Fort Meigs and Put-in-Bay for the weekend. They lived in tents and ate food prepared without modern convenience. He enjoyed interacting with spectators and sharing the things he learned about history.

"But eventually the kids grew up and the wives dropped out, and now it's just us boys with our toys," he said, and, right then a volley of musket fire erupted on the other side of the demonstration area, as if adding an exclamation point to the sentiment. The crack echoed off the monolith to the east and back west toward town, perhaps a quarter mile away. I wondered if the drunks in the bars could hear it.

"So do you ever wish you could do other wars, other eras?" I asked.

"I'm not as serious about it as I could be. Some guys spend all their money on details like having a period-accurate canteen made. I guess there's some people who switch back and forth, but that can get really expensive and," he paused, "it just doesn't feel right, abandoning one thing to do another one."

"What about the Civil War," I asked. "Would you ever do the Civil War?"

"Are you kidding me?" he asked as if he hoped I might be. "I wouldn't be caught dead doing the Civil War. The Revolution? Maybe. Maybe something like the French and Indian War. But no way. Definitely not the Civil War."

Dave smiled earnestly and excused himself, saying he had to get back to his crew. They were scheduled to do another carronade demonstration in a few minutes, and he wanted to be sure he was there to help prep the cannon. I thanked him and asked if it would be all right if I had a look around their camp.

"Suit yourself," said Dave. "But I'd be careful who you ask about the Civil War." He gave me another grin, and I half-expected him to wink as he walked off.

At just about that time, my old friend Marcus the park ranger came strolling up to me. As part of his summers spent working at the park, he had been trained to fire and demonstrate period weapons. I asked him what he liked best about doing that job and about the comfort of wearing so much wool under the summer sun.

"It's not bad," he said. "It doesn't really get that hot. Plus, there are a lot worse jobs I could be doing over break. I mean, look around. I've spent the last couple summers working on an island and part of my job was to fire cannons. I won't lie. It's really cool."

Marcus and I chatted for a few minutes, during which time he told me that, for an extra thrill at the end of a long day, the gun crews will load extra black powder into the barrel of the cannon. "The boom," he said, "is fantastic."

Boys and their toys.

Strolling among the dozen or so white canvas tents of the encampment, I couldn't help but notice the almost caustic contradiction between these simple shelters and the warren of high-tech, brightly hued tents on the other side of the monument at the Boy Scout camp. It painted such an interesting contradiction—we feel like we've come so far as a society, but our needs really have not changed much; a place to lay our heads and a roof over them, the occasional hot meal and some distraction, and we're pretty much happy. The Boy Scouts were set up at the base of the monument on the eastern side, while the period encampment was wedged between the demonstration area and the road leading into town. It was perhaps two hundred yards from the base of the monument, another two hundred or so from the place where I had rented my golf cart. Set under the shade of the only trees on the national-park property, the camp was tucked away, nestled, and I wasn't entirely sure if I was free to roam among the tents or not.

I followed my nose toward the smell of roasting meat and spent a few minutes talking to a man who was cooking a whole pig over a pit of blazing hot coals (they didn't have microwaves in 1813, yet another limit to my nostalgia) and a few more watching an older couple making wax candles based on instructions they had downloaded from the Internet. I was just about to abandon the camp and head into town for a beer when I noticed a middle-aged woman in full period dress sitting in an uncomfortable-looking chair and reading, of all things, a tawdry romance novel.

"Excuse me," I interrupted. "But I'm not sure your book qualifies as period-accurate."

She looked up at me without a smile and gazed from below her broad-brimmed hat with a look of mild annoyance. "I had to find something to do," she said. "He's the one who dragged me here. I'd rather be at home." She pointed to a man walking toward us with musket in hand. He was big, burly, and clearly middle-aged, and I wondered if he thought I was hitting on his wife. I stepped back,

The reenactors' camp–simple, austere, yet not all that different from the Techni-color din of the Boy Scout camp a couple hundred yards away.

almost unconsciously, and my eyes made their way to his belt and the ten-inch knife hanging in a sheath from it. For a long moment he just stared at me, sweat and dirt staining his face and his big, rough hands on his waist.

He introduced himself as Kenny, and the woman reading the book with Fabio on the cover was his wife, Linda. They were from Lakewood, a suburb on the West Side of Cleveland. Linda and Kenny were new to the War of 1812, though you couldn't tell it from their clothes and accessories. They both looked like they had been reen-acting for quite some time.

"We usually do the Civil War," said Kenny. "But we've been doing that a long time, and I've been promising that we would give this war a try."

"More like threatening," said Linda, in a way that made me think of a woman worried how she would explain such a dalliance into the lower class to her lady friends at the club.

"Either way, it's a break," Kenny said. "Just trying something new before we get back to the mid–nineteenth century."

Kenny was an experienced reenactor. There was not a drop of Farb about him, and he said that, despite her apparent disinterest in the exploits of the Madison administration, Linda has really enjoyed being a part of the community of reenactors. But I got the sense there was something a little subversive about their exploration into 1812. Kenny seemed to be enjoying it, like a star football player might enjoy spending the day playing soccer—he's not going to commit to it, won't take it seriously, but it won't hurt. Linda, on the other hand, seemed less comfortable with the less illustrious period.

I didn't want to push my luck talking to Kenny. Dave had been so adamant about not doing the Civil War and Kenny seemed so flippant about the War of 1812 that I worried about setting off some sort of class war. So I steered the conversation toward what I assumed would be a safe topic with a man like Kenny: weapons.

"Was it difficult learning to use those antique muskets?" I asked.

"Hell no," said Kenny. "It's really fun, except the government keeps sticking their nose in my business."

With that, he launched into a diatribe about the evils of government regulation of firearms that would have made Charlton Heston weep. I tried to mask my feelings about gun control—even antique guns—and nodded steadily to the gospel Kenny was preaching. After ten minutes or so, I found an excuse to leave, thanked him for his time, and wished Linda well when she got back to her era of choice.

Put-in-Bay can be a lonely place when you're a mere observer, and I spent the next two hours wandering idly around town. I read the historic plaques and took pictures of Perry's Victory and International Peace Memorial—my God, how I love typing that—and got an ice-cream cone at the Dairy Queen, which seemed to be staffed by the same Russians who had rented the golf carts. I looked at my watch and discovered that I still had another five hours to kill on the island but knew I would never make it. So I exchanged my ticket for the next ferry back to the mainland and sat on the lawn outside the park's visitors center to listen to the Toledo Symphony play its annual concert for the historic weekend.

My time was up. My circle tour was over. That night I would sleep at a hotel in Sandusky owned by my parents' neighbor, and in the morning I would head back to Avon Lake, collect my kids, and point my battered Jetta southward. I was tired, road weary, and more than a little lonely. The next time I got the idea to make a trip like this, I promised, I would do it with someone. Apart from Marcus and the reenactors, the people at Great Lakes Brewing Company, and a few other strangers I met along the way, I hadn't really spoken with anyone in a week. I had gotten it out of my system, and now, finally, it was time to go home.

I had learned quite a bit, though nothing I probably could not have learned from books or on the Internet. After his victory on Lake Erie, Perry joined Harrison to chase down the British and native soldiers as they fled Amherstburg east. He took part in the land battle at the Thames River, where Tecumseh was killed after an ambush by his warriors backfired. And after the war was over, Perry tried to press for a court-martial of Elliot. The snaky captain of the *Niagara* would escape scot-free, but Perry would continue to question his actions, or lack thereof, on September 10, 1813, leading to a rather public feud. Though the two would never meet on the illegal dueling fields with pistols at dawn, their feud is believed to have been at the heart of the duel that took the life of Stephen Decatur. Decatur had been a friend of Perry's and arguably the only man more famous than Oliver in the country. His heroism in the first Barbary War was legendary and continued through the War of 1812 and the second Barbary campaign. He was serving as the Navy Commissioner in 1820 when he was challenged to a duel by Commodore James Barron, the captain of the ill-fated *Chesapeake* during the *Chesapeake–Leopard* affair.

Decatur accepted the challenge, and on the morning of March 22, 1820, the two met on a field near what is now Colmar Manor, Maryland. Barron chose as his second Jesse Elliot, who had been a lieutenant on the *Chesapeake* during its run-in with the *Leopard* and a vocal critic of Decatur. Perry was unable to serve as his friend's second as he had died the previous August during an expedition to Venezuela's Orinoco River. He had contracted yellow fever from a mosquito and died aboard his ship, the *Nonsuch*. In his place, Commodore William Bainbridge served as Decatur's second. When the time came to fire, Decatur shot Barron in the hip and Barron delivered a lethal shot to Decatur's abdomen. Seeing that his man had mortally wounded America's greatest hero in an illegal duel, Elliot fled in Barron's carriage, leaving his wounded friend and mentor behind. He was chased down by Bainbridge and told to go back and get his friend.

To me this is further evidence of Elliot's character, and I can't help but think Perry was right to call him a coward or, at the very least, a man so hell-bent on achieving his own glory that he would willingly lose a battle for his country to create an opportunity to seek his own fame. Elliot went on to serve a long and controversial career in the navy, which ended with his death in 1845, twenty-six years after Perry's.

The whole thing seemed kind of unfair to me. I mean, here's Elliot—a real scoundrel—and he outlives two bona fide national heroes. He lived the same number of years after Perry's death as Perry had lived before the Battle of Lake Erie. How's that for some sticky math? I looked up the symptoms of yellow fever and found this passage on emedtv.com:

"The signs and symptoms of yellow fever can vary from person to person. In mild cases, some people have no symptoms, while others may have a fever, bloody nose, and a slow heartbeat. In more severe cases, symptoms can appear in three stages. Stage 1 usually includes things like a high fever, vomiting, and neck and back pain.

In Stage 2 the fever can end and some people recover entirely. Those who progress to Stage 3 will see their fever return and may experience jaundice, organ failure, or even death."

What a miserable way to die. I can picture Perry lying on his bunk, sweating profusely, groaning in pain and delirium. Here was a guy who had braved all challenges, stared into the face of certain death, and come out unscathed on the other side. A man of such remarkable bravery and guts that he faced long odds against superior enemies and had the tenacity to win. And it all came down to a mosquito. A freaking little bug. I guess at some point everybody's luck runs out. Maybe I should be glad that, so far, mine had eroded away in little bits—a closed museum, some bad brake pads. Neil Young, the seventy-year-old rocker who proclaimed that it was "better to burn out than it is to rust" might have been speaking about Perry. Because guys like him don't live like guys like me. They live harder, burn brighter, and, sadly, die sooner. In a way, I'm glad Perry's legacy is what it is, that he went before he got old or infirm, that he never lived to feel his mind go slack and his body fall apart. That's the cost of living in and for glory. Things end. For him, they just ended sooner than they did for other people. And that makes him perfect. Like a bug trapped in amber a million years ago, Perry lives forever, locked in the midday sun of September 10, 1813.

⁓22⁓

The Unfortunate

It's 3:15 A.M., October 21, 2009, six weeks after the conclusion of my grand journey, and I am watching my grandmother, my only living grandparent, die. It's close range, three feet between me and the bed where she's lying. I know that in the next twelve hours, she'll be gone—a hemorrhage in her brain will lead to severe swelling, impairing her brain, leading her to breathe her last breath. She will die. My parents were also sitting in the room—my dad on a foldout chair trying to sleep, my mom knitting on the other side of the bed and talking to the nurse about pulse-oxygen levels and the trends on the monitor hung over the bed. My uncle Roger and his wife Jean, and my Uncle Paul and his younger son, Mike, would be back in the morning. But dawn felt a long time away, death ticking closer by the minute, each second an eternity.

And in the morning, when it all happens and I am a grand-orphan for all time, I'll be on my way. But even now, in this time of need and family tragedy, I can't help but think about Oliver Hazard Perry, because the hospital I am sitting in is in Troy, Michigan. Four hours straight north from my home in southwest Ohio, and in the frantic rush to make it here—within the twelve to twenty-four hours the doctors said she had left—I passed a place that had eluded my course in my tour of Lake Erie: Monroe, Michigan.

In doing my online research leading up to writing this book, I had discovered that Monroe played a very important role in the Lake Erie campaign of the War of 1812, but sitting in this room, in the half-light from the intensive-care-unit nurses' station, I couldn't for the life of me remember what it was. I noticed a brown-and-white state-park sign announcing the exit for the Battle of the River Raisin battlefield on the way up to the hospital and remembered having read something about it in A. J. Langguth's *Union 1812*, but most of it was pretty foggy in my sleep-deprived mind.

There were two battles, actually. The first took place on January 18, 1813, and it was an American victory in which a group of volunteers from Kentucky drove back the British from their position at what was then Frenchtown, Michigan. This was payback. The Americans were pissed-off about how easily the English had managed to take Michigan from the tip of its index finger to Detroit, sixty or so miles from its wrist. Three days later the English, buoyed by the cold and sled-mounted three-inch artillery, laid waste to the American soldiers, cutting a wide swath through the Kentucky encampment. Or at least that's what the signs said along the quarter-mile blacktop path that marks the boundary of the River Raisin battlefield property.

I found myself standing along this path weary and stunned the day after my grandmother went into the ICU. My mom and I had pulled an all-nighter by her bedside, listening to her breathe, watching her make the slow journey from life to death. She had lived a good life. A life filled with grace and a sort of dignity that I have always admired, and I told her all this, whispered it in her ear, even though the doctors had said she more than likely couldn't hear me. She had been slipping away throughout the night. And though her vital signs were strong, it seemed to me that her mind and her soul had taken a head start.

Knowing that a funeral was imminent and understanding a need to get ahead on some work to be able to attend, my dad had decided not to wait for her final breath and the final beat of her heart. He was tired. Mom was tired. We were all tired. And it was time to go home. But what was supposed to have gone quickly was taking longer than the doctors had expected. We were told to rush to be by her side, but she refused to let go. Her body had known nothing but living for nine decades, and she apparently wasn't in that big of a hurry to stop. So I left with my parents, followed them through the hollowed-out industrial shell of Detroit and through the smoky air of the South Side until the brown sign once again caught my eye.

The day was getting late, the fall air crisp, and the blood-orange sun quickly falling behind the horizon, but I was this close. And with work and family commitments back home, I knew this might be the last chance I had to see the River Raisin site for a while.

Pulling off the highway, I followed the signs directing me toward the battlefield and visitors center. I had an idea, based on the prominent logo that appeared on all the signs, that the battlefield was more than just a curious attraction along the highway in southeast Michigan. This was a major source of identity for the small town of Monroe. Like so many of the towns I have visited in my life, Monroe is in part defined by the battles that took place there, or at least near there. The visitors center was in a small house designed in the Arts and Crafts style. It was closed, as I had feared, but a look inside revealed display cases and pamphlets designed in Microsoft Word and run off from a printer that was probably purchased with a donation from someone nearby or someone who had grown up there and wanted to give back to their hometown, if for no greater reason than the sense of place and nostalgia only your hometown can stir up. I know this feeling. It's the same one that inspires me to go to high school football games when I visit my parents. I just want to smell the fall in my hometown—the leaves, the crisp wind blowing in from the lake, the hot dogs warming in salty water. It is a smell that sometimes stirs me from sleep and takes my mind off the stresses of daily life four hours to the south and west, far from those Friday-night lights.

Walking around the small battlefield park, no bigger than most elementary school playgrounds, I got the sense that this history, these battles, are ingrained in the people who grow up in places like Monroe and Perry, Ohio, and Sandusky, and Vermilion. It's like the words to the alma mater that suddenly come to you one day on your way home from work and take your mind to a far-off place. The battlefield offers little to a visitor, and with the visitors center closed for the evening there was no one to answer questions, no source for further information.

I walked around for a few minutes and then returned to my car, where my weatherbeaten copies of *Union 1812* and Gerard Altoff's volumes about the Lake Erie campaign were stashed in my backpack. A quick search of the indexes revealed a couple of mentions of the battle, and I read how valiantly the Kentucky warriors fought and how their efforts probably delayed a British march into Ohio, allowing William Henry Harrison time to establish Fort Meigs and for Oliver Hazard Perry to construct his fleet at Erie—both events that would later lead to the Battle of Lake Erie. I read how those who fought and died near Frenchtown were the brave ones who stood up to a British force that had used the threat of native warriors as a weapon powerful enough to entice Americans to drop their arms and surrender their strongholds from the top of Michigan to its commercial center, Detroit. Those men who made a stand at the River Raisin were reactionaries; they leapt at the opportunity to defend their country and risked death or, worse at that time, the possibility of being torn to pieces and roasted for a sacrificial meal by Indians.

While the possibility that natives would show no mercy, no gentlemanly conduct, offer no quarter to soldiers, women, and children may have been overblown, the threat was sufficient deterrent for many. The British had won the war for native hearts and minds, leading Tecumseh to believe that siding with the redcoats would mean protection of freedom and people, property, and his way of life from the tyrannical imposition of American will. In short, the British had found the weakness of both their enemy and their ally and exploited them to maximum effect. Was it disingenuous? Was it cruel and unfair? Maybe, but it was also very smart. You can't hold intelligence against them; the British knew how to make the most of what they had and more.

The battle cry "Remember the Raisin" became ubiquitous throughout the Lower Great Lakes as volunteers and regulars, soldiers and sailors, began their uprising. In the long run, the battles of the River Raisin were relatively inconsequential. The loss of life was not great, and the loss of territory would eventually prove meaningless. But the idea that there were some Americans willing to make a stand, to sacrifice themselves not only for the protection of their homes but also their homeland, was significant. And it remains significant to this day to the people in and around Monroe.

The whole thing got me thinking about how we, as Americans, relate to the spaces we occupy and the history those spaces encapsulate. I know it would be impossible for the nation to preserve everything, but it seems to me that we ought to do a better job of maintaining and taking advantage of the spaces we do have. Sure, there are times when a place may overplay its hand when it comes to historical significance—simply being the home to the World's Largest Truck Stop (I'm looking at you, Iowa) does not mean you are a party to something monumental or significant. It means you are home to something kitschy and market driven. Does it really matter how large some thing is? Or how old? Isn't the point of laying claim to history an act of capitulation and embracing rather than a callous ploy for market share?

Over the years I have seen a lot of historic places in America. Places like Gettysburg, Pennsylvania, and Washington, D.C. Some are well tended and offer a world of wisdom and truth to those who will listen, and some are places so commercialized that they trample the memory of the things they exploit. Then there are places like Winchester, Virginia, where I lived right out of college, places where history is part of the zeitgeist, where remembering is important because it is the right thing to do. Monroe reminded me a lot of Winchester. The battlefield grounds, the park encompassing it, and the visitors center may have been small, but they were well maintained. And sure, there may have been a few hucksters who thought they could trade on the reputation of the battle, but I imagined for the most part that the past was a valued commodity. I could imagine retirees spending their Saturdays drinking coffee and tending the counter in the visitors center; groups of schoolkids going on a field trip to learn about something they couldn't possibly understand; and people like me, who reached a point in their lives when they decided it was time to pay attention and homage to the places around them.

I'm no sacred-soil protectionist, but I believe in the power of the past to keep us grounded. And caring for the past is a way of harnessing our nostalgia. I was feeling plenty of that while strolling around the blacktop path for the third time that day. I was feeling the power of memory as reminiscences of my grandmother came back to me in slow, undulating waves—her noodle soup, the way she managed to keep nine kids and forty-four grand- and great-grandchildren in line without raising her voice, the look on her face when she took me to the place where her relatives were buried, and how sharing that hilltop cemetery in rural Iowa with me seemed to mean the world to her. I wondered if the families—close or generations removed—of those Kentucky riflemen had ever walked these grounds and if the people of Monroe considered their memories to be family as well.

With the sky getting dark and my eyes growing heavy, with still another three hours to drive until I got home, I decided to leave the site of the Battle of the River Raisin, but before I went I walked over to the split-rail fence marking the edge of the riflemen's camp and repeated the battle cry that Perry and others carried with them. "Remember the Raisin," I said. Remember the war, remember the battles, and all those who have died.

Remember my grandmother, Martha Sophia Heimbuch. She died shortly before I got home.

⤳23⤶

The Final Destination

Maybe it was guilt, maybe it was a sense of missed opportunity, but I somehow managed to find myself in the car on the Wednesday after Christmas driving to Erie, Pennsylvania, with my dad and my nephew Jacob. It had nagged at me for more than three months that I had missed my opportunity to visit the *Niagara* and the Erie Maritime Museum during my circle tour. It wasn't that I regretted the decision I had made, but I had found reasons not to go, excuses for not making the trip despite having opportunities. Until, in the fuzzy days of post-Christmas hangover, I decided that enough was enough.

Jacob is the oldest of the grandkids and therefore the most likely to behave himself in a museum. He slept in the backseat on the two-hour drive to Erie while Dad and I talked history in the front, our periods of choice neatly dividing the journey. I was driving Dad's big GMC Yukon, and he was sitting in the passenger seat, Jacob behind him. He talked about Eisenhower as the last American president who put the good of the country above personal or political goals. As he spoke he stared straight ahead, not looking at me, not wanting me to look at him and divert my eyes from the road. On our last fishing trip to Canada seven and a half years before, we had been sitting in these same positions driving south through Minnesota when a truck on the opposite side of the road lost a tire, hub and all. He had barely gotten a word out when I noticed sparks coming from the opposite direction and in one fluid motion braked and changed lanes. The tire, which had been bouncing across the median in our direction, missed the front of our car by inches. Had I not hit the brakes or switched lanes, it would have hit us square, causing untold damage. I thought about that as we drove and how earlier in that trip I had managed to wrap around a tree a four-wheeler owned by the outfitter who was putting us up, flip over the handlebars, and knock myself unconscious. When I woke and my cousin helped me back to camp, Dad lit into me, the only time in my life I have ever seen him truly mad. He told me how reckless and thoughtless my behavior was, how I had "fucked" the outfitter because now he was down a vehicle. I don't remember him asking if I was okay, but I remember him swearing at me in the heat of the moment and hot tears forming in my eyes. Aunt Linette comforted me and told me Dad was so upset because he was worried about me, because I had scared him. When I dodged the tire on the way back home, he told me thanks and complimented my driving, a subtle atonement for his earlier behavior.

I think Dad likes Ike because he acted based on right and wrong, not popularity. He said as much as he spoke about the reluctant general, the reluctant president. He said he liked the way Eisenhower thought of America as being bigger than himself. In a way, that was the most romantic thing I had ever heard Dad say. Then, abruptly and almost exactly halfway to Erie, he asked me to tell him the story of Oliver Hazard Perry. It felt strange, telling my dad about history. That's not how our relationship had ever been. Apart from the rare times in college when I could tell him about something specific I had learned, he had always been the teacher, regurgitating the facts in a seamless, if slightly mechanical timeline. So when he asked me to tell him about the brig *Niagara*, I started with Perry's father, the sailor during the Revolution, then slowly, methodically, made my way to Oliver's years in the navy, ending with his early death from yellow fever. I was amazed at how much I had retained. Certainly more than the sum total I remembered from four and a half years of college history classes. My Perry lecture seemed to spring forth from some vault deep in the recesses of my brain. I finished just as we were pulling up to the Erie Maritime Museum and Dad gave a look, like "Well, let's go find out if you're right," before waking Jacob and the three of us trekked inside.

≈,≈

Erie, like much of northeastern Ohio, lies in the snow belt, an area famous for midwinter dumpings of snow blown down from Canada, and it had been snowing for a couple of days before our arrival. The parking lot was packed with cars and treacherous with ice and slush. I couldn't believe that so many people—hundreds, if my estimations were correct—were spending their winter holidays visiting the only other true Perry destination on Lake Erie. And I was surprised at the enormousness of the building. Easily a hundred yards long and three stories tall, the brick edifice looked old, but it had obviously been updated recently, giving it that nice ancient-meets-modern feel that I really like.

It didn't take long once inside to see evidence of the importance Erie placed on Oliver Hazard Perry, nor did it take long to understand what drew so many people out on a snowy morning. Inside the lobby, paintings and displays lionized the Age of Fighting Sail as men and women walked past from a long hallway carrying pieces of paper attached to sticks with numbers on them. Dad asked a passerby what all the hubbub was about and was told that there was an auction going on for homes that had been foreclosed on due to failure to pay taxes. The stubborn economy of the Oughts had hit hard in Erie as manufacturing slowed down and the city's largest employer—General Electric Transportation—had laid off huge numbers of employees because locomotive sales were down. It was nice

The Niagara, *fully restored in the early twentieth century and sailing the Great Lakes once again.*

to know that, should I have desired, I could have picked up some property on the cheap, but the reason gave my stomach a twist. We also discovered that, in addition to the Erie Maritime Museum, the building was home to the Erie Public Library and a sort of public conference center where the auction was being held. We visited the restroom, where I saw a man wearing a gray T-shirt with a photo of Geronimo and a few other warriors screen-printed on it. Above and below the photo read, HOMELAND SECURITY: FIGHTING TERRORISM SINCE 1492. A nice little jab at the white man that I found funnier than I probably should have.

We entered the Maritime Museum through, of course, the gift shop, which seemed to do a healthy business in T-shirts and posters, though the book supply appeared a bit picked-over. Probably the holiday rush, I hoped. Dad bought tickets from the woman behind the counter—add that to my tab—who seemed enthusiastic about having us, particularly when Dad did something I had never heard him do before. He bragged about my being an author working on a book about Oliver Hazard Perry. I wondered if years of my stories about getting free admission to things thanks to my press card had made him think he could benefit from the powers of the pen or if he was just genuinely proud.

"You guys are in luck today," the woman said. "Two of our best tour guides are in, and they really bring the museum to life."

Inside, the museum was not what I had expected. Maybe I had been tainted by my visits to other museums on this journey, but I had thought it would be plain—drop ceiling, a few paintings on the wall. So I was surprised when I saw a massive General Electric steam generator, perfectly restored and on display. We read the signs and found out the building was the former electrical power-generating plant for the city of Erie. When the city moved to a larger power grid, the building was abandoned and eventually donated for use as a museum and library. A combination of public and private dollars had been used to refurbish the site, and the museum still bore signs of its industrial past, including a fifty-ton overhead crane that loomed over us like a vulture waiting for our final breath. We only had a minute to stare up in wonder before we were greeted by a spry, diminutive woman in her late sixties or early seventies who introduced herself as Mary or Helen or something cute and grandmotherish. She began explaining the presence of the generator and the crane when an older gentleman with soft features and outsize ears rounded a corner and walked toward us.

"This is Jack, he's the best tour guide we have," said the matronly woman. "He's also my husband. He'll be taking you through the museum because my shift has ended."

With that, she turned and left almost as fast as she had come, and Jack Gold began his monologue about the generator afresh. I liked Jack right away, and not only because I have a soft spot for men with that name—my son and the editor of this book are both named Jack—but because of his gentle way of giving information without forcing it upon you. I remember visiting other museums where the docents and tour guides seem annoyed by your mere presence, as if visitors are the bane of their existence (and you know who you are, unfriendly tour guides). But Jack spoke quietly, evenly, as he led us through a display explaining the timeline of events that led up to the War of 1812, and he seemed a little nervous when Dad mentioned—again—that I was working on a book related to the primary subject of this very museum.

"Well I'm sure you know most of this," said Jack, "but just in case everyone else doesn't . . ." He continued his tour, showing us maps of the Old Northwest and how various Great Lakes conflicts in 1812 and 1813 related to one another geographically. When the time came for him to sit us down for a movie about the Battle of Lake Erie, I took Jack aside to ask him a few questions that had remained unanswered for me over months of study and travel. The first and, as it would turn out last, had to do with Perry's envelope.

As mentioned earlier, in the immediate aftermath of the battle, Perry jotted a message to General William Henry Harrison on the back of an envelope containing the most famous quote attributed to the commodore: "We have met the enemy and they are ours." Everywhere I had been thus far, these nine words had been prominent. They were painted on a wall in the basement of the museum in Vermilion; they were mentioned in signage at Fort Meigs and in the biography attached to Perry's papers at the University of Michigan; they were just about everywhere I looked at Put-in-Bay. So I asked Jack, "Whatever happened to the envelope?"

He stared over my shoulder with the kind of far-off expression made famous by Charlton Heston and said, "You know, I've often wondered the same thing. So a few years ago, I researched it, and I couldn't find a thing. No one seems to know what would have happened to it, but I've got a theory."

My ears perked up a bit as I nodded for Jack to go on.

"I think Harrison probably read it, crumpled it up, and threw it on the ground," Jack said, so plainly and matter-of-factly that the logic of his assertion was convincing. "It wasn't an official battle report—that he would have kept. It was just a scrap of paper, and the message was short, so he probably read it and threw it away. More than likely it had blood on it and water from the passage to Sandusky where Harrison was waiting. He probably didn't think much of it at all."

Jack was right. I knew that right away, but I couldn't help feeling a little cheated. For me, that envelope was as important as the Declaration of Independence or the Magna Carta. I felt myself getting angry at Harrison for not recognizing that importance. But the more I thought about it, the more I realized I probably would have done the same thing. Perry's battle report was the real information. The envelope was just an early-nineteenth-century text message or Tweet. The fact that those nine words, so perfectly aligned, so imbued with stoicism and heroism and all kinds of other -isms, carried through time to reach my ears and touch my heart, could not have been known by Harrison. Nor could he have been expected to care. I wondered for a moment how many other thoughts of such perfection, jotted down at moments of transformative importance, had been lost. I promised myself I would never delete another e-mail or text, just in case 195 years from now some kid wants to track down something my wife or my friend Kool-Aid sends me. It is better, for the sake of history, to be safe than sorry.

After the movie ended, Jack led us to what was easily the most horrifying and intriguing display in the place. Standing at eye level along a ramp was a reconstructed side of a War of 1812–era brig. As we approached, we were looking at the outside of the "ship" section, its gun ports open, the business ends of several cannons sticking out, and dotting the wood were what appeared to be several severe, though nonlethal, gashes. Jack explained that several years before, the Commonwealth of Pennsylvania—which owns the brig *Niagara*—commissioned a research study into the effects of various types of cannon fire on wood-hulled, square-rigged sailing ships. The idea was to build a replica of a ship and shoot at it to see what happened. This display that Jack walked us through had been that replica.

From the outside, it didn't look bad. A couple small holes, a couple maybe the size of a grapefruit, and a few that looked like the wood had splintered but had not been penetrated. Jack told us how looks from the outside could be deceiving. He played a video showing high-speed films of the cannon-fire test. Members of a military artillery squad fired period-accurate cannon from around a hundred yards into the side, and the video proved that the outside of the ship appeared relatively unscathed while the impact aboard the ship sent huge splinters—more than a foot long in some cases—exploding onto the deck. Styrofoam cutouts representing crew members were decimated without being touched by the iron balls, torn almost completely in half by the shards of wood hurled at them by the impact. Jack walked us to the other side of the replica and showed where the tiny entrance holes on the hull produced massive, gaping exit holes. It was impossible to fathom the destruction on board a fighting ship at the time. And these holes were made by just a few shots over the span of a half hour under controlled circumstances.

"Perry's flagship, the U.S. brig Lawrence, was shelled for a little more than three hours before he struck his colors and rowed to the Niagara," Jack said. "He suffered more than 80 percent casualties among his crew of more than a hundred men, and yet he remained unscathed." Someone from the small group asked if such high casualty rates were common among sailing ships at the time. "Most captains would have surrendered at between 30 and 40 percent losses," said Jack. "But not Perry."

As he said that, I felt a surprising nudge of pride, as if Perry were a close friend whose bravery was being praised to this group of strangers. I'd spent the past eighteen months with the guy after all. We were close.

Just then, I turned to a display case near the exhibit. In it was a small, ornately decorated and curved sword. The handle was intricate and, to my eyes, tiny, matching the scale of the entire weapon. Jack explained that, as near as anyone at the museum or elsewhere could tell, it had belonged to Perry and was the sword he received upon his commission as an officer.

"Where did it come from?" I asked.

"A family donated it to the museum," he said. "It had been in the family a long, long time."

"And you're not sure if it was Perry's?"

"We certainly think it was, but we can't prove it," he said. Like the envelope, it seemed that so many things in history could not be proved. I stared dumbfounded at the sword for a few minutes. It struck me that I was so overcome. After all, a few months earlier I had held letters written by the man, and yet being in such close proximity to what some believed was his sword felt so much more personal. Maybe it was that Oliver Hazard Perry had gained fame for things he had done while carrying that sword and not for his exploits with a pen, or maybe it was just that I could feel my journey coming to a close. But I was transfixed. I stared and stared until I heard Jack begin talking to the group behind me, breaking me from my reverie, but I knew that, of all the moments I had experienced in my chase, seeing that sword would be among the most powerful.

"This is the only cannon existing today that was known to have been used during the Battle of Lake Erie," Jack said. The long gun was sitting in the middle of a large open area beneath a replica of topsails from a brig. It had obviously been painted relatively recently and had obviously been through some hard times in the years since it saw battle. Giant pockmarks, like acne scars, littered the barrel and could not be concealed completely, no matter how many layers of paint were added. Jack explained that the gun was used on the HMS *Queen Charlotte*, one of the ships that riddled Perry's brig *Lawrence* with iron terror. For decades, perhaps more than a century after the war, it had been used as decoration outside a firehouse near Cleveland, where the elements, a lack of care, and time took a toll. But craftsmen at the Erie Maritime Museum had nursed it back to health and even hand-built a carriage for it to rest on. Apart from the brig *Niagara*, this was the museum's biggest showpiece. It was one thing to have maps and movies, quite another thing to have a really big gun. I thought of Marcus and the reenactors at Put-in-Bay—boys with their toys.

Jack made his apologies that his shift had ended and he needed to follow his wife home. He introduced Dad, Jacob, and I to his replacement, Tom. We shook Jack's hand and thanked him. He made me promise to send him a copy of the book—or maybe I offered—and I scribbled his address in the notebook I was carrying in my pocket. The other two members of our tour group also bid their farewells, leaving the three of us and Tom for the final, climactic experience of my grand adventure—a tour of Perry's victory ship.

The masts of the winterized Niagara. *When sailing, the ship includes forty additional feet of mast affixed to the top. The deck of the ship is covered in a customized canvas tarp to prevent damage from the harsh winter weather.*

My first impression of the brig *Niagara* was that it was small. It wasn't much bigger than the ferry that had taken me to and from Put-in-Bay, but with disproportionately tall masts that stretched more than a hundred feet into the stinging winter sky. During the warmer months, the brig—Tom explained that the vessel is a brig because of its two-masted design; ships, on the other hand, have three—trolls Lake Erie and other nearby lakes with summer crews and day sailors who part with seventy bucks to experience the way navigation and war were conducted for centuries before the internal combustion engine. But during the winter months, it is docked in the bay at Erie above underwater fountains that prevent the ice from wreaking havoc on its wood construction. Tom led us down some stairs and out onto the snow-covered dock, where the magnitude—or lack thereof—of the brig became even more clear. For one, it rides low to the water, no more than ten or eleven feet separating the gunwale from the surface, and two, it's narrower than you might expect a warship to be—maybe twenty-five feet across. The open deck—covered by a custom-made tarp that allows visitors to board and stand comfortably shaded from the elements—is like a bathtub. Maybe I had seen too many pirate movies, but I imagined a ship like this to be bigger, wider, and sturdier. It didn't even have a raised aft deck and grand old wheel. The brig was steered by a tiller—like an aluminum fishing boat—and its commander didn't issue orders from two stories above his crew like Columbus on a caravel, but from four steps up on a wooden plank. What a rip. Here, all this time, I had imagined grandeur and heft, and the reality was that Perry commanded a boat like an oversize canoe.

Tom took his time explaining the mechanics of the deck—how the anchor was raised, how oars were stored and could be employed by the crew to get over shallow banks, where the ventilation from the cook fire below came out and even (and maybe this was for Jacob's benefit) how crew members went to the bathroom. I listened, but given that we were the only people on board, I had myself a little amble.

Walking around the deck, I tried to picture everything I knew about the battle. For starters, the brig *Niagara* was commanded by Jesse Elliot, who was technically Perry's superior but was not given command of the Lake Erie campaign despite successes on Lake Ontario. As mentioned earlier, on September 10, 1813, Elliot had failed to engage the *Niagara* in the battle, the only ship in the Lake Erie squadron not to fight in the first disastrous hours of the conflict. He blamed the wind. Perry blamed his cowardice. But the *Niagara*, while not having been in the first stage of the fight, was certainly the ship that had won the battle. It was to the *Niagara* that Perry rowed when his crew on the *Lawrence* had been decimated. It was on that deck that he had climbed aboard and taken control from Elliot before ending the battle in a decisive fashion. It was on this ship that Perry, literally, turned the tide of the war.

I did my best to imagine that scene—Perry climbing over the side with his famous "Don't Give Up the Ship" banner in hand. I wondered if he punched Elliot or yelled, or if he just relieved him of his command and took his place on the slightly elevated board in the rear of the boat. I tried to hear the sounds of cannon, like Satan's Jiffy Pop, echoing for miles in every direction, and the fear and carnage made so real to every sailor aboard. I tried to imagine the smell of burned powder and the sound of victory cheers when the British struck their colors. I tried, but for some reason it wasn't vivid in my mind. It wasn't as clear as it had been that day on top of Perry's Victory and International Peace Memorial. Slightly disheartened, I rejoined Dad and Tom and Jacob, who was snapping pictures and shooting video with a digital camera he had gotten for Christmas.

But before we continued the tour below decks, I once again snuck off and, finding a break in the canvas that covered the entirety of the deck, pulled a rock from my pocket that I had been carrying with me since the day at the winery in Canada. I waited until no one was looking and threw it into the water near one of the gun holes. It was my contribution to victory, my shot fired from the deck of the brig *Niagara*, my reenactment. It might have been totally Farb, but it was also somehow gratifying. I smiled and rejoined my shipmates for the tour below.

Not to be self-critical, but my fat ass was not born to be a sailor, especially back in Perry's day. On the upper deck I had been fine,

Jacob and I have a go at pretending to be Perry and one of his men during the row from the Lawrence *to the* Niagara. *Even on a wooden cutout, the good commodore is blessed with fantastic hair.*

but the deck below was not intended for use by a man of my girth or height. For starters, the ceiling was claustrophobically low. Maybe five feet at its peak and without windows or light of any kinds. Tom led us to a couple of chairs and a bench set up for the tours and invited us to sit down for a chat.

"I think you gentlemen will be much more comfortable now," he said. He was bundled in a parka, and his salt-and-pepper hair was slick and combed. We asked him a few questions about life aboard the ship, and he explained that the crew would sleep in hammocks strung from the Hobbit-sized ceiling. The hammocks would be lined up in such a way that the sleepers would be nearly shoulder-to-shoulder, and when the boat swayed, so would they in perfect unison. By and large, life on the brig was lived above deck, except for those sleeping, the cook, and specialized crew members like gunners, who would sit below decks oiling their cannonballs every day to prevent rust. I thought perhaps they were being anal or prideful, but Tom explained that rust on a cannonball increased its circumference, thereby making it impossible to fit in the barrel of the gun. Dad raised his eyebrows in a "huh, I wouldn't have thought of that" expression, but I got an idea of the tedious existence of sailors in Perry's day.

Every day was the same duty, performed the same way in the same place. Every day was the same rations of food, the same smelly hammock, and the same tiny ship dotting the immensity of the ocean or a lake like Erie. With these guys being far from home, living on subsistence food, and performing the same tasks over and over, it was no wonder they were itching for a fight. At least Perry's men had the luxury of land. They got off at Put-in-Bay. They weren't on the lake all that long. Ocean-bound sailors and traders could be on board for months at a time in cramped, not-an-inch-to-waste quarters around a hundred or two other men who, like you, hadn't bathed in quite some time. I could feel my throat begin to close with anxiety. The deck we were on was dark, even under the pale orange glow of sodium bulbs. And there were only four of us. I tuned out of the conversation between Dad and Tom and thought about jumping ship. How could people live like this? What could possibly compel someone to choose life aboard a wooden sardine can that was freezing cold even in port? Perry must have really wanted all that glory if he was willing to put up with this.

That, or he was the size of Mini-Me.

We made our way aft—that's toward the rear for all you landlubbers—to the officers' quarters. The captain lived in a small room maybe six feet square at the rear of the ship. He had a desk, a bunk, some storage space, and enough room for one other chair that had to be dragged in from the officers' dining room. The other officer's quarters were about the size of the sliding-door closets in Rebecca's and my first apartment. And they opened the same way. Only slightly wider than the bed, they were open to the officer's dining room via latched wooden slats that made up the top half of the inside wall. Tom asked us not to go inside these quarters because they were being lived in by crewmen and itinerant craftsmen who worked on the ship.

On board the Niagara. *This is the brig's top deck, covered by a custom canvas tarp. I was stunned by how small it is and dreaded the thought of being aboard under fire.*

"Some of these guys who crew during the summer are sort of free spirits," he said. "They volunteer to live on the ship and provide a measure of security in return for free room and board."

Must be some life, I thought, if freezing your ass off on a dank, dark, crowded ship is a better alternative to finding a job for the winter. The officer's dining room was really just a widening of the hallway connecting the main part of the lower deck to the officer's quarters. Tom pointed out a small cabinet and said that it had once been home to the ship's dog that, like Perry, had survived the battle unscathed, despite having nearly been struck by a cannonball.

"During the battle the ship's surgeon used the officer's dining table as an operating room," Tom said. "It had the most space and the most light." Above the small table—roughly the size of an interior door—was a vaulted ceiling with short, wide windows that let light into the room. In the case of the *Lawrence,* the surgeon would have seen almost a hundred patients in this tiny space. Blood would have coated the floor like crimson gravy as cannon shot penetrated the walls and crossed right over (or through) the operating table.

"I can't imagine trying to work like that," I said.

"Me neither," said Tom. "I'm a retired doctor, so is Jack, and I can't even begin to think how they did it."

"What kind of doctor?" I asked.

"Pediatrician."

"From around here?"

"Not far, upstate New York."

"So how did you come to be a tour guide on the *Niagara?*" asked Dad.

"By accident, really," said Tom. "A friend of mine used to volunteer at the Presque Isle nature reserve, and when I retired he told me to come check it out. I did, but they didn't have any positions. One of the volunteer coordinators told me about the *Niagara,* so I came over here and signed up. Every Wednesday for almost fifteen years, I've been working here. Jack too."

I asked if he had always had an interest in naval history, and he said, no, he was an Air Force man himself. But growing up around the lake, he had heard of the Battle of Lake Erie and was glad that he had a chance to learn as much as he had. "I've come to think it's important to know about the history of where you came from," he said as we made our way topside. Before we climbed the stairs, he pointed to the wooden slats on one of the officer's quarters and said they were original to the brig *Niagara*. Those and a small piece of the keel were all that was left of the ship that sailed during the battle. The rest had been scuttled to the bottom of the lake, raised, and repaired, then allowed to fall into disrepair, then repaired and on and on for almost a hundred years before it was rebuilt for good in the 1990s.

"Why keep rebuilding it?" I asked, perhaps a touch cynically, but before Tom could answer I knew the reason. Because remembering is important. Remembering is how we build from yesterday today for a better tomorrow. Tom didn't have a chance to answer because Jacob had spotted a small, diamond-shaped prism hanging from the ceiling in one of the officer's quarters.

"What's that?" he asked like the elementary school student he was.

"It's sort of like a lightbulb," Tom said. "It lets light in so you can see in the dark." The top of the prism is flush with the upper deck and about the diameter of a baseball.

"How bright does it get?" I ask.

"About fifteen watts," said Tom. "That was bright enough to see and brighter than anywhere else on this deck." This place was darker than Sylvia Plath at midnight. It had to have been if the dimmest bulb on the shelf at Walmart would have been considered a luxury. Nope, the pirate life was definitely not for me.

We made our way topside and out into the crisp winter air. We thanked Tom and decided, after a few more minutes in the museum and a few more after that in the gift shop, that we'd better be heading home.

Once again, Jacob slept in the backseat, and Dad and I talked history as I drove. We both agreed that the excursion was worth the trip—the best day of the holiday season—and made promises to come back in the summer to sail on the *Niagara* for a day.

We were nearly home, tired, and ready to stretch out on the couch when Dad thanked me for taking him along.

"Thank you for coming," I said, and I meant it. I issued an appreciative thanks to Jacob for being such a good boy—and my, but he was. Twenty-some years before, Dad had taken me to the top of Perry's Victory and International Peace Memorial, and I had nearly thrown up over the side. Now, so many years—worlds, really—later, I had taken him to a place related to the same history. I don't know if he had known about Perry that day when I was young. He might simply have heard about the islands. He might have had a vague idea of who Perry was and wanted to learn a little more. Then again, he might just have been spending an afternoon with his family, helping them adapt to a new place. I couldn't be sure. But our trip to Erie, this whole escapade, felt like a circle coming around to completion. I was happy that he had been there, grateful that after everything, after years of distance and more mistakes than I could count, he was interested enough in me to be interested in what I was doing. Dad was never gifted with language or storytelling. He missed out on the day when God gave man the ability to express his emotions. Instead, Dad gives effort and time. He gave me that day at the monument, and it was the best thing he knew how to give, the best gift I could ever hope to receive.

"You told a pretty accurate story," he said, snapping me back to the present, to the interior of his SUV. "A good story." Heaven may as well have parted at that moment. I may as well have been standing on the precipice of Mount Everest. All day long I had been rattling off facts, all day long trying too hard to prove how much I had learned, to be the writer, to be the journalist, to show my dad that what I was doing was for real. And here, after exhausting my stocks of story and fact, after running out of things to say, he said some simple words, and I was validated. I had made it. I had grown up. I had become my father's son.

We went inside and settled in. I hugged Jack and Dylan and Rebecca, and we all ate dinner at my parents' house. Rebecca and I had planned on driving back to Cincinnati that night, but it had gotten late and I'd already had a long day. I was too tired to drive the 217 miles to our home. Instead, I asked her if we should stay. Get up in the morning and head back home. She was still on holiday break from school. I had no reason to rush. Please, just let me get some sleep. That night we put the kids to bed and settled onto the couch to watch a movie. Dad was lying down in his blue leather recliner, drifting in and out of consciousness. Rebecca and I were cuddled on the sofa about to do the same, when Mom came downstairs and said she thought Jack was throwing up. He had been asleep on an air mattress in my parents' bedroom, and she had heard him gagging and stumbled downstairs half-asleep to get us.

"I've got it," I said, and went upstairs to find my beautiful son covered in vomit, crying helplessly, exhausted and scared. Rebecca followed me upstairs and together we cleaned up Jack and the air mattress. He wasn't feeling well, so we decided to make a bed for him in the bathtub, and I told my wife to get some sleep. I spent the night on the floor next to him, holding his hand, helping him to the toilet when he got sick, wiping his face with a wet washcloth. I didn't sleep a wink.

In the morning, when Jack was feeling better and the house came alive, Dad came into the bathroom to find me sitting next to the tub. He asked about Jack and patted me on the shoulder. "Good job, Poppa," he said. "I'm proud of you."

⚞24⚟
The Last

That was pretty much it—a couple thousand miles, a few hundred pages, and a whole lot of typing. I learned some history, saw places I wanted to see, and managed to step out of my workaday life long enough to realize how good I really have it.

I suppose this is where I say what I learned, where soft music plays and a reflective, Doogie Howser–style voice-over pours out my insights. But I'm not Doogie Howser. There is no theme music, unless you count Miles Davis's *Kind of Blue*, which is playing on my iPod. I'm sitting on my couch in the silence of a winter storm. Rebecca and the boys are in Cleveland, and I have the place to myself. It feels good being home.

This is the part in *On the Road* when Kerouac sits on a pier in Jersey, asking his readers if they know that God is a Pooh Bear and reminiscing about his three-year journey across America. This is the part in *A Walk in the Woods* when Bryson makes a half-promise to himself to go back and hike the places on the Appalachian Trail he left untrekked. Those were important moments for them.

And I had a moment like that, a big ending to my journey. It occurred as I stood at the railing of the ferry heading back from Put-in-Bay. The sun was setting in that brilliant maroon-and-gold glow I have never seen equaled in beauty and sheer magnitude, and the water seemed to burn black on all sides. Looking behind me I watched Perry's Victory and International Peace Memorial shrink from its amazing size, inch by inch, sinking into the water and the horizon, and I knew that for me it would never again be a tall soap bottle. It would be a waypoint in my life, a marker reminding me of my first book, my first serious investigation into the past. And Perry would never again be just a picture on a beer bottle or a guy who lent his name to schools and towns and nuclear power plants.

Oliver Hazard Perry changed for me in that moment. He became, in the strangest way, a friend. And I sure as hell wasn't going to forget him. I still don't know what made me think of him when I wanted to write a book, still can't pinpoint his inspiration in my life, but maybe that's for the better. Maybe the reason is less important than the doing. It's like that with history. Maybe the reason we learn history is to remember. And maybe the reason we remember is the same reason we should take the time to sit on a park bench and gaze into the distance; maybe it's a way of meditating on the things we look forward to by looking at the places we've been.

I can tell you that, having learned more about him, I still see Perry as the kind of person I admire—brash, bold, daring. But I am no longer the kind of person I disdain, no longer content being a dream-addled wannabe. I am a doer, a traveler, a writer. I am, in some small way, becoming the person I've always known I could be, and I have Perry (and Kerouac and Bryson and Horwitz and a dozen more like them) to thank for that.

Lake Erie has always been a force in my life. My wife and I have been away for almost fourteen years now, and I still make time during each trip home to visit the water. Only now I can't gaze into the horizon and wonder what's on the other side, because I know what's there. I've stood and looked back. I have cheated myself out of that mystery, but what I lost has been more than replaced by having done something I've always wanted to do. And that horizon is now like a trophy, kept on a shelf in my mind as a reminder of what I did and the things I've yet to do.

I'd be lying if I said that I learned nothing on my odyssey, because I really did. I learned that you should never attempt a road trip without having your brakes inspected. I learned that McDonald's in Canada encourages recycling. I learned that people who follow their passions—whether it's reenacting wars or volunteering at historic places—are usually willing to share everything they know, to give away their knowledge for free. And I've learned that you need to be careful, to temper your expectations with regard to what others share. It's a form of nostalgia, sharing, and what they share is a gift that can't be bought, can't be replaced. Be careful how you receive it.

I learned that history is more than a bunch of facts and that the way we learn history in school is, well, pretty sucky and stupid. History doesn't die and go away. It may be a little harder to find the more time passes, but there are people who are willing to help. People like the staff of the Clements Library, like Valerie at the Park House, Marcus at the Perry monument, and Tom and Jack at the brig *Niagara*, Mary at the museum in Perry devote part of their lives to the preservation of the past so that it can impact our futures. I used to like history class, but I can honestly say that no book or lecture, no matter how good, ever made half the sense to me that the Battle of Lake Erie does now. Because I have seen the ships, touched the papers Oliver Hazard Perry wrote, stood at the edge of the water and let my imagination run wild, this fleeting incident that is usually no more than a footnote in history books is now personal to me.

I learned that history should be personal and that specific events or places or people don't have to fork from your family tree to become your own. My decision to write about Oliver Hazard Perry and the Battle of Lake Erie was made on a whim, but that whim came from a special place in my memory, a place where my dad took me in a time I can never relive. Trying to relive it, trying to retake those steps I took long ago, led me down a different path, a deeper, richer one. But I never would have taken a single step had my dad not shown me how. There can be nothing more personal than that.

At the conclusion of the Battle of Lake Erie, when the guns had gone silent and the dead and injured littered the ships, Oliver Hazard Perry reached into his coat pocket and removed an envelope. On it he scribbled his famous note: "We have met the enemy and they are ours: two ships, two brigs, one schooner, and one sloop."

He was talking about the British, the ships he had faced in battle, but after my experience of the last two years, I take part of that message to mean something else—*and they are ours*. All the men who fought that day, all those who have fought on other days, they are ours. They exist in our collective imagination, waiting to be explored. Oliver Hazard Perry belongs to anyone who has ever stood on the shores of Lake Erie and looked out at the water. He belongs to every person who has taken that rickety elevator to the top of his monument and witnessed the enormity of this tiny slice of the world. He and everyone else who has come before belong to us, just as we belong to those who will come after us, just as we hope to be remembered.

Perry went on to an early grave. Despite his heroism in the Lake Erie campaign, he could not possess enough courage, enough honor, to overcome the yellow fever he contracted in South America. He could not be braver than the grave. I think about him dying, just a couple years older than I am now. And then I think about him living, the life so much bigger than one I could hope to accomplish, and I am humbled.

My journey had a second ending, when things became clear, and it was in that moment I realized I had been chasing not only Oliver Hazard Perry but also my dad. It occurred just before we pulled into his driveway after our trip to Erie and again the next morning. Dad told me that I told a good story and, in the morning, that he was proud of me. He was interested in the story I told about

Perry, in the facts and trivia. But he told me he was proud of me when he realized that I had stayed up all night with my sick child. He was proud of the father I had become, and I realized that the thing I had been chasing was the image of myself as my father.

It can be hard growing up the only boy—my brother was adopted when I was twenty-one—in a household with a stoic man. My friend Fred likes to joke that there is a special place in heaven reserved for the sons of German fathers. But what is harder, I now realize, is to be that stoic man, to have your children afraid you won't be proud of them and to not know how to tell them that you are. I love my dad. I hope that much is vodka-clear after all of this. And I have come to realize that despite our differences—our political views, our careers, our abilities and acumen—there is part of me that has always wanted to be just like him and parts of me that already are. I may be the family's resident English major, but that doesn't mean we don't share something intrinsic, something innate, something that defines us beyond our résumés.

I made things hard on my dad. I resisted his advice growing up. I drew stupid lines in the sand when it came to my choice of career and my demands about how I needed to be loved. And I didn't show him the man that I was. I hid from him. I cowered. I should have stood up and demanded he wait for Rebecca to finish church before we left her home on spring break. I should have stood up about so many things. I also should have accepted him for who he was rather than demanding he be something else. I think he was waiting for that moment when I would do the things I needed to do because I cared about them, regardless of whether or not I thought he would be pleased. I think he wanted me to stop trying to please him, to stop trying to gain permission, to be more like him rather than work so hard to try to get him to like me. We've had a complicated relationship, like many fathers and sons. But it has gotten better with the passage of time. I have come to accept and admire my dad, to realize that the best way to make him proud is to be the best version of myself. When I was born, he didn't expect me to be just like him. He only wanted for me what I want for my sons—safety, happiness, the freedom to be what they want to be. If they can do that, then I will be, like my dad, a very proud father indeed. That is, perhaps, the best lesson he has ever taught me.

So that's what I've learned. That's what I know. Will I try this again? Maybe. Hell, more than maybe. It's pretty damn likely I'll set off on another chase. It will mean leaving home, and that will sting, but if it means being better when I am there, being more present and not spending so much time dreaming, then so be it.

And if I can offer one small bit of advice, one small nugget of wisdom to anyone willing to listen, one life-altering truth for the ramble-hearted, it would be this: go with an open heart and open eyes. Go with your dreams intact and your mind alert to every person, place, and thing you encounter. And always, always, always rent the golf cart.

About the Author

 **Craig Heimbuch** is an award-winning journalist and writer living in Southwest Ohio with his wife, the ever-patient Rebecca, and two sons, Jack and Dylan. He has been the managing editor of *Cincinnati Gentlemen* and *Cincinnati Profile* magazines and is editor in chief of manofthehouse.com. You can contact him at letterstocraig@gmail.com. No hate mail, please, though he is open to taking on a stalker.